GLORY DAYS

Stories of Growing Up in Lower Bucks County

EDITED BY
TERRY L. NAU

First Stillwater River Publications Edition
Library of Congress Control Number: 2021913480
ISBN: 978-1-955123-18-1
1 2 3 4 5 6 7 8 9 10
Edited by Terry L. Nau
Cover photos provided by Kathy Hull Ross and Carolyne Keefer Jones.
Published by Stillwater River Publications,
Pawtucket, RI, USA.

Publisher's Cataloging-In-Publication Data
(Prepared by The Donohue Group, Inc.)
Names: Nau, Terry L., editor.
Title: Glory days : stories of growing up in lower Bucks County /
edited by Terry L. Nau.
Description: First Stillwater River Publications edition. | Pawtucket, RI,
USA : Stillwater River Publications, [2021]
Identifiers: ISBN 9781955123181
Subjects: LCSH: Bucks County (Pa.)--Social life and customs--20th
century--Anecdotes. | Baby boom generation--Pennsylvania--Bucks
County--20th century--Anecdotes. | Suburban life--Pennsylvania--
Bucks County--20th century--Anecdotes. | Nineteen fifties. | LCGFT:
Anecdotes.
Classification: LCC F157.B8 G56 2021 | DDC 974.821--dc23

This book is dedicated to our parents,
who survived the Great Depression, helped win World War II,
and then raised their children in the post-war era,
determined to give us a better life
than they had experienced.

Table of Contents

(Chapter, writers and their hometowns)

Prologue: Terry Nau, Fairless Hills i

Chapter 1: Beverly Briegel, Oxford Valley 1

Chapter 2: Mike Chalifoux, Oxford Valley 9

Chapter 3: Merrily Evans, Fairless Hills 15

Chapter 4: Brian Delate, Levittown/Yardley 21

Chapter 5: Dan Nau, Fairless Hills 25

Chapter 6: Drew McQuade, Levittown 31

Chapter 7: Bob Keiger, Levittown 41

Chapter 8: Lisa Dubinsky, Levittown 47

Chapter 9: Denise Queen, Fairless Hills 53

Chapter 10: Arlene Bowling, Fairless Hills 57

Chapter 11: Bill Sheehy, Yardley 61

Chapter 12: Dave Anderson, Morrisville/Lower Makefield 67

Chapter 13: Lynda Cleveland, Fairless Hills 73

Chapter 14: Tom DiIorio, Levittown 77

Chapter 15: Wayne Marsden, Fairless Hills 81

Chapter 16: Tim Nau, Fairless Hills 85

Chapter 17: Jim Wysor, Fairless Hills: 89

Chapter 18: Barbara Cook, Fairless Hills 93

Chapter 19: Rich Dobos, Fallsington 99

Chapter 20: Barbara Welch and Ginger Lane, Levittown 105

Chapter 21: Ruth Hendry, Lower Makefield 109

Chapter 22: Sandy Dunn, Fairless Hills 115

Chapter 23: Gay Ormsby, Levittown 119

Chapter 24: Joan Marcotte, Fairless Hills 123

Chapter 25: Cindy Marcotte/Tom Mazenko, Fairless Hills 127

Chapter 26: Carolyne Keefer, Levittown 131

Chapter 27: Janie Griffiths, Fairless Hills 135

Chapter 28: Lorraine Goodwin, Oxford Valley 139

Chapter 29: Kathy Klein, Levittown 145

Chapter 30: Ed Quill, Lower Makefield 149

Chapter 31: Patti Sheehy, Yardley 153

Chapter 32: Nancy Milne, Lower Makefield 157

Chapter 33: Bob May, Levittown 165

Chapter 34: Craig Eisenhart, Levittown/Lower Makefield 169

Chapter 35: Jim Spahn, Yardley 175

Chapter 36: Don Bentivoglio, Levittown 179

Chapter 37: Hal Blaisdell, Levittown 183

Chapter 38: David Christian, Levittown 189

Chapter 39: Barry Miner, Fairless Hills 193

Chapter 40: Bill Thomas, Fairless Hills 199

Chapter 41: Barbara Hubal, Yardley 203

Chapter 42: Bill Wilson, Levittown 205

Chapter 43: Tom Wysor, Fairless Hills 209

Chapter 44: Mike Tapper, Yardley 213

Chapter 45: Terry Nau, Fairless Hills 219

THE BOOT CREW – Ron Meyers, right, began organizing gatherings at Puss 'N Boots Tavern that brought together Pennsbury High alumni, including Mary Weight, center, who passed away in 2016, not long after this picture was taken.

PROLOGUE
Old Friends Are the Best!

There is a tavern located on Trenton Road in Fairless Hills, PA called "Puss 'N Boots." This concrete structure has been in existence since the 1950s, initially attracting steel workers coming off the night shift at the U.S. Steel plant located alongside the Delaware River in Morrisville. These men would park their cars, have a quick beer, and unwind from a long night in the heat and dirt of their turbulent work place. Then they would head home, knowing their children had gone off to school and they could get an uninterrupted sleep.

As lunch time rolled around and a new wave of customers arrived, a lone waitress would serve hot dogs and French fries to go along with the beer. The crowd started to get younger in the late 1960s when Baby Boomers came of age. We didn't know it at the time but "The Boot" would remain a connective tissue in our community well into the next century. We young people of the 1960s would eventually become the old folks at the bar. We became the two friends from Bruce Springsteen's song, *Glory Days*, who meet outside their neighborhood bar and head back in to tell stories of their youth. The Boot is such a place and it has maintained its place in the community as a meeting spot for three generations of Lower Bucks residents and visitors.

All but three of the writers who tell stories in this book attended the Pennsbury school system. Elementary schools in the communities of Fallsington, Levittown, Fairless Hills, Lower Makefield and Yardley became the first meeting places for children whose parents had moved into the region after US Steel opened the sprawling "Fairless Works" mill on Dec. 11, 1952. There were also kids from the long-standing communities of Yardley, Morrisville, Lower Makefield and Oxford Valley who were born in the region after the war. We all grew up together in those schools, and we played in the rivers and creeks and woods that dotted the landscape of Lower Bucks during the middle of the 20th century.

Lower Bucks County consisted mainly of farmland before Benjamin Fairless and William J. Levitt began planning communities to house approximately 10,000 steel workers and their families. Beverly Briegel Sanders tells us in the opening chapter that a village called Oxford Valley existed along Route 1 in the location that became Fairless Hills. Local mail was postmarked to the nearby community of Langhorne.

The town of Fallsington got wind of the new housing projects and formed a Preservation Society in 1950 to protect the historic community, which had first sprung up in the 17th century. Most of its farmland was sold for profit but somehow Fallsington retained its identity. The inner village exists today as a throwback to what the area looked like before the suburbs took over.

Once the steel mill, which occupied 1,600 acres of land, began operations, life changed rapidly throughout Lower Bucks County. Never-ending highway construction projects tied the new communities together. Huge freighter ships filled with ore rocks churned up the Delaware River from Venezuela, sending waves splashing against the shore line. They docked near the mill, offloading a vital element for steel production. When the Blast Furnace melted those ore rocks down, red dust spewed from the mill's smoke stacks and settled on cars and houses within five miles of the plant. Billows of smoke constantly escaped the various Open Hearth and Blast Furnace stacks. Smoggy Pittsburgh had come to Lower Bucks County.

Even more than Levittown, Fairless Hills defined steel mill community, a company town, but business opportunities all over Lower Bucks would grow and diversify during the next 20 years. Fast-food restaurants like McDonald's and Burger Chef began to populate the main highways. A whole new way of living developed in these suburbs just 25 miles northeast of Philadelphia. Farmlands gradually were supplanted by more and more housing developments.

These new suburbs were a perfect spot to raise children as the 1950s took root. Families moved to Lower Bucks from all over Pennsylvania and surrounding states, joining long-standing residents of Fallsington, Morrisville, Lower Makefield, Oxford Valley and Yardley.

Children made new friends in elementary schools. They shared classrooms and ball fields, first banding together in school based on neighborhoods, and then meeting kids from other towns as they moved into junior high school and then high school. Sometimes they fought each other after school over silly things. Meanwhile, local school systems throughout Lower Bucks County grew by leaps and bounds. When Pennsbury students reached the outdated high school in Yardley, more than 1,000 teenagers crammed the hallways. The school board approved a new high school project in Fairless Hills that opened in 1966 to accommodate the Baby Boomer population explosion.

Somehow, 50 years and more have passed since we were high school students. A couple dozen old friends meet every few months for informal reunions at The Boot. Just 10 miles away, Pennsbury alumni often bump into each other at Yardley's Continental Tavern, whose existence can be traced back to the Underground Railroad slavery days of the mid-1800s.

There is a natural connection among Baby Boomers from Lower Bucks that produces easy conversations about memories we created so very long ago. We can't remember events that happened last week but some of us can recall details of sports contests from when we were 13 years old! Why is that? We hope this book of collected memories will help answer the question of why the best friends we have in life are often the ones we met in our formative years.

– TERRY NAU

WORKING MAN – William Briegel Sr. looks out on the farm he maintained for over three decades. The egg and poultry farm often contained between six and eight thousand chickens.

CHAPTER 1

In a Land Known as Oxford Valley. . .

By BEVERLY BRIEGEL SANDERS

*L*ong before the idea of a local steelworks was on the drawing board and the communities of Fairless Hills and Levittown were born, there thrived a small connected group of families in a village known as Oxford Valley. The Oxford Valley landscape was dotted with several working farms and an array of well-constructed, single bathroom homes with exteriors of clapboards or asbestos shingles with towering maple trees in their yards for climbing. Neighbors knew each family member well and shared their joys and sorrows as one. Many of these homes reflected historical memories like coal bins in the basements, a large central floor grate to heat the modest rooms, and familiar farmhouse porches where neighbors gathered on steamy summer evenings. It was not quite Walton's Mountain but it shared many of those treasured qualities of a simple life.

My grandparents, William and Elizabeth Briegel, lived in the Germantown section of Philadelphia with their three children, Marie, Frederick (my dad), and William Jr. My grandfather, often taking the family on Sunday drives to visit relatives in the countryside of the Langhorne-Oxford Valley area, decided to begin purchasing land in the area for an eventual farm. The initial purchase began in 1932 with ownership of what was known as the Oxford Valley Farms which extended from Bristol-Oxford Valley Road to Trenton Road to the Oxford Valley-Tullytown Road and eventually over several years acquiring a parcel just under 30 acres where he began raising chickens. Interestingly, my grandfather's youngest brother, George Briegel, claimed property at the corner of Big Oak and Oxford Valley Roads where he raised his family while driving the school bus for Pennsbury and becoming the head maintenance man at the new Medill Bair High School.

My grandfather's vision was that his sons would establish a working farm for their future. In time, my "PopPop" moved his family to Oxford Valley Farms while he began working for General Motors in Ewing, New Jersey; his children attended the Fallsington Schools. My dad and his siblings would graduate from Fallsington High School, donning the familiar orange and black colors, while tending to schoolwork, sports and farm chores. My father, "Freddy," was taught by two of

1

my high school teachers, Doris Kirby and Elizabeth Carfagno, with whom he maintained a life-long relationship until their passing, even serving as a pallbearer for Mrs. Kirby, wife of the Falls-ington Police Chief Franklin Kirby. My dad's favorite memories of school were participating in football, basketball, and baseball where he lettered in all three. While playing the forward position on the basketball court, he served as the team's captain. Post-graduation years, my dad continued playing baseball and basketball in local leagues where he connected with athletes from neighboring towns. With war on the horizon, my dad ran the Briegel Farm alone for several years when his younger brother, Bill, was drafted out of Penn State to serve as an Army Military Police. During those days, my dad was rejected from enlisting into the military because farmers were considered essential workers. My father worked the farm alone, with help from local farmers during their sea-sonal planting and harvesting times. My dad worked several years for Woolston Brown, who owned the property where the present Oxford Valley Mall and Sesame Place are located. When Farmer Brown ("Brownie") retired after the sale of his property, he returned to the planting and harvesting duties to help on the Briegel Farm properties from dawn to dusk.

Our Briegel Farm grew its own feed of corn and wheat for the chickens, having it prepared in feed sacks at the Spring Garden Mill in Newtown. As chickens age, they become less productive in laying eggs, so yearly, beginning in late winter and early spring, our incubator room was full of trays of fertilized eggs. I remember going with my dad to check nightly on the incubator tempera-ture as they awaited the arrival of hundreds of new baby chicks. You may wonder what happened to those older chicks…. Campbell Soup Company would send a truck to the farm for a pickup… HMM HMM… good!!! Campbell chicken noodle soup! Farming was a "never-a-day-off job" and many local farmers supported each other… George and Bill Lovett in Newtown, Bill Sterling, George Tidman and Howard Nelson to name a few. Snipes Farm in Morrisville was often the lo-cation for Fallsington alumni class picnics.

The official Briegel Bros. Poultry Farm sign went up in 1939 and it remained a working farm of six to eight thousand chickens for over three decades, but not without setbacks. Friday evening, October 15, 1954, our local area was scorned by Hurricane Hazel and the Briegel Farm took a hit… both two-story chicken house roofs blew off, a corn crib crumbled, and many out buildings were damaged. It was a challenging time for our family, but with the help of local volunteers and endless work hours, the laying hens were securely housed and operations went back to normal.

As my dad continued to man the farm alone while my uncle served in the Army, he balanced his work with sports and attending local dances in Trenton (grown-up canteen) where he met my mother, Anne Scott, originally a Scottish native and one of five girls. After a timely courtship, my father asked my mom to "join his flock" and with such an apropos proposal, she could not refuse. They were married in Trenton on November 11, 1942. The newlyweds established residency on the second floor of the Briegel farmhouse where they saved money to begin construction on their humble cape cod home on Oxford Valley Road (diagonally across from the now Austin Drive). My dad and his family worked after farm hours to frame our house so that by early 1948, we moved into the two-story, three-bedroom home surrounded by our farm fields on three sides and a narrow two-lane road in front… my address would begin as RD#2, Langhorne, then RD#2 Oxford Valley, and our final address, 301 Oxford Valley Road, Fairless Hills, where the narrow two-lane road gave way to a traffic-filled, four-lane street.

No matter what the address, life in that green-roofed, white cape house held countless memories. As a young child, I see the backyard scenery with fields of plowed farmland or rows of towering corn stalks… a great place for hide-and-seek until one day we lost one. We anxiously looked row after row for the crying victim, Lorraine Goodwin. Finally capturing her, we thought differently about the cornstalk maze. Local food shopping happened at Erwin's corner grocery store (now Pep Boys corner) where my mother and I would walk to purchase food items. Although the selection was limited, wooden shelves were stacked to the ceiling with choices. My mother would place her selections on the wooden counter where they were boxed for afternoon delivery at our backdoor. After work on the farm, my dad often stopped by the store for his favorite flavors of hand-dipped Breyers ice cream which, over time, gave way to pre-packaged half gallons of Breyers, occupying the majority of space in our freezer. A larger supermarket, offering greater selections soon opened in Penndel… the Acme Supermarket. For kids it meant hanging on to the shopping cart as your mother strolled the aisles. Daily living was beginning to change.

When the school bell rang for the Oxford Valley children, the Fallsington School would open its doors to a busload of eager learners. This was a time when parents instilled the importance of school studies and proper behavior. The children of the present-day Center Avenue and Oxford Valley walked to the bus stop at the intersection of the two Oxford Valley Roads where we loaded by oldest to the youngest. Some familiar names at that stop were Ronnie and Lee Robbins, Georgie Pape, Larry and Cathie Hill, Kathy Bond and Lois Goodwin. As a kindergartener in 1951, I was at the end of the line with fellow classmate and neighbor, Billy Eager. Kindergarteners had one seat on the bus, Billy, me, and Trenton Road pickup Russell Broadnix. For every day of my ride to school, that was my designated seat. The kindergarten class was held in the house across from the Fallsington School as space there was becoming more limited. The house was a great facility for kindergarten: a large meeting room with long red and blue painted tables and chairs with an open-spaced room for music and gym activities like learning to skip. The sandbox and art easels were housed in a sun-filled greenhouse, and when snack time came around, we lined up in the kitchen to receive a half pint glass bottle of daily delivered Greenwood Dairy milk and simple graham crackers. For recess we would run around the side yard since there was limited playground equipment. Kindergarten was only half day and so before noon we all boarded our buses for home. My bus was driven by one of my favorites, a sweet kind-hearted man, George Baker, who also happened to be a retired farmer. He watched carefully as each of us walked safely to our houses.

For several years, my backyard view remained farmland until in 1951 that vision would be altered by the Danherst Corporation's purchase of the neighboring farmland and where construction of prefabricated homes by Gunnison began. I vividly remember my mother remarking how in one day three or four new homes appeared along Andover Road as she looked out our kitchen window. This new concept would rapidly, and forever, change life for the Oxford Valley neighborhood. Families quickly moved in from western and upstate Pennsylvania to begin employment at United States Steel's new Fairless Works plant. By first grade, classrooms at the Fallsington School were overloaded and the Oxford Valley children found themselves attending school in what we termed "the houses" along Trenton Road. There was one house assigned for each grade with endless desks and chairs in each, and if a teacher had to send a message to another staff member, a selected student would wrap up in his coat and have to walk along the sidewalk to that designated "room," quite a personal intercom system. Some of my new classmates from the Fairless community were Linda Peebles, Nancy Trainor, and Ray Seig, all '64 PHS grads. New communities require new school facilities, so as second grade was beckoning, the Oxford Valley Elementary School opened its doors and welcomed more new children. As Wanda Klein '64 and I met at the bus stop, now on Route 1, we discovered that we were in the same class. We tightly held hands as we timidly tried to find our classroom in this large building. So many new faces and friends, Ruth Ann and Mary Beth Logan, Jean Kettler, Mary Lou Setting – all future PHS grads. As new sections of Fairless opened to more families, the Oxford Valley School was bulging. So Danherst built an iden-

EGGS FOR SALE – Briegel Poultry Farm preceded the development of Fairless Hills by two decades.

tical school, Fairless View, on South Olds Boulevard. Before the end of the second grade the Oxford Valley originals were transferred to Fairless View, where we completed our elementary schooling. From there it was on to the William Penn Junior High School for seventh and eighth grades. In 1960 we entered the new Medill Bair High School for ninth and tenth grades. To complete our education, we combined the Medill Bair and Charles Boehm students to produce a graduating class of 551 in 1964 from Pennsbury High. Although I never moved from my house on Oxford Valley Road, I attended seven different schools, all in the Pennsbury district, due to rapid development of the area.

As the communities of Fairless Hills and later Levittown grew, many local farms gave way to progress and land development. Fairless Hills Shopping Center, Fairlanes Bowling, the Eric Theater, the Fairless pool, and the little league "stadium" replaced local farmland. Times and lifestyles were changing and in the Oxford Valley Village, we witnessed this first hand. The 1930s and 1940s way of life gave way to the post-war era where jobs and financial assistance were created for returning vets and their families. These new amenities meant that access to a pharmacy in Union Supply, local doctors and dentists, banks, and bakeries were often within walking distance. Golfers enjoyed the nine-hole course at the bottom of Oxford Valley and Trenton Roads. Homes with television sets allowed many to share the same viewings. My neighbor, Earl Eager, opened a television repair shop and salesroom of Philco televisions; Mr. Eager also made house calls to work on television sets as they were much too big and heavy to move. Fairlanes Bowling, operated by Fred Lening, offered leagues for men and women and youth and became a popular place for weekend entertainment. The Briegel Brothers farm sponsored two men's teams on Monday and Wednesday nights where my dad and his brother and later my cousin, Billy, enjoyed the camaraderie of local neighbors. The Briegel Brothers Farm's long-time neighbors, Mareks, Tidmans, Hetzels, Weisenborns, and the Broadnix Brothers all survived the initial growth of the area. In fact, the novelty of fresh eggs became so appealing to many in both Fairless Hills and Levittown that during holiday times the egg room had customers standing in line waiting for weighed and polished fresh eggs—the business thrived better than my grandfather had envisioned. Fields of sweet corn and tomatoes and strawberries were grown to satisfy the need for fresh produce. We farm children grew up and left for college. Because none of the seven offspring of the Briegel Brothers wanted to pursue the laborious farm duties, the farmland eventually became prime real estate. In 1971, the farm was sold for development and my father and uncle sadly began closing down the operation of their livelihood for three decades and started planning for their next chapter. Not only would they miss the daily routine of running a farm but the friendships they had made with many customers. On his death bed, my dad spoke of having a great life because he was able to enjoy each day of work and time with his family . . . what a lucky man! Today our property is dotted with apartments and townhouses and while doing a drive-by, it is hard to recognize what was the forerunner of those buildings.

The Briegel brothers continued working for several years after their farm days. My Uncle Bill worked for the Central Bucks school district and my dad went to work for his friend, Willard Graeber, at Graeber's Lumberyard. My father and mother made a final move to join my family in Connecticut where we embraced the multi-generational household. My cousins and I continue to enjoy reminiscing about our days on the farm with cherished memories about all the wonderful people we met.

* * *

SPORTS FOR ME

In my early childhood, sports meant climbing the ladder on my swing set, running endlessly while playing a game of tag, and of course, learning to balance on a two-wheeler and practicing riding with no hands! Winter joy was meeting my Center Avenue neighborhood friends (Lois and Lorraine Goodwin and Cathie Hill) to work at creating the familiar snowman silhouette, building mighty snow forts, pushing the winter white into well-formed snow angels, and never leaving without the inevitable snowball fight. As our handmade mittens began to freeze and our nimble fingers turned red, one of our mothers would open the kitchen door and beckon us for some hot chocolate and a piping hot bowl of soup to warm us from our tummies to toes before venturing outdoors for a final round of frolicking in the waning snowfall, not knowing if it would last another day. Neighborhood games were an afterschool tradition in our Oxford Valley area... kickball, softball, croquet were backyard favorites... played tirelessly and never boring. Often a parent or two (Tom Goodwin and Peg Hill) would join in the activity to be a steady pitcher, an umpire, or just to challenge our skills and make the game more exciting. Children living in the houses and trailer parks along Route 1 would hear the shouts of joy and wander over to join in the simple pleasures of backyard play.

Early school days, sports were an energized recess of running around the playground to secure a swing or a seesaw spot or waiting in line to climb the highest slide. There were semi-organized games of kickball, softball and football... holding your breath, hoping to be chosen for one of the teams. At Fairless View my fourth and fifth grade teacher, Mr. Frank Robidoux, scheduled an extra gym class for his students each week. He taught us to play a line game of handball (wallball, as we called it). The line grew as our skills improved; the challenge was to be the last to compete with our teacher! In the Pennsbury School System, we were fortunate at the elementary level to have a designated gym class with trained physical education teachers (Mrs. Fritz, Mr. Ross and Mr. Sterling) at least weekly. We learned rules and positions of several sports, plus simple gymnastics, and folk dances. Unprecedented for the time, boys and girls each had their own locker rooms for changing into sneakers and shorts before lining up on those high gloss gym floors.

Sports at the William Penn Junior High School had a stronger presence in our weekly schedules. No longer was gym class a once-a-week special. Gym became a three or four day a week class with lockers, gym suits, squads, warm-up exercises, and team and individual sports. There was always a gymnastic unit with a gym filled with sophisticated gymnastic equipment. That scene is somewhat obsolete in today's gyms… high liability issues. At William Penn and Medill Bair, an inclusive intramural program was offered to all students wanting to play for enjoyment without feeling competitive pressure. Hockey, volleyball, basketball, softball. Take your pick. Seventh grade would be the first time I held a field hockey stick—that stick and I stayed together throughout my college days of playing. I learned the basics from Ms. Beebe and Ms. Baker at William Penn, and then played on the junior high and junior varsity field hockey teams under Coach Becky Hoffman, who prepped us for the next level of play under the renowned PHS field hockey legend, Cora Clinton. She always ran a structured practice, working on skills and strategies. During the summers, Pennsbury sponsored a pioneering field hockey camp where many schools sent players to learn the game from All-American and All-England team members.

As the fall season came to an end, many prepared for winter sports' tryouts. Pennsbury girls would have the opportunity to participate in a winter sport by trying out for cheerleading (year-round), the swim team, or the basketball team. In my household, basketball was the choice, a game I played with joy instilled by my dad. However, refreshing my thoughts of those early games, I remember they were rather uneventful games. Six players per team, three guards and three forwards and neither allowed to cross the center line. Then a BIG change occurred: now one guard and one forward were permitted to play full court. That team member was known as a ROVER. I continue to love women's basketball, but regret that I never had the opportunity to play the game on today's court.

Spring sports' season arrived and the echoing of umpires calling strikes and balls resounded on the girls' softball field as team members took their turn at bat. Other girls had the chance to play on the boys' tennis team as a girls' team did not exist then. Some female athletes prepared for the track invitational events. The female sports scene was dramatically changed when Title IX was passed by our federal government in 1972. However, I felt privileged to have been part of the Pennsbury athletic program in which the diversified sports offered to girls were superior for our era.

Continuing with field day competitions at Charles Boehm and Medill Bair, each school held their annual day of Orange versus Black. At Charles Boehm, it was called Gymkhana and at Medill Bair, Bairlympiad. The entire day teams would compete in individual and team events with opening exercises organized by each team's cheerleaders and welcoming speeches from administrators and team captains. The cheerleading squads earned points with their artistic entrance, original songs and cheers, all centering around the overall theme. In the evening a schoolwide dance culminated the day's activities.

In 1962 Jack Dale and I were elected Bairlympiad's Orange Team captains, competing against the Black Team and their captains, Joyce Lisbinski and Tom Mazenko. However, three days before Bairlympiad, Jack fell backwards and hit his head while trying to set a long jump record during gym class. An ambulance arrived on the scene and Jack was driven off to be checked for a concussion. It was determined that Jack had received a concussion and would not actively be able to participate in our field day activities. Jim Barnes was chosen to replace Jack as Jack watched from a lounge chair on the day of Bairlympiad. Jimmy joined in and accepted his leadership role.

During the preparations for the '62 Orange Team Bairlympiad at my home on Oxford Valley Road, where team members gathered and diligently prepared props and constructed an entrance barn for opening ceremonies, a hair-raising event occurred. Cheerleader Jayne Griffiths '65 and team member Bob Haviland '64 took a break from the preparations to try their prowess at bareback riding on one of my cousin's horses. Unfortunately, the horse sensed the strangeness of the riders and took off through the backyard fields of the Briegel farm. This simple pleasure turned into a runaway experience for the two riders clutching to the reins as my worried dad chased after them. The two riders and runaway horse flew through the field and turned onto the farm property with a swing set in their path when Jayne fell off and Bob, in true cowboy heroics, jumped off to save her (or possibly himself, too)! This incident certainly played into our Bairlympiad western theme. Surprisingly, Jayne continues to enjoy horses today.

Besides team sports at Pennsbury, students, cheerleaders, and staff looked forward to the March extravaganza of the annual Sports Nite… Orange vs. Black… designated girls' and boys' nights with team competitions in creative relay races, original class dances, cheerleading, extensive artwork including massive murals, patron sales, and sportsmanship. In a dramatic revelation of the victorious team, the Sports Nite Queen would rustle her orange and black shakers as the two teams anxiously waited for the Queen to raise the winning-colored shaker over her head. Would it be ORANGE or BLACK?? The winning team would go into a frenzy of shouts of joy as cheerleaders did cartwheels and mascots enticed the audience into jubilant celebration. Begun in the 1950s, this tradition has continued throughout the decades. As an aside, Jack Dale and I were bestowed the honor of representing our team once again, this time, thankfully, no concussion! Jack and I were Black Team captains, opposing Bob Peresta and Joyce McCann serving as Orange Team captains.

The exceptional Pennsbury sports program offered multiple opportunities for both male and female participants to enjoy athletics, both as team members and as individuals, and to acquire skills for lifelong passions. I am grateful to have walked the halls of these schools during this era.

* * *

(**POSTSCRIPT:** *Beverly Briegel Sanders spent 40 years in the education field while raising two children and two step children. She especially enjoys spending time with her seven grandchildren. For the past several years, she has divided her time between Connecticut and Florida while grateful for an active lifestyle. A yearly highlight is the annual girls' shore weekend with Pennsbury friends in Stone Harbor . . . a true blessing of friendships.)*

AERIAL VIEW – This photograph taken in 1960 shows Route 1 running down the lower left and Fairless Hills homes and streets on the top right.

CHAPTER 2

Mike Chalifoux Worked Hard on the Farm

By TERRY NAU

M ike Chalifoux's memories of growing up in Lower Bucks County are pretty unique. His family history dates back to 1935 when his grandparents, William and Katherine Gallagher, purchased a farm along the Lincoln Highway, right where Fairless Hills is located today.

"My grandfather bought the farmland from the White family, who were cousins of Samuel Snipes. The Snipes owned a huge amount of land in Falls Township and sold some to the Whites. Their land was over by where Strick Trailer Company was built. The land we bought from the Whites was considered Oxford Valley at that point in time. Langhorne was our post office. Our land ran from Route 1 almost to Trenton Road, from creek to creek," said Chalifoux, who was born in 1946 and became a working member of the Gallagher farm crew before he could shave.

"My father, Dick Chalifoux, married Virginia Gallagher. The Gallaghers were a big family. My mother had three sisters and two brothers. Their farm had cattle and pigs, and also grew toma-toes, corn, wheat and potatoes," Chalifoux added.

"In 1949, my grandfather sold most of his farmland to the Danherst Corporation, which was part of U.S. Steel and would build Fairless Hills. A lot of people seemed to think my grandparents were rich. I don't believe they were. They were uneducated and probably didn't get their best price from Danherst. After they sold most of their land, they still had the land along Route 1. In 1954, the barn got blown down during Hurricane Hazel. I was very young at the time but remember watching from the kitchen window as grandpop, dad and my uncles removed livestock from the barn. My grandfather decided to build a restaurant and a trailer park along Route 1. He wanted to take advantage of how the area was becoming more populated. Everything was named Gallagher's . . . the restaurant and the trailer park. At one point, we even had a hot dog stand where the current Delaware Valley Animal Hospital is now. If you remember where Graeber's lumber yard was, that was part of our property. They bought the land from my grandfather for $10,000. I think he sold the Amoco gas station owners their land for $10,000, too. That must have been his price for every-thing."

9

"After selling off land to Danherst, my grandparents rented what was left to farm to Bill Sterling and when I got old enough, I worked for him," Chalifoux said. "Most farm work and field work was okay but the real fun was baling hay and straw. Picking potatoes wasn't bad because the diggers did most of the work. Tomatoes were a lot of work. They had to be hand-picked and put into baskets, loaded on to wagons, and then loaded into the truck that would take them to the markets. We had two big accounts – Stokely Van Camp in Trenton and, of course, Campbell's Soup down in Camden. Sterling's farm also had some apple orchards. You might remember those orchards because as kids we would sneak in there and pick some apples."

The original Gallagher's farmland plot can best be viewed in a 1960 aerial photograph shown at the beginning of this chapter.

"If you look at the top left of the photograph, that is Sterling's farm and the apple orchards," Chalifoux said. "My grandparents' home is below that, the one with six windows showing. That house was built in 1860 and it was considered a mansion at the time. My grandparents sold it late in their lives and it is now the main office for the trailer park. You can also see part of Fairless Hills in the far right portion of the photo."

While kids his age were growing up playing in the streets and fields of Fairless Hills, Mike would get up before dawn to perform farm chores.

"We had to get the cows milked every morning," he recalled. "I had a couple of cousins but they weren't much help. There were a lot of cousins who were girls and I guess they did what girls do. I became sort of a handyman. By the time I was 12, I was helping to put in a septic tank on our property. They brought in a bulldozer to dig out the hole and then I went into the hole and started laying the cinder blocks on the floor and the walls."

"One of my uncles, William Gallagher, had a job building homes on Woodbourne Road. We didn't see him much," Chalifoux added. "My father and another uncle, Bob Gallagher, were Falls Township policemen. I think Falls Township had five cops at the time because the population was pretty small. Before Fairless Hills was built, there might have been 500 people living in Oxford Valley. We had to drive to Morrisville to shop for groceries."

Danherst put up a cyclone fence along the border of the remaining Gallagher Farm land to separate it from the Fairless Hills development. "I couldn't even swim in the Fairless Hills pool or use the golf course because we weren't considered residents," Chalifoux said. "But for some reason we could play on the ball field. I had to go to Penndel or Morrisville for a swim. Most of the time, I was either going to school or working on the farm. I didn't have many friends my age. Well, I did become friends with Ed Quill, who lived on Woolston Drive, about two miles down Route 1 from the farm. Ed's family had a little store in Morrisville and sometimes we would drive down there and get a soda. But we didn't do much together because I was so busy working. I actually lived on the farm with my grandparents. My parents bought a home on Chelsea Road, a stone's throw away from the farm, and sometimes I would stay with them, but I had to get around that darn fence first."

At an early age, Chalifoux received a pretty good education in the life of a working man.

"I was the only kid who worked on the property," he said. "If a water line broke, it was usually up to me to repair it. If a sewer line backed up, it was my job to get it flowing again. We were always building something around the restaurant and the trailer park. I remember tarring the roof of the restaurant. We had a coal truck that would come by and dump coal in the basement of the house. My job was to make sure our furnace was covered up so all that soot wouldn't get in.

"There was another job we did often," Chalifoux added. "A railroad car would drop off 2,000 bags of clay that weighed 50 pounds each. We would unload those bags and haul them over to Hulmeville to a wallpaper company. That was a lot of work, hard work."

The restaurant became a regular stop for truckers in the 1960s. Bill Gallagher hired go-go dancers to keep the truckers entertained.

"We were the first place in Lower Bucks to have go-go girls," Chalifoux said, chuckling at the memory. "That happened because one of the customers said this would be a good way to make lots of money. When I went into the Army, my grandparents rented my room out to the girls! I was living in a tent 90 miles north of Saigon at the time. By the time I got home, the girls were living elsewhere. My family sold the restaurant sometime in the 1990s."

NO LUCK – Mike Chalifoux joined the Army to get away from work at home and ended up serving in the Vietnam War!

Chalifoux joined the Army in 1966 "because I just needed a break from all the work." The Army made him a truck driver, sent him to Germany and then to Vietnam.

"I started out driving trucks in a place called Dian, not far from Saigon," he said. "I had to bring (dead) bodies to Long Binh for processing back to the states. But that was only for a few weeks. The Army decided to transfer me north of Saigon to a place where helicopters were refueled. My job was to bring in those barrels of fuel and get the choppers ready. I was never hurt over there, thank God."

Looking back, Mike reflects on his unusual childhood in nonchalant fashion.

"I can't complain," he said. "What can I compare it to? I only knew the farm. Same for Vietnam. I just did what I had to do. One thing I learned growing up on the farm was to think for myself. I learned how to work, how to do a job. I already had confidence in myself before I went to Vietnam."

RIDING HIGH – Merrily Evans shows off her bicycling skills for her father, Dave, who casts a shadow into this faded 1950s photograph.

CHAPTER 3

Fairless Hills Unlocks Visceral Memories

By MERRILY EVANS

*J*ust saying the name Fairless Hills unlocks visual, visceral memories. And they aren't dim. Maybe it's the product of aging, but at times I can wend my much younger self through the rolling streets of my past—Andover Road, Austin Drive, Fairfax, Trenton, Chelsea, Waltham, Wyandotte—with an ease that surpasses my ability to use Google Maps. Not just the names of the streets come back but with them the topography, a topography ingrained from miles I walked or pedaled. I remember flying on my green Schwinn across Oxford Valley Road, down Andover, past Mary Jane Buchanan's house, across Trenton Road (yes, mom. I know it's dangerous; I will stop) through the golf course toward Cindy Marcotte's home and Fairless View. My good friend Vicky Hadden lived on Austin Drive so that route was even more familiar and meant crossing the creek. It was a trip made longer by my obsession with cycling past Alan Maxwell's house in the hopes he'd be outside. He never was. To encounter someone special in those days before cell phones was fortui-tous. Finding people in the fifties and sixties was an art, nonchalantly clandestine. We all knew where to look. But more on that later.

In 1952 our family came from Uniontown, even then a tired town south of Pittsburgh, when my father began his job at the Fairless Works. I am not exaggerating when I recall that scene was bleak: there wasn't a shrub or tree in Fairless Hills when we pulled up to 207 Andover. The old Plymouth was crammed with my grandparents, my parents, my 2 year-old brother David, our dog Freckles, and me. No seatbelts, of course. That's what fathers' arms were for. I was only five, but I remember my mother crying when we slowed to a stop in front of the house. And from the early pictures, I can see why. This was not the lovely suburban home I know the young wife had envisioned. The Danherst Corporation had constructed the stark one-story, pre-fab Gunnison homes of Fairless Hills in a hurry to lure and to accommodate the newly hired steelworkers and their families.

These houses were called *Magic Homes*—I'm guessing because they magically appeared on the now barren horizon. But magic they weren't. The walls were plywood and the tile floors asbestos. The kitchen cabinets were metal; you could conveniently see them as you entered the front door. Once inside, from the wide picture window you could peer into the house across the street. No need to be curious, though: it looked just like yours. And these three-bedroom boxes were close together. Danherst had made excellent use of the denuded farmland. From the carport I could almost touch Billy Peterson's house next-door. Back then all these houses looked alike. I remember a friend's mother told me that her son once came home from school to the wrong house and fearfully watched a family not his own eating dinner in what he thought was his kitchen.

Over the years the desolate landscape of Fairless Hills improved. Homeowners added porches and garages and extra bedrooms and patios. Lush hedges and backyard fences separated the lots. Robert Frost was correct: these fences did make good neighbors. Mud became grass. The whir of the weekend lawn mower is the soundtrack of my earliest memories of Fairless Hills. Gardens flourished; spindly trees grew tall. The willow planted by my grandfather the year we moved in became unwieldy, its roots wrapping around our water line, so it had to be removed. I loved that tree. In its prime I would climb to its top where I could hear the cars racing at Langhorne Speedway and just about see the drive-in theater on Rt. 1.

Although the houses of Fairless Hills were once quite sad, the streets and the community were not. Our small "company town" was well-planned and inviting. Most of all, it engendered a child-hood autonomy that I doubt was the primary objective of the municipal planners. They had created wide, sidewalked winding lanes with enchanting names borrowed from English villages. These quaint-sounding street signs beckoned to us kids. And we followed. We amused ourselves in many Truman Show-esque places—the modern Olympic-sized swimming pool, Lake Caroline, Queen Anne Creek, the playgrounds at both elementary schools, a golf course, the Little League Field, a shopping center featuring McCrory's and Union Supply, and Fairlanes, our bowling alley. Best of all, just shy of 2 square miles, Fairless Hills was walkable. Or bikeable. One of my most vivid memories is of biking up Oxford Valley Road after a long hot day at the pool. My goal was always to get to Andover Road—at the top—without having to stop and walk my bike. Walking one's bike was giving in. I would be hot and tired after that trek and since we had no air-conditioning, I would flop on the cool tiles in front of a fan in the kitchen.

What I marvel at now is how we managed to find each other without texting. An adolescent ESP directed our wanderings from pool to playground to the shopping center. I don't recall ever really planning these meetings—they seemed to happen serendipitously. Maybe their spontaneity is part of what made these encounters so memorable and exciting. In the summer, the hub of our community was definitely the swimming pool. My friends and I lived at the pool. I cannot hear *Will You Still Love Me Tomorrow, In the Still of the Night,* or *Chances Are* without being immediately immersed in that usually quite cold water. And I do mean immersed, since in the 1950s dunking the girls must have been a rite of passage for the boys. Like skinny sharks, the boys would move in packs. Some perfected the "swimming under water to grab the legs" technique—or at least they thought they did. We girls knew they were coming. I remember we could have easily escaped these pool rituals, but we girls knew the game, too. Like much of what would come in the future, this pre-courtship game was one we willingly played. Looking back, I remember that we shared the pool with our mothers, who kept to their own spot near the baby pool. We stayed as far away as possible except to ask for money for a Town Cake—two glazed chewy graham cracker rounds with marshmallow in between. I can see my mom in a quintessential '50s pink two-piece. She was so young and so pretty. I did not know that then.

Winter weekends in Fairless Hills found me hoping for weather cold enough to ice skate on Lake Caroline. Everyone came. Ice skating was, and still is, a multigenerational sport. There were fires, s'mores, and headlights for night skating. If the temps were frigid enough, we could even skate on the creek that meandered through the golf course. I cherished my white skates with their red yarn puffy tassels and bells. I religiously dried the blades and snapped on the skate guards. Two of my rare athletic successes occurred on Lake Caroline: I learned to skate backwards, and I became brave enough to join in the often calamitous crack the whip. I was always fearful of being catapulted over the falls which, although barely 2' high, seemed to cascade at least 12' to the creek below. So much of what I remember seems larger in the past.

As the oldest daughter of a baseball fan and devoted Little League coach, and unlike most preteen girls in Fairless Hills, I spent almost every evening of the season at the Little League field with my dad. The field sat in the shadow of a water tower between Austin Drive and Center Avenue (behind my good friend Lorraine Goodwin's charming, non-Gunnison, house). The field was just one street away from Andover Road—close enough to hear starting lineups. On game days my mom had dinner ready at 4:45 so when dad came through the door from daylight shift, we could eat and be at the field by 5:30. My brother David was four years younger but because of his August birthday and his great fielding ability (he played 2nd base and pitched), he was bumped up to play with the older boys. This meant my little brother David was on the same team with boys my age. Boys I liked. Boys I was afraid to talk to. Dad gave me the job of team manager which meant I got to type the roster. On my mom's old Royal upright, a bulky beast of a machine, I hunted and pecked every name. I had a clipboard. I was sure I mattered to the team. I did not. But being at the Little League field all those summer evenings was a significant part of my early years. When I returned to Fairless Hills for our 50th high school reunion and looked out of my hotel window, what did I see but the water tower! Honestly, within seconds I was back on that dusty field. The names of the teams that played on all those hot summer evenings in their ill-fitting, scratchy wool uniforms popped into my head: Women's Club (our team, in maroon), USW (in black), Danherst (blue, I think), John Melvin (green), VFW (yellow/purple), and Fire Company (appropriately red). I once got to don the Women's Club uniform for a girls vs. guys game. Somewhere I have a photo of my mom, Joe Baron's mom, Denise Queen (our team's ringer) and me. In my memory I got a hit.

I loved baseball, could field a ball like a boy (said my dad), and once won the high school softball throw, but I was too timid to try out for the team. I am sure those enjoyable years prepared me to love the decades I have spent on bleachers cheering on my own four children. Above all, those evenings at the Little League field allowed me to see my dad in ways I might not have otherwise. His life, like those of so many steelworkers, was at times quite hard. It was during those summers, when he was coaching that team, that I think he was the man he most enjoyed being. He genuinely loved being able to pass his passion for the game and sportsmanship on to my brother and his team. I imagine on those warm summer evenings he felt a sense of accomplishment that working in the mill didn't offer. I have a framed photo of my dad with his players gathered around him on the day Women's Club won the championship. When I want to see my father young and happy, I look at this picture.

If the steel mill was its catalyst, Pennsbury School District, renowned throughout the state for its educational excellence and state-of-the-art facilities, was the backbone of our community. In grades K-6 we walked to either Fairless View or Oxford Valley. We attended William Penn in 7th and 8th and Medill Bair in 9th and 10th. This progressive (only two grades in one building) approach to education fostered our social and academic confidence. Only after years of teaching have I realized the emotional benefits of separating young 7th graders from their much more mature 10th grade peers. At the time this pedagogy was lost on me, but I knew I felt secure among my friends in the classroom. In our junior year, however, this comfortable world was disrupted when we boarded buses for the high school in Yardley. Just riding a school bus comes with its own anxiety triggers— who will sit with me? Will I sit alone? Am I cool enough to sit in the back? (I wasn't). Like entering a school cafeteria without a designated friend group awaiting at your special table, riding a bus each day can be upsetting. At least it was for me. Although the kids I met were welcoming, and some like Gail Zoerner and Susie Smith became close friends, I never again felt as though I fit in the way I had in Fairless Hills. While I was eager to get to know these new peers, I perceived their lives as very different from mine. And indeed, they were. Most of their fathers were professionals or solidly middle-class, not laborers at the steel mill. Their home lives were not governed by the vicissitudes of shift work or strict budgets that necessitated making hard choices between getting braces or saving for college. In my insecure adolescence I exaggerated the perks of this higher socio-economic milieu. What I glimpsed on my bus ride to the high school told me a story of a life I was definitely not living. I was in awe of the stately stone homes nestled behind treed, manicured lawns; I longed to live in a house with a second story. In retrospect, I think the abundance I saw overwhelmed me. Of course I now realize that monetary comfort is not synonymous with happiness. At 15, however, I was fairly sure it was. To compensate I devoted myself to my studies. My parents valued academic success above all. Both avid readers and interested in the arts, my parents extended their meager budget to expose my siblings and me to museums and historic venues. We toured Washington, D.C. and Gettysburg, where my father told us Civil War tales while we tramped past the monument marking Pickett's Charge. My hardworking parents knew that only by attending college would my siblings and I be able to escape economic uncertainty. Our conservation of paper and food and products was not borne of lofty idealism but rather of necessity. We recycled before I knew what the word meant. My efficient mother kept a large manila folder crammed with letters and advertisements hanging in the utility room. The blank backs of all these papers were mine to use. I rarely drew or made notes on paper that did not have advertisements on the other side. As I grew older, I realized that the private drawing classes I took at the Fallsington Art Center meant my mother probably wore her winter coat for another year. I have never forgotten these lessons and acts of love; they have shaped my parenthood and my life.

I would say now that leaving Fairless Hills to attend high school in Yardley marked the end of my childhood naivete. As often happens when we evolve beyond our egocentric visions, I realized that the world around me had begun to change. The Fairless Hills of the iconic '50s—Friday night canteen (a must!), the Fireman's Fair, backyard barbecues, and poodle skirts—gave way to madras shorts, Jackie O sheaths, and Weejuns. My own family changed, too. In 1961 my little sister Beth, a blonde sprite who would delight and challenge my parents when David and I left for college, was born. Fourteen years my junior, Beth's special memories of Fairless Hills are different from mine. The community, like the times, was transforming. In these fast-paced years we traded our bikes with plastic streamers for driver's licenses. Escaping our community's boundaries, we ventured over the *Trenton Makes the World Takes* bridge to go to the movies in another state. We drove north on the beautiful and winding River Road to New Hope. I took a train to Philly to dance on American Bandstand. Now the world beckoned, and we excitedly followed. I think because I never lived in Fairless Hills again after graduating from college, my memories of childhood, adolescence, and Fairless Hills have merged. I cannot think of one without conjuring the other. And because I didn't return, Fairless Hills stayed the same, preserved in my mind like a chrysalis in amber. As I write these sentences, I turn that stone over and over in my hand, each turn releasing a memory. There are so many. And while we all recall different events and faces and names, those of us who grew up together in this community share a palpable bond, one I imagine we will forever revisit. Although not luxurious by any means, these seemingly idyllic scenes of our youth in Fairless Hills were rich beyond measure.

* * *

POSTSCRIPT: *Merrily Evans Schweers lives with her husband Bill and their Italian Spinone Ulysses in Mt. Lebanon, a suburb of Pittsburgh. She is the mother of four children: Jennie and Jeff Baron (their father is Joe) and Ben and Dylan Schweers. Merrily is a retired English teacher who now tutors students for the SAT/ACT and edits their college essays. She has lived in a two-story house for the last 50 years.*

DANCE PARTNERS – Brian Delate hooked up with his favorite girl at age 12, Linda Seaman, to participate in the Friday night Canteen dancefest.

CHAPTER 4

Dancing With Your First Girl on Canteen Night

By BRIAN DELATE

I'm now twelve years old and have an incomprehensible crush on a girl. And of course, she has no idea. In general, I feel invisible to girls. Our family lives in Levittown – the section known as North Park. In North Park every street starts with letter 'N' and we're on Neptune Lane. In third grade I became fascinated with astronomy. Oh, Man, we live on a street named after a planet!

Okay, so who's the girl? It's Linda Seaman. She's pretty and I love to see her – especially when she's not looking. I like her eyes and hair, and she seems sure of herself. She's also quiet and seems kind. I don't have a clue with what to do with my chaotic feelings. Plus, I possess the self-esteem of Laurel or Hardy – take your pick. Penn Valley is the elementary school. Most of the time I hate it. My reading's terrible and I never seem to catch up. I daydream, too, which frustrates my teachers. Needless to say, my grades and report cards reflect my lack of accomplishment.

All of us love the music at this time – Elvis, The Drifters, The Coasters, Gene Pitney, Freddie Cannon, etc. So, in late spring after the weekend and back in class I hear the other kids talk about Canteen. 'Hey, what's that?' 'That's the dance on Friday nights, you dope.' Hmm… I think I wanna go. I'm glued to American Bandstand after school and love it, but I don't know how to dance. I need help, but who do I ask? I know, the other Linda – Linda Huntsberger. Our families are close and they live around the corner. Linda's a couple years older, advanced and knows everything. Linda and her mother teach me to jitterbug and follow simple box steps to slow dance. Hmm… I like this.

That's it, I'm going this Friday night. 'Hey, Brian, you've got to get dressed up -- a jacket and tie.' Oh, well. Thank God I've got a clip-on bow-tie. Friday night – Canteen starts at seven and it's still light out. As we wait for the doors to open, the boys cavort together and the girls chatter away. I'm overwhelmed – this is unknown territory. Everybody seems to know what they're doing – I don't. Before I left the house, my dad handed me a dollar, way more than needed for sodas and chips.

So, we all pour into the gym, which is lit up like a car show. What's the first song they play? *'Please, Mister Custer, I don't wanna die…'* What? That's stupid -- who wants to dance to that? Okay, time for a soda. I get a bottle of coke – yes a bottle. Then I become a wall-flower. Fold-out chairs are set up along the walls. Good idea. An older kid sits up on the stage and plays 45s on a turntable with speakers. During school the gym serves as an auditorium.

Some of the girls jump up and dance to *Palisades Park*, by Freddie Cannon. *Walk – Don't Run* by The Ventures plays and I find myself next to Linda. Without speaking, our eyes give each other the green light and we're suddenly dancing. *Wild One* by Bobby Rydell quickly follows. So, we keep dancing. Oh, my God, this is neat! The ice is broken and I love it. So, it's dance, dance, dance. I'd dance with other girls, but would end up with Linda again. Then we slow-dance. It's magical and her hands are soft. I love Canteen!

Fast forward a couple weeks and Linda's parents come to watch the goings-on. Such nice people. Her dad brings one of those new-fangled Polaroid cameras and takes pictures of us. Sure, why not?

At most every Canteen there's a dance contest near the end of the evening. Linda and I decide to try our luck. The first time out -- whoa! We make the first cut, but that was it. The next week we do it again – same thing. Then the following week I feel the impulse to really let loose and I do. They're playing one of my favorites, *Fingerpoppin' Time* by Hank Ballard and the Midnighters. My feet and body take off like James Brown. Linda's a great partner and goes with it. We make the second cut and the third cut. What? Now, we're one of three couples on the dance floor for the final. The teachers or older students no longer judge. The winners will be decided by applause from all the other kids surrounding us. And it's close, really close, but we don't win. Wow! It's so cool to stand out and feel free.

To finish the night, Linda and I slow-dance to *Angel Baby* by Rosie and the Originals. Jeez, I wish I was a better talker, especially with Linda. So, just as the dance ends, I say goodnight to Linda. Our eyes celebrate what we did. I'm about to leave when three older boys I don't know very well block my path. One of them says, "You like to dance, don't you?" "Oh, yeah, I do." He leans in, "We don't like the way you dance, do we fellas?" His buddies smile darkly. "We don't like it, 'cause you dance like a nigger.' " One of the other kids steps in and jams his finger into my chest, "So, knock it off." They wait for a response. I freeze. "Okay, you've been warned." They leave and I'm shattered.

I don't tell Linda or anybody else what transpired. After that I shield my wilder impulses. Decades later, as a professional actor in New York at The Actors Studio, I would work with a tough Japanese director, who'd say, 'the nail that sticks out is the one that gets hammered.' I got hammered that night and it took a couple years, after we moved to Yardley, before I'd enjoy dancing again.

Here's the kicker – after all this time, last year Linda (Seaman) Simoncavage and I connect on Facebook. What a nice surprise! She remembered our dancing and not long ago sent me a picture her dad took of us at Canteen. What I described sounds bitter-sweet, but I'll focus on the sweetness. Thank you so much, Linda!

PS — Just prior to the pandemic I started swing-dance classes. Why not?

SUMMER OF 1967 – Daniel Nau Sr. stood with his sons Danny, Terry, Larry and Tim Nau for a photograph taken by his wife, Olive Nau.

CHAPTER 5

Lower Bucks, Good Preparation for the World

By DANIEL J. NAU, JR.

*L*IFE IS THE GIFT! It finds the necessary energy to assert itself whenever and wherever conditions allow. I view my coming of age in Lower Bucks County through this prism, enabling me to live in a free and demanding environment.

When my mom and dad brought us to Fairless Hills in 1952, I was 10 years of age. Our town was just then coming off the drafting board of the Danherst Corporation's architects. It would become a self-contained development housing thousands of United States Steel Corporation workers largely transplanted from steel mills in Western PA. My father foresaw that the Homestead Mill, where he worked as a Second Helper, was inefficient and would eventually be shuttered so he applied to go to the Fairless Works where he would quickly be promoted to the job of First Helper.

One year or so after we came to Bucks County, more than 1,000 people lost their jobs in the steel belt around Pittsburgh. Thus began the monumental decline of the steel industry in the Monongahela Valley and the ascendancy of Fairless Works on the other side of Pennsylvania. The Delaware River provided easier access to huge ships stocked with ore from Venezuela than did the land-locked mills around Pittsburgh.

In Lower Bucks County, farmland located around the existing town of Fallsington was largely sold off to Danherst Corporation and the Levitt Brothers, who built Levittown at the same time Fairless Hills was rising out of the ground. This led to rapid changes in the demographics of the area as thousands of new families moved in. There was little infrastructure so initially the company store model was applied and a general company store was established on Trenton Road, which ran parallel to the Old Lincoln Highway (Route 1). I believe this economic system worked on a credit model until a worker's next paycheck became available. The song "Big John" in 1961 reflected the control this model exercised on communities and individuals. Dad and mom bought their house from the Danherst Corporation for a down payment of around $100 with a monthly mortgage of $86. What an interesting period of time.

This was the Cold War era environment in which I grew up. McCarthyism, the Korean War, and Russian Communism generated many conspiracy theories and general fear and anxiety, not unlike today's fears of hidden agendas and subversive forces. I have read that President Truman's advisers at one point felt there would be nuclear war within a month.

My brothers Tim, Terry, Larry and myself were very fortunate to have loving and involved parents, Olive and Dan Nau. Olive was a gregarious, kind and compassionate person. Most of all, she was intellectually motivated. She had earned her high school diploma in the middle of the Depression, and passed her love of learning on to us. When many other women were being phased out of their jobs after the war, Olive worked for American Bridge in Trenton (as a Keypunch operator) and at General Motors. She worked in payroll at Strick Trailers on Route 1 in the 1960s before finishing her working career in a similar job at US Steel's office in Trenton after our father died in 1969. I learned my love of gardening and my empathy traits from her example. Mom was good, beautiful, ever loving, and forgiving. Olive had great strength of character and compassion as a worker and a person.

Mom and dad worked as a team to ensure their children were cared for and healthy. The path to their goals was often complicated by real life struggles. In the 1951-52 period, President Harry Truman attempted to nationalize steel production facilities in the United States as the country fought a new war in Korea. In 1952, the US Steel workers' union went on strike for 53 days, settling on July 24th. Even in these difficult times, mom and dad provided for us. They had uprooted their lives in the Pittsburgh suburbs to move across the state and start all over again. That took courage!

Dad was a remarkable man. He was devoted to his position of First Helper (managing one of the eight Open Hearth furnaces and supervising the staff under him) and often turned down supervisor positions because he liked what he was doing. Dad was passionate about what he did. He felt so grateful that he had won Olive's hand in marriage and treated her with love and respect. He had a passionate relationship with his hometown teams, the Pirates and Steelers, and often followed the Pirates on Pittsburgh radio station KDKA at night in our cozy home, the sound of announcer Bob Prince's voice wafting into the adjoining rooms.

One of dad's great passions was hunting and, by extension, his hunting dogs. He loved the outdoors especially well in the small game and deer seasons and involved each of us in this love. He and mom supported whatever sport or other activity we kids were involved in as we grew. Dad did have a temper and he could become upset with us individually when we screwed up. His blood pressure would rise in a hurry! However, he would quickly regain self-control. Dad had a rule that his sons never went to bed without knowing that he deeply loved and respected us. He loved taking day trips through Bucks County in his car with his boys pestering him at nearly every turn. Dad was definitely a family man. He valued his word, was an honorable man, and had a well-developed sense of humor. He was a story teller. An unfulfilled ambition was to travel domestically and even overseas but family and his beloved wife "Ollie" came first. We lost him to heart disease in 1969.

My brothers and I were indeed fortunate to have parents who valued education. My cousin Ronnie and I were the first of the Naus to graduate from high school and college. That was one of my parents' overriding goals. Dad dropped out of middle school in the early days of the Depression and never forgot the sacrifices everyone made in that time of his life. The Depression never left him. He was forever reminding us to turn out the lights and often said, in jest, "What do you think, we live in a barn?"

I gained so much life knowledge from my parents and from growing up in Bucks County. The sense of being supported in a new and growing community, having good schools and a beautiful natural environment contributed to my being an optimistic soul. From my parents I learned a number of traits that have sustained me in my long life. From dad I learned patience and the need to never leave emotional issues unresolved. From him, I inherited an incredible sense of wonder for the natural world. Perhaps because of his unfulfilled desire to travel, my wife Elaine and I have travelled to four continents and 35 countries. Further, from my mother I inherited gardening as a hobby and life interest, a sense of wonderment in the world, and an ability to be interested and respectful of each person I met; and to respect their lifestyle choices and formed opinions. This served me well in my career as a psychologist and psychotherapist.

While growing up, I played a lot of sandlot baseball and football in the fields near our home. We played against big kids like Frank Strang, who was a starting lineman for Pennsbury's football team. I remember playing sports with Joe Stefanik and my next-door neighbor, Larry Marsden. I took a job at the Shop Rite grocery store when I was 14. I became a cashier and then front end manager before heading to college. In our family, mom and dad both worked hard, and I guess that work ethic carried down to their sons. All four of us worked hard throughout our lives.

In the late 1950s, I participated in the Civil Air Program that was located in Bristol. Early in 1960, I began experiencing a terrible pain in my gut. Our family doctor came to the house, looked me over, and decided I had a ruptured appendix. I needed immediate surgery. After graduating from Pennsbury in June, I enrolled at Penn State but came home after one semester when our father suffered a major heart attack in January 1961. I worked at the steel mill to help mother make ends meet. A year later, I went back to school, this time at Methodist College in Fayetteville, NC. As a student, I took a side job as Student Pastor at Asbury Methodist Church for two years. I completed my B.A. degree in 1966.

Even though I was nearly 25 years old, the draft board pursued me and I served in the Army from 1967-69. I went to Fort Sam Houston for medical training and pretty soon I was off to Madigan General Hospital in Tacoma, WA, where I sometimes worked with soldiers who had been wounded in the Vietnam War. In my spare time, I pursued my master's degree in Clinical Psychology at Pacific Lutheran University in Tacoma. After I left the Army, I did course work towards a PHD in Psychology at the University of Victoria, in Victoria, BC. But I never could complete my dissertation. My son Jonah from my first marriage still lives in the Tacoma area and has provided me with four grandchildren and one great-grandchild.

I met my wife Elaine in Victoria, B.C, where I was lecturing in Psychology. We have been happily married for 42 years. Elaine is kind, remarkably intelligent, beautiful, and loving of me. I have been a psychologist in prison and youth centers, taught University and practiced psychotherapy. We live in Bedford, N.S., Canada.

***

We come from our families and they shape how we grow. Bucks County was a positive experience for me. Because so much of Fairless Hills was uniformly designed, it offered conformity and familiarity in the Cold War and post-McCarthy era. I rebelled against conforming to social and cognitive norms. I also became suspicious of authority. I became interested in liberal thinking and perspectives. I recognize in retrospect that I had some minor learning disabilities but I studied hard and overcame most of my difficulties. I had supportive teachers at William Penn Junior High and at Pennsbury High. I was shy but I could talk up a storm. I regret not having a sister as I might not have felt so awkward around the fairer sex.

What I have taken away from my formative period in Bucks County is the kindness and helpfulness of the people I encountered and the friends that I made in my formative years. I loved walking the fields and woods of this unique place. The dogwood trees and mountain laurels in their majestic blooms; wildflowers and creeks; fishing; the beautiful changing of the seasons; the stone houses, the river rides and the wonderful little towns of Upper Bucks County. These images, and those of my family and friends, linger with me wherever I go.

I wish I could have shown more of my love of my parents in their living years. Dad died young at 53 before any of his sons could know him from an adult point of view. I lived on the west coast in the 1970s and most of the 1980s and did not see mom as much as I wanted, but she did come with me and Jonah to Europe in the late 1980s, before she became sick. We visited her ancestral home in Wales. Mom passed in 1996. Her surviving sons often speak of her, and our father, with love and appreciation. I am almost 80 years young now, and will always be grateful to my parents for the gift of life they gave to their four sons.

THE MCQUADE CLAN – Gathering for a family photo taken by Andrew McQuade Sr. were, front row, left to right: Rosemarie and Mark McQuade. Second row: Alice, Kathy and Franny McQuade. Back row: Drew, Joe and Mary Alice McQuade.

CHAPTER 6

Seven McQuade Kids in One Levittown House!

By DREW McQUADE

M y heart forever pumps at 15 Robin Hill Lane in the Red Cedar Hill section of Levittown. My soul still hovers in the room I shared with my brother Joe. My brain houses the library of childhood memories nestled away in a dimly-lit corner. The shelves are full of both tender and agonizing moments.

The library is always open. Admission is free. It's up to me to open the door.

There's a haze in the first two years of my life in the Germantown section of Philadelphia my parents called the projects. My memories start to clear some three months before my third birthday after landing in Levittown on Oct. 20, 1953.

Andy, the decorated Marine turned accountant, parked his Studebaker in the carport of the new digs he and Alice bought for about $9,000 with the help of the G.I. Bill. Kathy, 3, and Joe, eight months, joined me and my parents on the adventure, followed later by Mary Alice, Franny, Mark and Rosemarie.

Inside the house, memory streams flash.

My mom, champion-caliber vocalist and jitter-bugger, and my sister Kathy, my protector and 13 months my elder, often chased me around the living room after school at St. Michael the Arch-angel elementary, trying to get me to dance with the Lloyd Thaxton show on TV in the background.

I preferred Thaxton's sit-down dance, "without leaving the chair, no need to go anywhere." My mom and sister wanted me on my feet.

In other unsuccessful chases, there were those moments my mom futilely tried to catch any one of us with a kitchen utensil after we did something wrong. We stopped laughing after she said those six ominous words: "Wait till your dad gets home."

We thought "uh-oh" but that was generally the end of it. My dad was firm, fair, easy-going and tired when he got home from government work.

My mom really never wanted to catch us or hit us. She wanted to take care of us. In my case, she wanted me to have a day off from school, so we could watch soap operas in anticipation of our favorite, silly, recurring story line: a character gets amnesia.

The McQuade Hall of Fame chase involved Joe trying to catch Fran as they ran down the steps. I was coming from the other direction. Fran's face hit a step before I could catch it. All I got was one of his teeth plus blood and saliva in my hands.

With seven kids scrambling to hide from chores, we were outside more than inside, including the time I snuck out the bedroom window onto the roof and dropped to the ground on my way to see a girl in the night.

"Where did you go?" said Joe after I climbed back in hours later. "Go back to sleep," I said, weary after hoisting myself up to the roof and thankful I was caught by my loyal brother and not the former drill instructor downstairs. If my dad had caught me I most likely would have gotten one of his lines.

"You'd forget your head if it wasn't attached," he would say. Or, my favorite, "I could see you doing something as a lark but if you keep doing it there's something psychologically wrong with you."

Fortunately, I was never given a Rorschach test. My dad clearly wasn't Ward Cleaver. He was mild-mannered, however, with power behind the smile and a dry sense of humor. He coached every baseball team Joe and I played on.

Coached Franny as well. Took Mary Alice, Mark and Rosemarie to their various Girl Scout, Boy Scout, dancing and bowling activities.

Took us every Easter to Bristol's Silver Lake to get a portrait of all the McQuades with their hair disheveled by the wind. I have ample evidence.

He drove the family to the Jersey shore on vacations. He piloted the Dodge with push buttons up-state to places like Scranton and Hazleton when Kathy was in the Belles and Beaux baton-twirling troop.

She taught me how to twirl in case an impromptu parade ever popped up.

I distinguished myself in a scheduled parade when I was in the Lower Bucks County Drum and Bugle Corps. An appendectomy at 10 ended my career as a drummer, highlighted by a surprise solo, a noisy one-note affair as I tripped and fell on top of the drum during a July 4th parade on the Levittown Parkway.

With drum sticks akimbo, I faceplanted with a flourish. Both the drum and my feet were too big for any semblance of a smooth march.

I was with friends the other time I faceplanted. We were racing on our bikes down Ridge Avenue after a trip to Hillborn's convenience store near Five Points. Both the handlebars and front tire twisted. I went air born, with my arms lagging. I landed on my front teeth in front of the house where my classmates, the Morin twin sisters, lived. Their mom came out and cleaned the blood off my chipped teeth.

Most of the forays outside were without pratfalls. There were plenty of Catholics, hence plenty of kids. Before the adults got to really know each other and constructed barriers, defying the early no-fence rule, there were spacious backyard palettes to paint joyous moments.

Levitt & Sons planned the suburban oasis of houses, schools, pools, recreation and religious sites and the spacious Levittown Shop-a-Rama as Nirvana. For kids, it was.

When it snowed, next door neighbors and amateur architects Rich and Larry Knorr constructed solid forts with high walls and special compartments for backup ice-ball ammo when opposing marauders got too close.

Tommy Boyce lived on Red Cedar Drive next to the creek (pronounced crick), a convenient place to ride his ancient toboggan. With hands on the wood curved up in front to chest level, we would fly down the hill through the stick weeds we called punks and zip across the frozen water.

Once an angry adult appeared at the top of the hill above the creek after one of our contingent's blind snowball volleys over a thicket smacked his windshield. He got his hands briefly on a couple of us, but we knew the terrain. The guy went sprawling down the hill onto the ice as we scurried away.

We should have had remorse. Instead we were proud of our aim and escape. We were still knucklehead kids.

In warmer months, we were infantry for hours, through the yards of the Woods, past the Sims, up the little hill of the Foleys, over the lawns of the Chericos, Caputos, Zalots, all the way to the house where Joey Williams lived and beyond. The battlefield stretched as far as the little soldiers with plastic machine guns could see.

We played kill the man with the ball in those yards and touch football in the streets. Touch football was as close to tackle as possible.

Once we played soccer in three fenceless backyards. Tony Verano, whose father was born in Italy, was the only one in the neighborhood with knowledge of the sport. He taught it to us. With our American know-not, it resembled kill the man with the soccer ball. Our feet sliced air, limbs and sometimes the ball.

Tony's older brother Joe was the leader of the Red Cedar Hill Gang. He was a nice guy with serious clout behind the grin. We were glad he liked us and happy to live across the street. It was the '50s, so the gang was more akin to the Jets and the Sharks than the Bloods and the Crips. When they danced with rivals, they were all fists.

In the early years, Levittown was more Mayberry than mayhem.

It was peaceful at Wistar pond, catching carp or sunnies with just a string, hook and bread. I can still hear the zit-sit sound the burning plastic made when it hit the ground in an opening in the woods behind houses on the drive. We got the plastic from the leftover pieces after extracting toy Army men from packaging. The actual Army men made for perfect zit-sits as well.

The woods were an escape to an alternate universe. Joe and I held our breaths when we saw Gary Goodwin try to swiftly scale a tree and then flail through the air and land, groin first, on a giant log. There is residual pain even now from those who witnessed the plop.

It was devastating when I saw my first death in a quarry not far away as they drug a kid turned purple out of the water after he dove out of a tree into the unknown.

I can still hear his brother's ungodly screams.

In stark contrast, the rewarding clink of the chain net after a swish still resonates. A bunch of us wore out the cement below the wooden basket at Thomas Jefferson Elementary School. We played every day for years. Rain was no barrier. If it snowed, we shoveled and took jumpers. One of the games, called Utah for some reason, was a free-for-all with the losers leaning against the wall of the school as the winner pelted them in the butts with basketballs.

It doesn't sound like fun but it sure was.

Joe and I played baseball in the driveway for hours, sometimes with friends, pretending we were Mantle or Mays, stopping briefly that one time he was catching too close and snared the backswing of my bat full in the face.

Bloodied and fast, he sped screaming down the street with me plodding in pursuit, yelling, "Don't tell." That wasn't necessary because my loyal brother never ratted me out. The fact it was an accident might not have held up under parental interrogation. I was supposed to be the responsible older brother.

We mostly played the traditional sport in season. Football in the fall, hoops year round and in summer, Little League ruled. Joe was an all-star on every team he ever played on. I wasn't Joe. In my first stint as a pitcher at 9, I beaned my best friend, Don Boone. I was quickly shifted to Siberia, also known as right field, where young weak talent is often banished.

Over time I grew in size and but never overwhelming skill in baseball, making the all-stars for the first and only time at 15 as a first baseman on a Senior Little League team.

I proved the doubters right, setting a record by striking out three times in the all-star game.

I fared slightly better in football. I grew from weight football as an 80-pounder at 11 to a linebacker and backup tight end on the St. Mike's championship team in eighth grade. As a freshman at Bishop Egan High School, I tried out for weeks in the legendary football team's version of Parris Island and shortly before the season started I was still waiting for my uniform.

That team had future NFL running back Larry Marshall and future Penn State starting linebacker Gary Gray. There was no room on the roster for the future pro football writer at the local paper.

I was never officially cut. I could catch a pass but not a hint right away.

Being a kid wasn't all fun and dejection. Started working at 12 as a Philadelphia Bulletin paper boy. It was an adventure biking past the teeth of some dogs and trying to ferret out customers hiding in the dark behind curtains while ignoring knocks on the door on collection day.

At 15, Don and I walked to Burger Chef and applied for jobs. Don lasted a couple days. I lasted about five years and made lifelong friends.

I learned a few things that have never left my brain. The Big Shef is spelled with an S and is considered a banquet on a bun, a fact I used in speech class after a classmate touted Gino's excessively. I had planned to talk about a lever after learning all I could about it in an article.

Triggered by the opposition, I tore up that idiocy and crafted the masterful oration on fast food.

The jingle still plays on a mysterious loop in my head:
"For 15 cents,
A nickel and a dime
At Burger Chef
You eat better
Every time
For a nickel and a dime
Will get
French Fried potatoes
Crisp and fresh
Or the greatest 15-cent
Hamburger yet."

One Burger Chef incident later became a bedtime story for my son Dan. Lenny found a giant watermelon in the back, cut it in half, carved out enough to make a helmet, wore it up front and waited on customers as juice rolled down his cheeks past the seeds that had stopped.

Customers were not as amused as the employees.

I had my first romance at Burger Chef. In my exuberance, I foolishly told an Egan classmate her name was Barbara. Cries of Barbie Burger took on a life of their own. Even teachers brought up her name and included the adjective. They were priests and clearly had as much fun as classmates in the alliteration.

When I played in the intramural championship basketball game as a senior, every time I touched the ball I heard the refrain: "Bar-bie Bur-ger, Bar-bie Bur-ger."

She had already dumped me. Truth never got in the way of group degradation at an all-boys school. To be honest it was pretty funny back then. The opposing team had no idea what was going on.

I was mostly a non-descript wise guy in high school. I started school at 5 at Thomas Jefferson public because the Catholic school didn't take kids that young. I imagine it was getting crowded at home, too. My claim to fame in first grade was a non-speaking role as a tree in the Sherwood Forest.

From second to eighth grade I attended St. Mike's. In fifth grade I upped my acting chops, playing a gangster in a play I wrote and they still let me present it. I died melodramatically against the bookcase. At Egan, I was a face in the crowd and a flower on the wall at dances.

For the most part, I soldiered on in anonymity. I did, however, make the local paper, which published almost everything back then, including the details of me breaking my pinkie at 13, while diving into my sister's back at Brook Pool.

Then there was the infamous story on the front page of the Bucks County Courier Times detailing the only incident of note on Mischief Night. A group of ne'er-do-wells marched through Red Cedar Hill, grabbed a dummy off a porch, carried it to Red Cedar Drive, tied it up to a pole, where an archer shot a fiery arrow into its chest.

The police had no suspects. Neither do I in case the statute of limitations is still in place.

Wound up working at that paper for 12 years after graduating from Penn State. Married the smartest and kindest woman I know. We have an extremely talented son who blossomed into a fantastic writer.

I retired as the assistant sports editor after nearly 30 years at the Philadelphia Daily News. My parents are both gone. My dad at 53, mom at 74. I lost two of my sisters, Kathy at 55 and Mary Alice at 60. Lost my brother Fran at 56. You expect parents to die but only a person who has lost a sibling can understand how devastating that is. Imagine losing three.

Adulthood adds serious sadness to the residue of happiness from childhood. I can still be that kid, in my thoughts, however, anytime I want. I can play baseball today with my brother Joe in the driveway of 15 Robin Hill Lane in the Red Cedar Hill section of Levittown.

I just smiled after writing that last sentence.

QUIET MAN – Andrew McQuade joined the Marines at age 16 and was fighting on Guadacanal within a year. He hardly ever spoke of what he saw.

My Father Never Spoke About Fighting in WW II

By DREW McQUADE

(EDITOR'S NOTE: Many parents in our neighborhoods were World War II veterans. We rarely heard their stories. For this book, Drew McQuade shares the story his father never told him. Andrew McQuade represents all the war-weary fathers we knew in our neighborhoods who kept their stories to themselves.)

Memories can be disjointed, yet soothing fragments of reflections when you age, piercing the clutter in your brain with a peaceful pause.

There's a photo of me that forever makes me smile.

I forget about it, then I come across it and just beam when it's found again, a recurring comfort of a child, safely in his dad's arms on a street in front of a home in the Germantown section of Philly.

We are both looking out to the next second and the future beyond that. As I started my life, I had a man of strength and character who had my back as long as he lived.

There are also splices of my life that forever make me a little sad with joy on the fringe.

In 1976, in the middle of my dad's nine-year fight with debilitating leukemia, I took him to the All-Star Game at Veterans Stadium.

The former Marine drill instructor marched in baby steps as I helped him up the ramp to our nose-bleed seats in left field. We laughed like we always did at games, cutting up the people in the stands, shaking our heads at the concessionaires with idiosyncrasies. We cheered when Phillies' Greg Luzinski hit a home run below us even though we didn't know it was gone at first because of the angle.

Figures. We were in left field. It landed in the left-field seats but our vision was such that we only knew that because of the reaction of the fans.

It didn't matter. For a brief moment in time we mostly laughed amid the joy of a relationship that lasts forever.

Three years later, he was gone at 53, much too young to leave his wife and seven kids with faint memories that sweep in and out with no set schedule.

He was a man of few words and lyrics. When he sang it was either the first line of the Marine hymn, "From the Halls of Montezuma," or an obscure line from a strange diddy, "When Frances dances with me, holy gee."

There was little to sing about for years. After endless blood transfusions and innumerable hospital stays you could merely touch his arm and a purple blotch would appear a short time later. He had an incalculable strength forged as a kid.

I learned a lot about his time in the service after he was gone. As a kid, I was too much involved with myself. He did mention once that he landed on an island in the South Pacific and seconds later half his unit was dead. End of conversation.

He didn't expound on that horrible image. He never talked specifically about his time on Guadalcanal or Peleliu Island where his courage led to a medal for bravery from the Secretary of the Navy and a letter from the Commandant of the Marine Corps expressing his "deep appreciation" of his "devotion to duty and gallant action."

To this day I can't fathom being a teenager, running on a tightrope in hell.

"All who survived would long remember the horror they would rather forget," said former Marine and author Eugene B. Sledge about the first Marine division on Peleliu.

We had heard our dad was 17 when he enlisted in the Marines. I found out later he was actually 16. My grandparents signed a paper backing up that lie so he could do his duty. At 17, I couldn't decide what to say to a girl as I dead-flowered against a wall. At 17, my dad was making life and death decisions in the muck and mire of an island cemetery.

The McQuade siblings knew their dad as the rock. Yes, he was a war hero and a drill instructor in the Korean conflict during the second part of his Marine stint, but he wore his toughness beneath an armor of quiet contemplation.

I can't ever remember him curse. He taught through example to be kind.

Growing up in Levittown was heaven. Having supportive parents left us free to absorb the positives. My dad was the unpaid but willing driver down the shore and to so many activities for such a brood of kids.

He was a manager and treasurer of the Levittown Pacific Little League for decades. After my parents used the GI bill to help buy a house in the Red Cedar Hill section of Levittown, my dad graduated from La Salle college night school with a degree in accounting. He later became a CPA and never stopped putting figures onto ledgers.

I can't really hide from my batting average for the Joe's Pizza Little League team or my much-improved numbers on the Senior Little League team my father also managed. I still have the books my dad kept.

There is accounting for good and bad stats. My dad saw to that.

He was stereotypically conservative for an accountant, rarely letting his former red hair down. One exception involved my goofy request at the start of our 18-game Senior Little League season.

"If we win our first 17 games, can I pitch the 18th?" I asked.

Knowing full well I beaned my best friend in my first and only pitching stint, five years earlier as a 10-year-old, my dad still answered, "Sure."

A man of his word, I was on the mound for the 18th game of a season.

I was a first baseman. When I was permitted to impersonate a pitcher, I threw hard but straight down the middle. Once opposing batters shook off the fear, they swung to delight.

It seemed a risky move. My dad knew we had five really good pitchers. One of them replaced me in the third inning. It was a perfect season in so many ways.

My dad knew what to do and when to do it. He had a job once at a place that delivered dry cleaning and at the end of the first week he had to attend a meeting where everyone was forced to stand and sing the company theme song. He turned and walked out of that place forever.

One of my favorite memories is a fuzzy scene on the sideline of a basketball game at the Chester Y, where Penn State Delaware County played its games.

He drove 50 miles to stand awkwardly on the wall next to a giant congo drum at the end of a line of hip-shaking dancers who backed my team by rocking the building with soulful chants.

No one went to those games, except a CPA and conga line members. A disinterested Y employee might glance as he walked by.

Someone had to keep the stats, "my" stats. My dad was a cool, faithful, reliable guy with a dry sense of humor, who loved his wife, kids and numbers.

Without visible protestation he attended activities where kids twirled batons, played drums and bugles, did boys and girls scouting, played baseball, basketball, football and even bowled.

If he could guide a platoon during war, he could handle seven manageable kids. Most of them, anyway.

We all have flaws. We also possess the same pieces of my dad's makeup. A respect for others and a kindness we know we should always have in our pockets.

I was first to the hospital the day he died. Saw him struggle to breathe as he went past on the gurney. Somehow he hung on until all his kids could get there. It took hours.

We said goodbye, then put our memories in that special place that opens up whenever we want.

BUDDING MUSICIAN – Bob Keiger tried his hand at football but ended up playing trumpet in the Pennsbury High School band.

CHAPTER 7
Idyllic Life Shielded Us from Some Harsh Realities

By BOB KEIGER

I was born in Trenton, NJ and lived there until I was 5. In 1952 my parents bought a home in Levittown (Tanglewood Lane in the Thornridge section). My first memory was shortly after we moved in. I was sitting on the front "lawn" eagerly anticipating my father coming home after work. As his car approached I jumped up and waved enthusiastically only to watch him drive right by our house and pull into the driveway of another house two doors away. Every fourth house in Levittown was identical. I was crushed. And that was likely the most disappointing thing I ever had to confront growing up in Levittown.

To say this was an idyllic environment is an understatement. I went to schools that were never more than a mile or so from my home from third grade through 10th grade. All the dads went to work in the morning and most all moms did not work outside the home. They were there when you got back home from school. But as it turned out, as comforting and safe and protective and fun as it was, it also shielded me from understanding a lot of important things going on all around me. In hindsight I would not trade it, though. I still have life-long friends from growing up there — in fact many are among the closest and best friends I have ever made. And indeed that is priceless.

I knew nearly every kid in Thornridge and quite a few from the adjacent neighborhoods. We all went to school together and through sixth grade we all walked there — protected en route by the outdoor AAA school safeties at intersections and once we were inside the school by the hallway safeties. And if you were a safety, you had better show up at your post on time, adorned with your brilliant, gleaming white safety harness and badge otherwise you might get a demerit from the captain. As a safety you also had another duty — just before lunch you had to retrieve the milk from the school refrigerator and bring it to the cafeteria. And that job led to getting to eat early. And for your 35 cents you got the hot-out-of-the-oven first serving of hot dogs (all-time favorite), baked beans and stewed tomatoes followed by the beautifully wrapped frozen chocolate, vanilla and strawberry block of ice cream. Life was good.

My mother lived in that Levittown house for 68 years until she died in March 2020 at nearly 104. Her next door neighbor was still the same neighbor from when she first moved in and the neighbor next door to her (and coincidentally the house my dad drove to) is also still there after all those years.

My maternal grandmother and grandfather emigrated from Italy in the early 1900s. They lived in Morrisville for most of their lives. My mom was the oldest of five children. We would have dinner at my grandparents' house at least once a week and the entire family would generally be there on Saturday or Sunday night and every holiday we had a family picnic at one of my aunt's or uncle's homes. Neighborhood and family bonds were extremely strong. That kind of stability just doesn't seem to occur very much anymore.

We were the Baby Boomer generation — there were probably 30-40 kids my age within a 10-minute walk of my house. After school we all played outside — either in the neighborhood or at the school playground. But we had to be home before the street lights came on. Everyone had a bike, all the boys played football or baseball and through elementary school the girls were generally absent from play except as we got to the sixth grade when birthday parties with spin the bottle and post office were discovered. That was a game- and life-changer.

Organized sports revolved around baseball and football along with basketball and bowling. No soccer, lacrosse or hockey. I had a 1956 Mickey Mantle baseball card that made this great sound when you clothes-pinned it to the spokes of your bike — just guessing that sound is worth maybe $10,000 today. Did I mention it was a great sound? 1960 was the year our area's Levittown American team won the Little League World Series in Williamsport. Half the players lived within a few streets of me and I went to school with them every day — many remain friends even now. I also remember being in a bowling league on Saturday mornings — I was even allowed to ride my bike to the Fairlanes bowling alley but I had to walk my bike across Newportville Road because of the traffic. On Saturday mornings the lanes were completely filled with kids. There was a lot of time we all spent in the company of friends.

Music was also an important part of my life. Fortunately, the Pennsbury school system had a remarkable music program. I was encouraged to play the trumpet in fifth grade and I stayed with it through high school graduation. Our high school Stage Band amazingly got to play on the Tonight Show and at the 1964 Newport Jazz Festival. And again the marching band, stage band and concert band created many opportunities to spend lots of time with friends.

But there were other things happening during this time from which I was sheltered. In 1957, the Myers family moved to Levittown. They were the first Black family in all of Levittown. While I remember that happening, I also recall that it was not talked about at all in front of kids. Sometimes when I walked up to a group of adults talking, I had a sense that the Myers' were the subject of the conversation, but the talk ceased whenever we were near. It was indeed a protective, white environment in Levittown. While I can't recall any regrets growing up then, it is clear now that this extremely happy childhood also had its downside as well. I felt like I had been completely shielded from the struggles and agony of Black folks just trying to live their lives. I don't recall any conversations either at home or in school about racial injustice. It wasn't until near the end of high school in 1965 and Bloody Sunday on the Edmund Pettus Bridge that I really began to become aware of the serious racial issues in this country. Since then I have continued to grow to own not only my own complacence and responsibility but also the responsibility of my ancestors.

Levittown was one of the first totally planned communities. Churches, schools and recreation were all designed as central to adjacent sections. Each section had a name — Thornridge (where I lived), Birch Valley, Vermillion Hills, Magnolia Hill, North Park, Elderberry, and Pinewood in our part of Levittown, which also sprawled over into Bristol and Middletown Townships. All the street names in each section began with the same first letter as your section. That made it easier for you, the police and the fire department to find your house.

Our summer life centered around the community pool. William Levitt built a pool and baseball field for every 10 or so neighborhoods. You either walked to the pool or rode your bike — we never had to be driven anywhere. And this was yet another place to be with your friends.

As we moved through junior and senior high, our schools also sponsored weekly dances during the school year called canteens. Girls mostly fast-danced with other girls (except for the really cool guys who led the way in breaking the gender barrier). Pretty much all the guys talked with one another on the sidelines while the girls were dancing with one another. But it was the slow dances that brought most of the boys onto the floor, encouraged by the delightful prospect of getting really close to some girls.

The most important rite of passage was getting your driver's license. The prospect of that freedom was giddying. But back then most families had a single car so advance planning for car use was mandatory and never guaranteed. At the same time your driver's license also became a central point of negotiation and punishment hanging over your head like the Sword of Damocles. The day I got my license, I went to visit a girl, stayed past my required allotment of time, came home a little late (my words and recollection) and immediately had that precious "ticket to ride" yanked out of my wallet (which by the way I had just finished making in shop class). And that leads immediately to shop class — what kid today knows anything like this? Outside of our regular classes we were assigned three supplemental classes — 12 weeks or so each. We all had music and art but the girls went to home economics and the boys went to shop. They made the cookies and we made the containers for them. I recall having wood shop, metal shop and even making a leather pocket book (in addition to my wallet) for my mom. As I recall that pocketbook remained safely stored and protected from deterioration by any harmful light or weather in the back of my mom's closet.

Then there was the telephone. A Levittown house was maybe 800-1,000 square feet — at most you might need two telephones. One on the wall near the front door and kitchen and one in your parents' bedroom. Needless to say, neither of those spaces was conducive to sweet talking a girl for any length of time. How humiliating to have to sit or lay down on your parents' bed to ask for a date.

Some people see the Great Wall of China as an important historical structure. But it pales in comparison to the section of US Route 1 — the original Post Road extending from New England to Key West — where it separates Levittown/Fairless Hills from Yardley/Lower Makefield. And yes — I have exaggerated its importance. But, it was the geographical and political boundary that separated the east side of the Pennsbury school district from the west side. School populations were exploding in the Baby Boom generation and it was a challenge for the school system to keep up with their classroom needs. In seventh grade, ALL students from both sides of Route 1 were together in the same building. That ended in eighth grade, when a new school (Medill Bair Junior High School) was built on the east side of Route 1 and the Pennsbury students on the east side were separated from the Pennsbury students on the west side. That lasted until 11th grade when friendships were reclaimed as we all attended Senior High. While there were clearly some socio-economic differences between the east and west sides of Route 1, when all the kids got back together with former school friends, it again became a unified group with friendships reclaimed through the years of separation. It was like we all came home — and we demonstrated you can do it again. As an aside, our graduating class of 1965 was the last senior graduating class from the OLD high school building. The following year they opened a NEW high school building — one with no windows that somewhat resembles a prison.

In 1965, the Pennsbury High School Senior Prom was held in the school gym as it had been for years. And to this day, that tradition has endured — it is still in the school gym with decorations constructed by the students. In 2004, the prom was awarded "Best Prom" by *Reader's Digest* as part of their "America's 100 Best" feature. I think the stability and longevity of such a tradition of something as simple as a high school prom, speaks loudly to the bonds that have been created and sustained and strengthened through all these years. It is truly amazing.

My generation grew up at the beginning of the commercialization of children — McDonalds, Davy Crockett hats, Matchbox cars, Trix cereal, MAD magazine and the Barbie doll didn't get their starts until the mid to late 1950s. The TV show Disneyland, Captain Kangaroo and The Mickey Mouse Club arrived in the mid-1950s. Annette Funicello was my first TV crush! The Supreme Court did not rule school segregation unconstitutional until 1954. And the mid-1950s saw Congress investigating links between TV and violence and juvenile delinquency and the publication of that historic best seller "Why Johnny Can't Read." Our "screen time" pretty much started in the 1950s. In 1950, there were about five million TV sets in homes and by 1960 there were about 55 million.

So what was it that created these long standing relationships? Was this time the 'golden age of childhood?' Was it just a simpler place and time? Was it really a safer place to grow up? I'll leave that to others to figure out. In the meantime, I will keep track of all my long-time friends and meet them at the next reunion and share a beer with them at the Boot. Cheers.

RIDING HIGH – Lisa Dubinsky got to ride a little pony when she was very young.

CHAPTER 8

Levittown Wasn't Quite Perfect!

By LISA J. DUBINSKY

My grandparents, and probably a good portion of other original Levittown kids' grandparents, were immigrants. Mine came from Eastern Europe – Czechoslovakia, Austria, and Hungry. My best friends' grandparents were Italian, Polish, and Irish. Some of our parents were bilingual, having learned their parents' native tongue growing up, as their parents learned to speak English. Most of our Dads were WW II veterans, and their plan was the typical American Dream – home ownership for their family. Developer William Levitt made that dream possible – for *some* folks!

In the early 1950s, Levittown was growing by leaps and bounds into an enormous mega development. The town was not your typical town with a courthouse and a main street. Instead, it was split into a multitude of "sections" so that visitors and locals alike would have a prayer of being able to find someone's house. Our family's first Levittown home was in the "North Park" section, and it was there, between the ages of 2 and 12, that I made my fondest childhood memories.

I learned to skate and swim and most importantly, ride a two-wheel bike on the very safe sidewalks of North Park Drive. Once I had mastered that, and at a pretty young age of 6 or 7, I was even permitted to ride my bike around "the block." The block was actually a huge loop passing several side streets. My folks were not worried since the trip did not require me to actually cross any of those side streets. I often stopped to visit with friends whose houses were along the way. I could head out in an easterly (or westerly) direction, be gone for quite some time, and because of the layout of the loop, return home in the same direction in which I had started.

We lived right at the entrance to North Park. My first school, Manor Elementary, was within eyeshot of our house, and there was a crossing guard to safely spirit us kids across the busy Penn Valley Road. My parents could literally watch me from the time I left the house, until I entered the school's front door. They could have, but they didn't need to, and I doubt they did. The 1950s were a different time, and Levittown felt super safe for all of us. The school was a great hangout space, especially in the summer. I picked blackberries from the bushes that grew by the creek next to the school. I made art projects and took field trips with the summer recreation program there. I also practiced my baton and marching skills with the "Levittown Twirlers" in the school parking lot.

As a kid growing up in Levittown, I could not have had a happier existence. My world was probably less than a square mile, yet it had everything I could possibly have hoped for as a kid. There was no Disney World yet to bug our parents to take us to, but I had church fairs, a community pool I could ride my bike to every day, and an enormous expanse of green space in which to play.

Because Levitt had prohibited fences of any kind, our large backyards merged into a huge parklike setting, complete with fruit trees that had planted behind each house. If the fruit was ripe nobody minded if you snagged a peach, a pear, or an apple from one of their trees. Our house even had a bonus grapevine. The grapes were sweet on the inside but the skins were tough. The neighborhood kids knew they were welcome to squeeze the grapes and suck out the juicy pulp, but they had better not leave the skins on the driveway or they would hear about it from my Dad.

We were all welcome to play wherever we wanted — and we did — in everyone's yard, whether or not they even had kids. We played dodgeball, tag, kick the can, and my particular favorite — "murder-in-the-dark" — a game we invented to discourage younger siblings from pestering us to join in. In our carports we hung blankets from clotheslines to create "curtains" and put on talent shows – singing and dancing atop picnic tables which doubled as our "stage." When it rained, we colored and crafted, played with our Barbies and chalked up those same carports.

No one ever had to tell us to go outside and play — if anything our parents had a hard time dragging us in for meals. No matter whose front yard or back yard or carport we were playing in, we all knew when our Moms called it was time to wrap it up and go home. However, we usually played deaf prompting our Dads to come out and give a loud whistle. Somehow, we all recognized our *own* Dad's signal and knew that now we had better hightail it home. When we got a bit older, we were spared the indignities of being called like cattle, and were actually allowed to stay out until the street lights came on.

Growing up in Levittown, we rode our bikes constantly, but always on the wide sidewalks, which the developer had the foresight to provide. Unfortunately, one of his other designs could have potentially created a problem for folks later in life. What we kids called "creeks" located in the various sections, were actually drainage ditches that were often filled with standing water, and in the summer loaded with mosquitoes. Our townships would periodically "fog" the area with chemicals intended to kill the nasty critters. To us kids it was a form of entertainment. We would jump on our bikes, and while remaining safely on those wide sidewalks, pedal as fast as we could to ride in the cloud of DDT. Neither we nor our parents knew at the time of the potential danger of this practice.

It was a very different time. If you got in trouble in school, you got in even more trouble when you got home. Parents did not challenge the teachers and your friend's parents did not hesitate to correct you if you got out of line at their house. If you were lucky, they just corrected you and didn't mention it to your parents.

In fourth grade my parents switched me to parochial school. The exciting part was that I got to ride a bus to school, which made my two best friends jealous. I loved my years at Saint Joe's. Thanks to the patience of the Bernadine nuns, I became a decent speller, developed a life-long love of reading, and mastered some award-winning penmanship. I got to make even more friends, play intramural sports, and be named captain of the cheerleaders. I thought I was really cool until the basketball coach pulled me aside to advise that I was cheering for the opponents. And it took me quite a few years to realize that when I sang in 8th grade Glee Club, I actually couldn't sing! I was flattered when the handsome male director told me that "the pretty tall girls stand in the back and sing very softly." For that whole year I believed I was a pretty, soft singer - when in fact I was just tall!

In November of my eighth-grade year, my family moved from my beloved North Park to a bigger house in the Vermilion Hills section of Levittown. I was disappointed to leave my friends and the only home I could remember. And I was upset to learn that there would be no more fun bus rides to school because the new house would be within walking distance. I took my last bus ride on moving day morning, armed with directions how to find my way home. It was on that very same day that I saw a nun cry. I remember Sister telling us to "Stop working; we need to pray because President Kennedy has been shot." I remember feeling sad and scared for him, but also worried that I might forget and get on the bus again. That afternoon I found my way to my new home, and was met by my mother in tears. Boxes and furniture were everywhere. My Dad had obviously made hooking up the TV a priority so they could follow the news. Looking back, November 22, 1963 signaled the end of my blissful Levittown childhood. I had just turned 13 a week before, but on that day, I had to face the first of life's very real tragedies. Up until then I had been not even been allowed to watch "The Untouchables" on TV because my parents felt it was too scary for me.

The very next summer I met a really nice boy-next-door type who actually lived down the street. He too had grown up in Levittown. Time flew by for us – high school, college, Air Force, marriage, moving, jobs, baby and eventually back home, where we bought our first house in the Lakeside section. We noticed that although much had changed over the years, much had remained the same, and we were thrilled to give our young son a Levittown childhood, similar to the one we both had enjoyed. Then one day tragedy struck and I found myself a young widow. My just turned 14-year-old son most likely left behind his blissful Levittown childhood around the same age that I had, some 20 years earlier.

Fast forward many more years. I am remarried and living in Virginia, where jobs had taken us, and where we decided to retire. When I finally had some free-time I was able to pursue my passions. For years I worked as a Court Appointed Special Advocate for abused and neglected children and volunteered at a furniture bank. Now I feed the homeless and volunteer in the memory unit of a nursing home. The most important thing I do is to advocate for racial reconciliation and for social justice. However, I once was too embarrassed to tell my fellow advocates my terrible truth. A truth that even I had been ignorant of most of my life. I had lived in Levittown, PA — where the developer and the lending institutions had made home ownership possible for returning World War II vets . . . but only if they were white! When I finally confessed my secret to my Sisters of color, they were kind. They forgave my ignorance, and they schooled me on red lining and on systemic racism. Sadly, they had known about Levittown's covenants years before I did.

I spent the months of May through September 2020 (in the midst of a pandemic) back in Levittown caring for my ailing mother, in the same house she moved into on that tragic November day.

Despite her failing heart, she was sharp as tack and tuned in to the times. She was still the Mom that all my friends had wanted — kind, compassionate, and generous as always. And I discovered during our many conversations that my 97-year-old mother had also become an advocate. She was particularly sympathetic to the immigrants at the border, because as she put it: "For goodness sakes, my parents were immigrants too; they only wanted a better life for their family!" To my surprise I discovered that my mother was well-versed in social justice, climate change, and was an even more diligent recycler than I was.

I just had to ask mother as she neared the end of her days. Did she know about Levittown's covenants back in the 50's? She said she knew that fences were not permitted, and you weren't allowed to hang wash outside on a Sunday because that was what the neighbors talked about. She claimed she had not read the contract's small print and said she did not know whether or not my Dad had. They had never discussed it. They were just young and jumped at the opportunity to own a reasonably priced new home with no money down. She told me she learned of Levittown's illegal covenant, barring sale or rental to anyone other than whites, when a young Black family moved into another part of town in 1957. She said she was horrified, saddened, and embarrassed by the way that innocent family was bullied and threatened. I had to ask her, "Would you have moved here if you had known *everything* ahead of time?" She thought for a moment and replied, "Levittown had so much to offer our family. I think I might still have come, but I'd like to think that I would have fought to change things!" You and me both, Mom, you and me both!

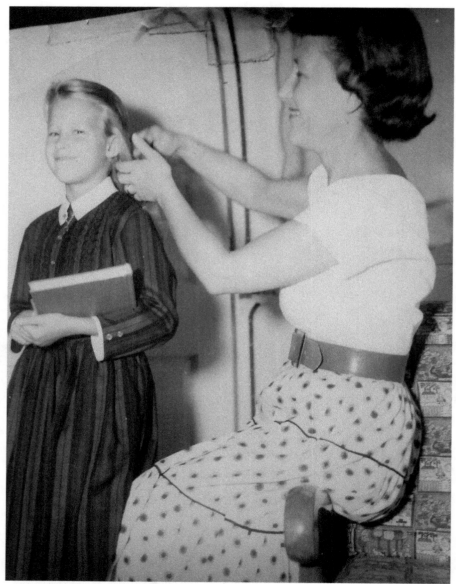

MOM'S JOB – Denise Queen's mother, Eileen, brushes out her hair in a photo that appeared in the Levittown Times.

CHAPTER 9

The School Bus Stopped for Denise Queen

By DENISE QUEEN

My family came to Fairless Hills in 1952, just as the new community was being built. My father, Frank Queen, transferred from Donora Works in western Pennsylvania to the new Fairless Works Steel Mill in the southeastern corner of the state.

At first, we stayed in a house on Andover Road, I believe. It was temporary housing because our home on the corner of Olds Boulevard and Austin Drive wasn't finished yet.

I attended kindergarten, first grade and maybe even second grade in the sample houses on Trenton Road. The schools weren't ready yet as the community slowly developed in those early years, building homes and schools one section at a time. In those early years, all the land below Trenton Road was still wetlands, in its natural state.

My first best friend was Arlene Bowling. We met in fourth grade. Her family moved to Fairless Hills from Roanoke, Virginia. I loved her southern accent. Arlene lived on Trenton Road, not far from my family's home. We rode our bikes all over, and didn't come home until dinnertime.

Our claim to fame, in our minds, was when we took the train to Philadelphia, and went to see the American Bandstand show that played on Philadelphia television every weekday. Dick Clark was the host, and the guest when we visited was Patsy Cline. We were disappointed, because country music wasn't a hit with teenagers in the north.

My bus stop conveniently was located on the edge of our home's property. I went to Oxford Valley Elementary School. Our bus driver was the most lovable man, George Baker. We walked down Olds Boulevard to school from seventh through 10th grade. It was less than a mile to William Penn Junior High and Medill Bair. For our junior and senior years of high school, we took a bus from Fairless Hills to Yardley, only about five miles in all. We made so many new friends during those years.

In those simpler times, it was always exciting to ride your bike behind the truck spraying a fog to kill mosquitos. Not the smartest thing to do, what did we know back then? The Oscar Meyer Weiner truck was another hit. The driver was usually a little person, he threw us plastic Weiner Whistles that we would love to use.

Winters we went ice skating on Lake Caroline. Our dads would turn on the headlights so we could skate at night. Summers were spent at the Fairless Hills swimming pool. When we were old enough the best job was to work at the pool. I worked in the Concession Stand. Dick Spickler, Sandy Dunn, Jimmy Wysor and Bernie Hentz were lifeguards.

My biggest memory that still makes me laugh came when Dick and Jimmy thought it would be great fun to lock me in the walk-in refrigerator. However, when they decided to let me out, I was sitting on a milk can that we used to make frozen custard, just waiting for them to let me out. Dick loves to tell this story to this day.

We had the Fairless Hills Shopping Center as the center of our social life. It included the Fairlanes Bowling Alley in addition to the Pool, all located within 100 yards of each other.

We always seemed to have something to do when we weren't going to school. The Hugh Carcella Union Hall on Trenton Road regularly held dances. In the summer, we couldn't wait for the carnivals to come. There were two. One was held at Bishop Egan High School across from the Levittown Shopping Center. The other was at St. Francis Cabrini on the other side of Fairless Hills.

We also had a chance to roller skate at Skate A-Rama in Levittown, and movies on Saturday at the Towne Theater, where you hoped your boyfriend would show up, too. Of course, these were still the days when your parents drove you. My mother, Eileen, often hosted card games for her friends at our home. I was fortunate to have wonderful parents.

My first car was a 1957 Chevy, Aqua and White, huge! My father made me learn to drive a stick shift, so I would be able to drive anything. He also showed me how to change a tire, which I have never done, and never will. We did the same thing with our children, with an exception for the tire changing.

And of course, who doesn't remember Friday night Canteen? You attended the school you went to, in my case the first was William Penn or as Arlene reminded me the first was in sixth grade at Oxford Valley. I think it cost 10 cents to get in, or maybe the cokes were 10 cents. Everybody went, the boys on one side of the gym, the girls on the other. Teachers chaperoned, and I think a teacher acted as DJ. I had to be on my deathbed to miss canteen.

I attended Rider College after high school, rooming with my Pennsbury classmate, Gail Zoerner. I went to college despite my Mom telling me girls don't need to go to college. So, as part of the Medical Secretary degree, I needed to take a general math course that was pretty much all algebra. I never took algebra in high school. My teacher saw that I would struggle with math, and recommended that I take a general math course rather than algebra. Needless to say, I did not fare well with my Rider math course.

I got a job at U. S. Steel in the Rolling Division the summer after my first semester. I was enrolled in a two-year Medical Secretary program at Rider. When I saw how much money I was making at the Steel Mill, I quit school. So much for math! That was a bit of a regret, but I met my husband Jeff. We will be married 54 years, have four children, and eight grandchildren. Guess who keeps the books! Not so bad at math after all.

I was always surrounded by friends. My bridesmaids were Arlene Bowling, Gail Zoerner, Betsy Marozzi and Elaine Karpowitz, all good friends from Pennsbury and Lower Bucks County, where we grew up and created lifelong friendships. Jeff and I now split time between our homes in the Poconos and Idaho. Life is good.

GOING DANCING – Best friends Denise Queen and Arlene Bowling posed for a picture before heading to Canteen on a Friday night many years ago.

CHAPTER 10

Bowling Family Came North from Virginia

By ARLENE BOWLING

My Dad, Luther Bowling, came to Pennsylvania from Roanoke, Virginia to work on the construction of the new U.S. Steel plant, Fairless Works, as an electrician out of the Trenton Local. Dad rented a room in Trenton while working on the job in Morrisville. After a while and much coaxing, he talked my Mom into moving the family, temporarily, until the job was completed. When the job was completed, we kids; brother Adrian, class of 1957; sister Juleece, class of 1959; sister Joy, class of 1962; brother James and myself, class of 1965, did not want to leave during the school year.

When we first came to Pennsylvania, we rented a mobile home on Rt. 13 in Morrisville (moving to three different properties). Fallsington Elementary is where I started my education with Pennsbury Schools. I attended classes there from first through third grades.

Our family moved to Fairless Hills when I was in the fourth grade. That is when I met my new best friend, Denise Queen. One thing that stands out in remembering those days was the wonderful deli bologna on Mrs. Queen's homemade bread with Gulden's mustard! We only had yellow mustard at my house.

I remember Friday night canteens at Oxford Valley Elementary. (Can't recall if we had it in fifth grade or just sixth grade.) John and Dottie Vislosky were our chaperones. They were such a wonderful couple! Denise and I visited their home quite often since their house was just down the street from both Denise and myself.

Sixth grade was when some of the students from Levittown attended classes at Oxford Valley. We then moved on to William Penn for the seventh and eighth grades, where we were integrated with some of the students from Lower Makefield, H Section of Fairless Hills and more Levittowners.

Ninth grade moved us into Medill Bair for ninth and tenth grades. I remember running for Student Council Treasurer against the very popular Eddie McGurk!! What was I thinking!!

Then on to Pennsbury Senior High School where we were reunited with the students from Charles Boehm. This was a time to rekindle friendships that began in seventh grade.

Looking back, some memories linger in my mind all these years later. Remembering the summer days at the Fairless Hills pool, riding our bikes, walking, walking . . . and more walking, Landy's Restaurant and its tasty crushed cherry sundaes, roller skating at Rollerama, Fairlanes bowling alley, Levittown's Elderberry Pool, winter ice skating on Lake Caroline and the lake in North Park, and bonfires.

Each step along the way from Fallsington Elementary to Pennsbury Senior High School brought new friends, new teachers, and new experiences. We loved every step along the journey.

READY FOR FUN – Before heading out on the Delaware River to waterski, Ron White, Bill Sheehy, Rich White, Betsy White, Jeanann White, Rob White and Sally White gathered around their boat.

CHAPTER 11

The Adventures of Yardley's 'River Rats'

By BILL SHEEHY

For children growing up in the '50s and '60s Yardley was Mayberry. The boys were Opie, the cops were Barney Fife, everybody had an Aunt Bee and our dads were Andy Griffith. As a small town, the Borough kids shared a common experience of life on Main Street. But, for a few, there was a magical slice of Americana within this small community. An era that came and went in a span of a few years during the 1960's, most residents were unaware of the carefree rascals who traversed the Delaware River between the Scudder Falls Bridge and the Railroad Trestle. The events and challenges of those blissful days has indelibly shaped my life, I believe for the better.

The River Rats were a group of freewheeling boys who would be considered feral by today's standards. By 1961, we had speed boats that filled our summer days with endless adventures. The five boats ranged from 14 to 16 feet long with 25-40 horsepower outboard engines. The Captains of this flotilla were the White Boys: Robbie ('63), Richie ('64), Ronnie ('66); Billy Sheehy ('65'), Calvin Day ('65), John Hoffman ('63), and Skippy Garlits ('62). No adults were involved whatsoever. We bought, sanded, painted, varnished, maintained the engines and fueled our boats with money we earned.

Ronnie and I learned to waterski together from Skippy's flat bottom skiff with a 25 HP engine. It was April of 1960 and the water was so cold our lips were blue. Always the better athlete, Ronnie, age 11 (Pennsbury High School and University of Pennsylvania wrestling) got up after several attempts. I remember Seventeen as my number of tries. I was age 12. Our bodies shivered as we felt the cold wind, but it did not matter. We had learned to waterski and owned the bragging rights thereto.

That evening Mom asked us how our day went. Beaming, I regaled the family with my triumph. "Skippy taught us how to waterski." They congratulated me without a trace of alarm for the dangerous elements involved. I suspect that if today someone spotted two boys in the fast-moving current without a safety jacket, struggling in the freezing water, they would call 9-1-1. The parents would be explaining to a judge in Doylestown a reason not to charge them with "Child Endangerment."

Once I got a taste of boating, I negotiated a deal with Dad. If I earned half the money, he would give me the balance. By age 13 I had saved enough to buy a $350 boat. Unaware the trailer was not included; it was unceremoniously dropped off in our front yard. With the help of Ronnie and two sisters, we lifted the boat onto two wagons attached to a rope and dragged it to the boat ramp. It was the start of four fun-filled years.

All of us worked multiple jobs. We caddied at Yardley Country Club, bussed tables at the Yardley Inn, cut grass and shoveled snow. We never asked our parents for money or advice. These were our boats and none of their business.

By late afternoon, jobs complete, we grounded our boats south of Afton Avenue and wadded to shore carrying a five-gallon tank. The Esso station provided $0.32 per gasoline, candy bars and cold cokes. Next door was a Hot Dog joint with an open flamed grill proudly called Dirty Bill's (now Charcoal Steaks & Things). We were good until nightfall.

Over the years we became good slalom skiers. Richie and Calvin were the best at spraying the water up to eight feet with their bodies almost horizontal with one hand on the rope, the other skimming the water. On sharp turns, usually between Sue Smith's (Class '65) dock and the Railroad Trestle, we would pull as hard as possible using the centrifugal force to get us parallel to the boat. Then, as the slack increased, we had sunk slowly into the water awaiting the inevitable jolt of the towline. A wise guy driver could turn inward exacerbating the dilemma. That cruel action would practically yank your arms out of the socket. Yes, we were all wise guys, but also revengeful drivers.

Sue Smith's family dock was a focal point for waterskiing because it was in deep water. Once we became confident, we naturally wanted to show off to Sue's attractive friends who were frequently sunbathing there. We would stand on the dock with the ski leg hanging over the edge, the towline wrapped in a loop on the dock. With the boat positioned a few feet from the dock we would yell: "Hit it!" As the line drew taut, the skier jumped off the dock with the boat almost at full speed. Suspended in air, the challenge was to land on one ski. Any misjudgment was an easy way to look foolish, the results were mixed. This recklessly macho behavior can only be explained by raging hormones.

Since it is easier to get up on skis sitting on a dock, we taught new skiers from there. When you have a boat, friends want to tube or ski. Helping someone learn to waterski was a daunting task. Typically, someone would get up for 25-50 yards then fall. They struggled as the detached skis drifted in the current. A novice has no idea how to put them on or become positioned in deep water. This required us to help by holding the beginner in place, skis up. When the line became taut, command the driver to accelerate. It is a process that requires patience and kind encouragement. But when they finally feel the thrill of "standing on water," it was as much fun for the River Rats as our pupils.

For friends who did not have the desire or patience to learn how to waterski, a fun alternative was tubing. We took this to an art. Guests were on our turf and we controlled the outcome. The equipment used depended upon the expectations of the rider. For the non-adventurous, we used a truck tube with the rider sitting upright to assure a pleasant but uneventful experience.

The opposite of "Mr. Nice Guy" treatment was given to those who sought an unexpected thrill or with a trace of hubris. Using a small aluminum saucer typically used for snow sledding we started out slowly with wide turns as they adjusted to the sensation of racing atop the water on their abdomen. With confidence established, we would push the throttle to full speed and sharply turn in a tight circle. This accelerated the rider to the outside and guaranteed they would eventually hit the wake at maximum speed. The high velocity catapulted the unsuspecting victim airborne for several seconds followed by violently sending their body skipping across the water with arms and legs flailing in every direction. Yes, it was hysterical. No, it never got old.

After watching a waterskiing exhibit on TV at Cypress Gardens, I wanted to learn how to waterski backwards and to do 360 degree turns. I bought a pair of "trick" skis in 1963 and Ronnie and I spent hours learning how to pivot. Without a rudder, the falls are harder because your feet fly sideways. Eventually we could spin several times in each direction and ski backwards on one leg. Our final gimmick was to ski double with the trick skier backwards on the shorter line crossing under the slalom skier with raised arms. A feat nobody cared about except us-that was enough.

In the early spring, the water was high enough to take our boats northbound to New Hope. The barrier was Scudder Falls a few hundred yards north of I-95. Hitting a rock caused the shear pin to break off which immediately stops the propeller. Replacing it was routine. The threat is losing control of the boat in choppy water and crashing into the rocks splitting the wooden hull. After many unsuccessful attempts, we found the solution: There was a narrow passageway in the concrete wall and the water gushed extremely fast. Initially we approached at half speed; the result was to hit bottom as we drew too much water. Undeterred, we decided to throttle at maximum speed with someone hanging over the bow. This higher plane in the transom gave us enough clearance...it worked. From there, it was smooth sailing. Eventually, we "jumped the Falls" while towing a skier. In retrospect, that was daredevil even by the standards of a testosterone-driven teenager.

Every July 4th Lambertville held a water show. It involved boat races and a waterskiing competition. Ronnie and I cajoled the sponsor, who serviced our boats, to allow us to do a "Water Show" on our trick skis. We were accustomed to smooth, glass like conditions. The choppy water from the boat races made it impossible to turn around without catching a ski in the wake. We fell multiple times. Eventually, it calmed down just enough for Ronnie to do a few 360s while I skied slalom alongside awkwardly holding on for dear life. Although we were disappointing not to do our "patented" backward cross-over trick, it was a day to cherish.

The last time I used the boat was the week before high school graduation in June 1965. Suffering from a severe case of senioritis, a group of classmates organized a "Skip School Day" to go waterskiing. My partners in crime were: John Lutz, Jeff Konover, Dan Roup, Ross Burgess and Bob Larson. Since I couldn't drive the boat in front our house, we arranged to go to the Penn Warner Quarry in Tullytown — a little smelly, but deep.

I told my parents that I needed to pull the boat out of the river because I was selling it. Then, parked it behind the garage out of sight. Danny Roup had a boat hitch on his dad's station wagon. I told Mom I'd be late because I was playing golf after school and Danny would drive me home, then boarded the bus. After signing in at Home Room, Danny and I drove to the back road behind the house. We physically towed the boat across the lawn and hitched it up. Off we went.

My dad, uncharacteristically late for work, was walking to his car and spotted our boat being hauled away. He rushed to call the Yardley Police. A cop shows up and he completed a full report for the "stolen" boat (I'm laughing as I write).

We all rendezvous. Armed with a case of beer and cooler full of hoagies, we have a blast. It was a cloudless day and everybody skied. I had an opportunity to exhibit my waterskiing tricks. It is perfect. So far.

We deposit the boat back behind the garage and Danny drops me off in the driveway. Arriving home, Mom anxiously tells me she need to discuss something important but wants to wait until Dad gets home so they can tell me together. In her motherly tone, she then notes that I am badly sunburned but thankfully doesn't press the issue. After all, I was "golfing". I suspect the school had discovered our truancy. It is perplexing because Mom is upset, but her consternation was not directed at me. What is going on?

When Dad came home, we convened in the living room. To paraphrase:

Dad: "Billy, I have some bad news. Somebody stole your boat."

I'm obviously stunned by this twist of events. I thought I was in the clear. I needed to stall and think of plausible alibi.

Me: "Oh yeah, how do you know? What happened?"

Dad: "I saw the thieves towing it down the back road. I filed a report with the Yardley police, hopefully they'll find it. I'm so sorry, Billy."

The gig is up! How do I possibly explain that the boat has magically reappeared behind the garage? Checkmate!

Me: "Nobody stole the boat. I used it skiing today."

Mom, looking confused said, "That's strange, the boat was gone this morning, not after school.

I looked at Mom and sighed, "I played hooky today. Danny and I were towing the boat away. It is now behind the garage."

Long pause.

Dad sat back in his chair and exhaled. "Well, that explains everything."

My parents were so relieved that the boat was not stolen they lost focus over their obligatory feigned outrage that I skipped school. I suppose, compared to all my shenanigans over the years, this was too low on the "Bad Boy" scale to raise any wrath.

I am not sure how, but we all got caught. That week, I explained my role in the caper to Assistant Principal, Mr. Barnhart without repercussions; sold the boat for more than I paid; moved to Lower Makefield; went to the Senior Party with Nancy Ent, my face peeling from sunburn, and graduated. Later, I taught Nancy to waterski using Ronnie's boat. She was my favorite student. I had not spoken to Calvin Day about our mutual experiences until the 50th High School Reunion. We laughed together, sharing a memorable and unrepeatable slice of Yardley history.

WINTER GAMES – Dave Anderson, top left, plays in the snow with Tom Piper, Roger Anderson, Pete Glen and Mark Anderson.

CHAPTER 12
My Deep Morrisville Roots

By DAVE ANDERSON

O ur Ferry Road neighborhood in Lower Makefield Township near the Morrisville border had a lot of boys around my age. In our area there were the three Glen boys who lived six houses down Ferry Road from us. Classmate Jim Glen was born less than two months before me and our mothers often chatted as they walked us in our strollers.

One corner of the Glen's yard was pie-shaped, making it an ideal layout for baseball games. When we started breaking windows in their house (which was in left-center field) with hardballs, we switched to softballs. And when we started breaking windows with softballs, we switched to wiffleballs. I paid for my share of broken windows.

Along the first base line was a hedge. On the other side of the hedge was where our classmate Myles Fisher lived from sixth through 10th grade and then moved to Iowa. Up the street a few houses was the home of the Piper brothers — Cole (Class of '64) and Tom (Class of '68). Then further up the street was our house. Across the lane was Doug Cook's (Class of '64) house. Further west on Ferry and also behind us on Arborlea Avenue there were more boys around my age.

We socialized through pickup games of baseball, basketball, football, ice hockey, card games, flipping baseball cards, flashlight tag, sleep overs, riding bikes, building go-carts and something called Mumblety-peg. Then there were the things we did which were outside the box ... most notably when a bunch of us decided to go into the woods to saw down trees while perched on the higher limbs. There were enough trees that they only fell to about a 45-degree angle and lodged in another tree. This was lots of fun until we got up in a tree that had a bee's nest near the bottom. Those who were sawing got stung by the swarm first and as the rest of us scattered down, we also got stung, some a lot more than others.

We had also played Cowboys and Indians in those same woods in many a younger day.

To make a little money, we put on a roller-skating show, a circus, and then made and sold candles one holiday season. I then became a paperboy for the Trenton Evening Times, typically making $15 a week with tips ... good money when candy bars and a pack of baseball cards were

5 cents. In spring of my junior year I went to work at Clover Leaf Dairy in Morrisville after school for 85 cents an hour. I mostly made ice cream cones. That job came with a free dinner … usually a cheeseburger, fries and cherry coke. Then I got the call from Cole Piper to go to western New York at Chautauqua Institution to work for the summer of 1964. Generations of his family had spent summers there since the early 1900s. And up there I was making one dollar an hour and typically worked 10 hours or more per day. Paying my own room and board, I still came home with about $500. And it was a great summer with water skiing in Lake Chautauqua and dancing almost nightly in the high school club . . . the first summer of the Beatles.

In addition to spending so much of my time with the neighborhood boys, I also had all my Anderson aunts, uncles and cousins in Morrisville … one male cousin seven years older and four female cousins closer to my age. We also had our Anderson grandparents in Morrisville. There were get-togethers for holidays and picnics in the summer. On Thanksgiving there was always the Morrisville vs. Bristol traditional football game with cousins as cheerleaders telling how the game went that year. In my grandparents' house, temporary tables for the kids to eat at extended into the living room. Same on New Year's Day. We kids played a game before dinner we called huckle-buckle-beanstalk which involved hiding a small object while others kept their eyes closed. When you saw the object, you had to sit down and say huckle-buckle-beanstalk. Whoever found the object got to hide it next.

My mother and father both graduated from Morrisville High School. Mom got her diploma in 1940, one year ahead of Dad. Mom and Dad performed on stage in high school and Dad was also a cheerleader. Both sang very well. Dad went to Scott Field in Illinois to become a B-24 radioman who eventually flew 35 missions over Germany after D-Day. He then came home and married Mom. Dad still had Army time to serve so they lived on a couple of Army/Air Force bases in the South before returning home.

Dad grew up a block off of N. Pennsylvania Avenue (where we attended the annual Memorial Day parade – always on May 30 before 1971 – my birthday) in Morrisville. No school on my birthday, but a parade, bikes with red, white and blue all over, and baseball cards making noise in the bike spokes were plentiful.

Morrisville is named after Robert Morris, who financed a significant part of the Revolutionary War. The house he lived in – Summerseat — was later occupied by another Declaration of Independence signer, George Clymer. Summerseat is now a museum and sits adjacent to the old Morrisville High School, which burned down when we were kids.

When Mom was about to graduate from eighth grade at Edgewood School, she was given the choice of attending either Yardley or Morrisville High School. A tour of each was given. As she knew a lot more of the kids in Morrisville, she chose her hometown school.

Mom and Dad both attended Morrisville Presbyterian Church before and after it moved to its present location. My Dad's ashes are at the present location and my Mom's will go there also. Born in 1923, we're fortunate to still have her with us.

The house my Mom, her two brothers, myself and my two brothers all grew up in was only a few blocks away from the line separating us from Morrisville Borough. That location had everything to do with my life's course. The house on West Ferry Road is on a double lot on the corner where it meets Cherry Lane. It was built in 1923/24 by my maternal grandfather and grandmother . . . Emily and Norman Conover. Emily volunteered with the Red Cross during WWI. Her main job was to inform families of those who had died.

Norman Conover's mother, Annie, lived in that house until her death in 1944. She was born before the Civil War and had come from Lambertville to that house when it was built, as did my Conover grandparents, my Mom and her two brothers. Norman died nine years before I was born, but I feel I know him well as he kept a daily journal from 1924 until 1930. He served in England during WWI in the 228th aero Squadron and married my grandmother after the war. He came home on the Mauritania, running mate of the Lusitania, which had been sunk by a German U-boat in 1915 off the coast of Ireland, killing nearly 1200 passengers and crew members.

I was a pallbearer for my other three grandparents . . . and attended my paternal grandfather's 100th birthday celebration in 1993. We called him Pop. Pop (Bill Anderson) was on the Board of Education in Morrisville and for a while he was President of that Board. He once told me that he was all for Morrisville and Pennsbury school systems merging, but that he could never get enough Board members to agree. My grandmother Ethel Anderson (Mom) and Pop were also the treasurers at Morrisville Presbyterian Church. My dad would be there to help them count the money right after Sunday services. In my teens while I was trying to complete my coin collections, I would be there with them looking for the ones I was missing. During my senior year at Pennsbury I was President of the junior deacons at church where our main function was to help pass the collection plates during the services.

When we were about to have our 50th PHS reunion, I did a bit of research on the history of Pennsbury. The system was formed in 1948 as the state was encouraging the merger of smaller local systems. Of the places that were asked to join, Morrisville and Tullytown did not. Tullytown eventually joined in 1964. Morrisville has attempted to join in recent years, but Pennsbury has declined the offer.

When the Delaware River flooded in 1955, my parents walked me down Ferry Road to where the water was, above the canal where we fished. This was a pretty steep slope. Riding down Ferry Road on a sled towards the river was a wonderfully long and fast ride in the days before salted roads became associated with snow storms. When I was a bit older, I started riding my bike to the Morrisville swimming pool which was adjacent to the Delaware River in an area known as the Island.

I earned my Junior Lifesaving status in that pool and spent many a summer day there swimming with friends from Ferry Road and other places around town. The Little League ballpark was close by with the outfield wall painted in letters that proudly reminded people that Morrisville had won the 1955 Little League World Series. The team's star player, Dick Hart, went on to play in the Milwaukee Braves' farm system and then switched sports, becoming a starting offensive guard for the NFL's Philadelphia Eagles.

In ninth grade at Charles Boehm, I went out for wrestling and did OK, but turned my attention to gymnastics and more specifically the side horse in 10th grade. Small change it seemed at the time, but the chain of events at Pennsbury was to determine much of my path through life. Our coach, Russ Neiger, took us to the Naval Academy and to West Point to compete against the first-year classes' gymnastics teams there. We beat the cadets at West Point. It was on those trips that I decided I wanted to attend an Academy. I landed at the Coast Guard Academy where I also competed on the side horse for four years and was co-captain of the gymnastics team in my last year.

Then came 26 more years in the Coast Guard. Had I lived my childhood a few blocks to the south, I would have attended Morrisville High School. In those days Morrisville High did not have a gymnastics team, nor did it have an honors math program. Those two programs at Pennsbury were instrumental in my being accepted to the Coast Guard Academy. And the honors math program at Pennsbury was largely duplicated during my first year at the Academy, which allowed me to concentrate on other subjects, especially two that had me struggling.

When I have had the pleasure of talking to history majors at Pennsbury in recent years around Veterans Day, I make certain to let them know how the school's Honors program helped me in college. Hopefully that will enhance their understanding of the value of the education they can receive at Pennsbury.

The highlight of my life began in my senior year at Pennsbury when my wife, Janet, and I started dating. Over the past 57 years, we have enjoyed a wonderful life together. We have seven grandchildren from daughters Lynn and Julie and our son, John. We still greatly enjoy getting on the road to see our family. Indeed, for the past 25 years we have been together with our children and grandchildren at a resort near Disney World which has greatly facilitated the grandchildren knowing their cousins who live in different states.

My grandparents and their generation are all gone now, except for Mom. She and Dad moved out of the Ferry Road house in 1988 and over to Holland, PA into a new townhouse. Dad died there in 1997 and a few years later Mom moved into an apartment at Attleboro Retirement Center in Langhorne where she still resides in her own apartment.

My oldest Anderson cousin moved out towards Charles Boehm Junior High. His sister died about a decade ago. The cousin closest my age, Carol, lives outside Trenton and her two sisters live in different parts of Maryland.

After my Dad's funeral service Carol commented how we didn't see much of the family any more. I decided to start an annual Anderson Christmas dinner at a restaurant which will have been doing since 1997, except for a COVID year and one snow storm year. So, we have now seen my cousin's kids and grandkids grow up and fly from their nests. Carol's oldest son lives near us and we see them a few times a year. One of my brothers lives near Bucks County Community College where his wife teaches. He is also one of the drivers at Attleboro and another retirement center in Newton. My other brother went to college in Ohio and still lives in Ohio. I have been taking Mom out there for the first weekend in December since 2006. We are there when his clan goes out and cuts down their Christmas trees at a place that has a horse drawn wagon for carrying your tree back to where it is put into the net for placement on top of their cars.

Janet and I have been in Reading since I retired from the Coast Guard in 1995. But memories of Morrisville live on in my heart.

FAMILY AFFAIR – Chuck, Bruce and Neil (Bud) Cleveland kept a good eye on their sister Lynda during the early days in Fairless Hills.

CHAPTER 13
The Magnetic Qualities of Steel

By LYNDA CLEVELAND MILES

Most of us who are sharing stories of moving to the brand new town of Fairless Hills have one thing in common. Our families were drawn there by the newly constructed mill built by the United States Steel Corporation, aka US Steel.

The move was one of several new beginnings for me during that time. After losing my Mom when I was three, I was blessed with a new one when my Dad remarried a year later and we moved from Western Pennsylvania to Ohio.

Shortly after, my Dad was given an opportunity to work as a supervisor in the coke division of the Fairless Works. Off we went on an eastward journey. In 1951, our house and the entire town was nowhere near completion so we were lodged temporarily at the Hotel Hildebrecht in Trenton, N.J.

For me, this period was similar to living in a Disney fairy tale. The hotel was quite posh in those days and home to many inaugural balls and celebrity guests. I had a fabulous time there. Hotel dwelling was forever to be one of my favorite pastimes. I don't remember how long we stayed there but since I wasn't really living in a fairy tale, eventually the time came for us to leave.

Our permanent home was still not completed, so, while we waited, we were moved into a house that was ready for occupancy. While living at 115 Andover Road, I attended kindergarten at a house on Trenton Road. Mrs. Spickler was a fine teacher and school was going splendidly until my brother Bruce and I both contracted whooping cough and had to be quarantined in a bedroom.

My memory doesn't afford me the knowledge of a timeline for this period but we grew bored and resorted to some mischievous behavior. My oldest brother, Chuck, was in the Air Force fighting the war in Korea. We found his red Mario Lanza vinyl records in a closet and thought it would be cool to melt them over the vaporizer.

Also, during this time, I remember certain streets were still dirt and sidewalks were wooden planks. Church service was held in a barn near where St. Frances Cabrini is now located.

Finally, in 1953, our new home was ready to inhabit. 731 Edgemont Rd was located on a dead end and beyond that was a huge playground. The house was surrounded by woods. What a great place to play in those early days. I met my first best friend, Patty Hamilton, who lived close by. We spent our days designing chalk houses in the street and playing in them, swimming in her pool, running through my sprinkler, and playing cowgirl on the small hills at the playground.

We lived near the Fairless Hills Model Homes on Route 1 and would have a grand time playing house in those, as well. Our first Halloween in the house was a vivid fun memory. It seemed as if the entire town took part in a Halloween parade and then gathered in the parking lot of the afore-mentioned Model Homes for music, cider, and snacks. I'm not sure why but this never happened again.

Spending mornings at the Pennsbury summer playground/camp was a highlight of the summer. From 9-12 we would learn a variety of crafts, songs, and fun games. Occasionally, there would be special theme days. The "crazy hat" contest was a great memory. My favorite counselor, Rosalie Doetsch, met and began dating my brother, Neil (Bud). I enjoyed some special treatment during that period because of my connection and thoroughly enjoyed it! They eventually married and in November, 2020, celebrated their 64th anniversary.

While the town was still expanding via church and schools, those of us who attended Catholic school, were bused to schools in nearby towns. My brother Bruce attended Holy Trinity in Morris-ville while I attended first and second grade at Our Lady of Grace in Penndel. In 1953, St Frances Cabrini School was established. This was my third and fourth grade venue. I acquired several awe-some friends during this time. Recess was especially fun since there was a small creek located at the border of the school yard and my best friends and I would play some imaginative games there.

For fifth grade, I was sent away to an all-girls Catholic Boarding School in Westchester County, N.Y. and remained there until high school graduation in 1965. Sadly, I lost touch with all my pa-rochial school friends from Cabrini but I still remember them all with great fondness.

Days in summer were also spent swimming in the new Fairless Hills Pool. As a young girl, I looked forward to the time when I would be old enough to attend the dances that were held there every Saturday night but when that time came, they had ceased to be. We couldn't wait for Field Day each summer which was held on the property behind the pool. This consisted of various races, contests, and food. We also had fun for a few years at the Fireman's Carnival by the banks of Lake Caroline, complete with fireworks over the water. The lake was an attraction during the winter also. Meeting friends for an afternoon of ice skating was one of my happiest memories from that time.

Of course the new Fairless Hills Shopping Center was also a huge part of the early days. We all loved shopping at Meyers Stationary Store and having fries and cherry cokes at Landy's. I bought my first record at Stahl's Camera Shop and my first Lime Rickey (non-alcoholic of course) at Yards Department Store soda fountain. Yards was the Company Store, I believe. It was located in the spot that Big C would later occupy.

There were a few unique aspects of growing up in a town that was built for the US Steel work-ers. The influx of so many families moving to the area caused a housing shortage so, creating it was a necessary solution. US Steel Corporation arranged to have the houses built and financed them, thus making it a "company town." My family life revolved around a monthly paycheck and three work shifts at the mill. Most of us had but one car in those days so when my Dad was working second shift (4 pm-12am), we were usually obliged to stay home. Often, friends' parents would take turns chipping in to drive us to movies or parties. I remember well the long 54-day strike in 1952 because my Dad, being in management, had to stay at the Mill during this period.

In those early first days of our new town, I never realized just how unique it was. Its namesake, Benjamin Fairless, said he felt it was the most impressive thing about the steel plant. It was a totally different kind of "company town," where individuals could own their own home for $1,000 down and around $85 a month. Eventually, it was thought of as a development in the suburbs and owners from every walk of life would move there but it was the magnetic properties of steel that caused its birth.

MAT MEN – Tom DiIorio, top left in second row, wrestled for Medill Bair with a bunch of his friends. Front row, left to right: John Dishaw, Cliff Owles, Joe Reiley, Julian Kalkstein, John Friemann. Second row: Coach Jesse DeEsch, Tom DiIorio, Joe Fioravanti, John Coutts, Dick Spickler, Charlie Stevenson, Mike Wilson and Coach Harry Gallagher.

CHAPTER 14

Glory Days Over
But The Memories Remain

By TERRY NAU

"Glory Days well they'll pass you by
Glory Days in the wink of a young girl's eye
Glory days, Glory Days."

— *Bruce Springsteen*

While Tom DiIorio was growing up in the North Park section of Levittown during the 1950s and 1960s, he made many friends. An extroverted youngster who passed easily from one group to another, Tom served as a magnet for unsuspecting students every September as the school year began anew. He accumulated friends from Levittown, Fairless Hills and Yardley, winning them over with a funny joke or his uncanny knack for creating mischief. In a huge high school class of 725 people, Tom stood out as an energetic soul who wasn't trying to make the Honor Roll, or go to college. Tom just wanted to have fun.

One of Tom's earliest memories was watching older kids from his neighborhood excel in sports, including a big, strapping fellow named Vern Von Sydow, who became a big football star for Pennsbury High.

"I remember Vern," Tom admitted. "He went on to play football at the Naval Academy. We looked up to those older kids. My sister Diane graduated in 1960 from Pennsbury and married Vaughn Ward, who was a star pitcher for the varsity team. Sometimes I would go to his American Legion games in the summer with my sister, over at Island Park in Morrisville. I got to see some really good baseball players like Dick Hart and Danny Napoleon. Dick Hart hit a ball out of the legion field into the Little League field. That was quite a shot in those days."

Lower Bucks County was a feeding ground for young athletes in the 1950s and 1960s. Dick Hart would sign a professional baseball contract but eventually switched to football and became a starting offensive guard for the Philadelphia Eagles. Danny Napoleon signed with the New York Mets and played briefly in the big leagues. Morrisville won the Little League World Series in 1955 with Dick Hart leading the way. Levittown American would capture the same tournament in 1960 with many of Tom's classmates and friends playing key roles.

"Levittown American was my league," DiIorio said. "We had a really good all-star team in 1959 when I was 12 years old. But we didn't have the pitching that the 1960 team had with Joe Mormello, Jules Kalkstein and Tucker Schwartz."

A sociable youngster, DiIorio found several lifetime friends living not far from his family home on New Pond Lane.

"We moved to Levittown in 1954," he recalled. "My father, Thomas DiIorio Sr., was from Langhorne and my mom, Anna, came from Bristol. Dad worked for the Lower Bucks Water Authority. When we moved in, I became friends with Eddie McGurk, who lived five houses up the street from me. Betsy Marozzi lived across the street. Jack Mack lived a couple streets away. We also had friends from the Elderberry section who we first met at Penn Valley Elementary School – Harry Mervin, John Friemann and Joe Reiley. Dwight Kerr lived on Primrose Lane in the Pinewood section. I became good friends with Ronnie Clunn in seventh grade."

These youngsters had a knack for "busting chops" at an early age.

"I remember in fourth grade when Harry first came to class at Penn Valley," Tom said. "When he walked into our classroom, Eddie started laughing. The teacher wanted to know what was so funny and Eddie told him, 'We finally have a kid in our class who is fatter than me!' That was the way we got along. Right from the start, we kidded each other."

Mervin and McGurk would always be two of the bigger kids in school as they grew up, sharing an unspoken bond. Eddie was even more of an extrovert than his friend Tom, and became one of the most popular students in the Class of 1965 at Pennsbury.

"I loved growing up in Levittown," DiIorio continued. "Sports were a big deal. Some of us played football for the Am Vets team in the Pop Warner League," he said. "Jack Mack played quarterback. Dwight Kerr and Dave Neeld were our halfbacks. I played split end. This was a league based on your weight. I was between 100 and 115 pounds in those days. The bigger kids in our neighborhood, like Eddie McGurk, could not play for our team.

"Those were the 'Glory Days' for me. Because I could run fast, the coach installed running plays for me, reverses and end-arounds. I also returned punts and kickoffs. One time, I scored five touchdowns in a game. We got to play tournament games in North Carolina, Florida and Connecticut."

DiIorio focused on Pop Warner ball while his classmates tried out for junior high and middle school football teams. When Tom finally went out for the varsity in 11th grade, he couldn't get any playing time.

"I think it was political," he said. "I hadn't played in the system and the coaches didn't want to give me a chance to show what I could do. I decided to focus on wrestling instead."

Tommy never took school too seriously.

"My mother asked me one time how come Jack Mack comes home with all those books under his arm and I never have any books," he said, chuckling at the memory. "I told Mom that I had study hall at school and did all my homework before I came home."

DiIorio was one of the most popular kids in school despite his aversion to classroom work.

"We weren't bad kids," he admitted. "We liked to bust chops and play practical jokes on our friends. Some people thought I was a hoodlum because I hung out with a couple of tough guys but I just felt like I got along with everyone. People invited me to parties because I was a good dancer."

It was not uncommon to see DiIorio jitter-bugging with Ginger Lane, Roberta Eisenstein and other female classmates during co-ed portions of physical education class. The 1960s were the early days of American Bandstand on Philadelphia television. Dancing was almost as big as playing sports or getting good grades in school.

And his skills on the dance floor certainly dazzled the girls.

"Tommy learned to dance because his sister and her friends used to watch 'Bandstand' at Tom's house and he was the only boy so he had to dance with all of them," said Liza Hamill, one of his classmates. "It made Tom FAMOUS. When he was going out with a girl named Karen – can't remember her last name – they'd start dancing at Canteen and everyone would just stand around in awe. All the other boys would be standing in the corner and there would be Tom and Karen, dancing like they knew what they were doing."

Tom married young and became a father very quickly. He is a great grandfather now who proudly posts pictures of his children, their children and their children's children on Facebook. Great grand dad is a pretty cool guy, still, but there is a sadness to him because of the friends he has lost. Joe Reiley was the first. He died in his middle years from a rare disease that put him in a wheelchair in his 40s. Tom and his friends always made a point to visit Joe until the end.

Ed McGurk succumbed in 2019 from cancer linked to Agent Orange exposure in Vietnam. Tom, Harry Mervin and John Friemann always visited when Eddie needed cheering up. Harry lost his battle to cancer in April 2021. Tommy was with him two days before Harry died. He has always made it his business to keep in touch, to visit his friends, and offer support.

"I feel like I am the glue that holds our group of friends together," he admitted a decade ago over a beer at Puss N Boots, the local tavern for Pennsbury alums. And slowly, his group is getting smaller. Even Tom has battled health woes of his own. But he soldiers on, missing his friends, showing open emotion at their funerals, and holding on to the remaining friendships that still guide his days.

Glory Days are gone but their memories remain. Tom might even dance to the tune at his next high school reunion.

FRIENDS FOREVER – Tom DiIorio, Ed McGurk and Harry Mervin had a lot of fun over the years.

TOO CUTE – Looks like some parents got Linda Secor, Larry Nau, Pam Burke and Wayne Marsden to sit still together for a quick photo in the mid-1950s. They were all neighbors on Cardiff Road in Fairless Hills.

CHAPTER 15

We Grew Up During Simpler Times

By WAYNE MARSDEN

In late 1954, my father, Ted Marsden, left McKeesport, PA and drove 300 miles east for work at the United States Steel plant in Morrisville. He stayed at first in a boarding house in Trenton. Many years later, I recall hearing the story of Dad talking to my mother, Dorothy, over the phone, telling her that the houses in Fairless Hills all looked the same. Mom told him, "Well, just buy one."

Dad chose a house at 244 Cardiff Road because it had a fire hydrant that would identify which house was his. Mom packed everything, including her three young children and climbed aboard a greyhound bus headed east. My older brother Larry was 11 years old at the time. Sister Donna was nine and I was five years old.

I made quick friends with Larry Nau, who lived next door. We were both the same age and the youngest children in our respective families. Larry and I were kindred spirits. Our mothers watched us for a while and would jokingly refer to us as "gasoline and matches." We could get into trouble almost without trying.

There was always something new to explore in our neighborhood, especially in the woods that remained on Sterling's Farm, just 150 yards from our front door. We built forts and tree houses, played ball or picked strawberries from the untended farm fields that bordered the neighborhood. We participated in apple fights in the orchards that still stood behind Collingswood Road. We also had a few BB gun wars in those woods. If we were feeling brave, we crossed Route 1 and ventured into the Five Mile Woods. You could get lost in those trees!

We often slept out in the Falls Township Recreation field, one street over from Cardiff. Our group of friends included Steve Secor, Denny and Jordy Brown, Bob Seanor, Larry and myself. We were the younger kids in a neighborhood full of teenagers who were a few years older than us. Kids paired up according to age groups. The sleep outs could be fun, and a little dangerous. Sometimes we climbed the water tower, which was 180 feet to the very top. Once you got to the top, you could see miles in every direction. Occasionally, we would leave our tents at 1 in the morning and ride our bikes to the Fairless Hills swimming pool, climb the fence and take a late night swim.

BEST FRIENDS – Wayne Marsden and Larry Nau remained close until Larry's death in 2012.

We played midget football in an organized league. Our team was called the Danherst Eagles. Danherst was the company that helped build Fairless Hills. We lost to Kiwanis in the championship game but our coaches — Mr. Jackson and Mr. Arnold — took us to Greenwood Dairies on Route 1 in Langhorne for ice cream to cheer us up. Greenwood Dairies had the best ice cream and the biggest scoops in all of Lower Bucks County.

Times were so much simpler then. When we were 11 or 12 years old, it was nothing to take our 22-calibre rifles, sling them across our shoulders, and shoot rats at the dump behind the Hi Hat Diner on Route 1. What would people think today if they saw kids walking down the street with rifles? Like I said, we grew up in simpler times.

In 1964, Larry's parents took us to the World's Fair in New York. We left from their deer hunting cabin located in the Pocono Mountains, not far from a little town called Marshall's Creek.

Entering New York City at the age of 14, we began to realize there was a big world outside the small one we occupied in Fairless Hills.

As we turned 16 and earned driver's licenses, our friends began to travel in different directions. We started dating girls and driving the family car when allowed by our parents. We began to dream of owning our first car. I have fond memories of dances at Hugh Carcella Union Hall down on Trenton Road. We also went to dances at the Edgely Fire Hall in Bristol. On the way home, we stopped at Landy's Restaurant or a pizza shop in the Fairless Hills Shopping Center.

We cruised the Levittown Parkway, hitting all of the hamburger joints – Gino's on Route 13, the Red Barn in Morrisville and the Steer Inn on Route 1. The fairs held at St. Michael's Church and at the Fairless Hills Volunteer Firefighters Hall also were a lot of fun.

Looking back, thinking of when we were young, makes me feel emotional about those sweet memories. Like a lot of youngsters, we did not realize those were the good old days. We were lucky to grow up in such simple times.

I cannot express enough the gratitude I feel for my parents, who made a courageous decision to uproot their lives and move across the state, away from their own home, to give their children a better chance at life.

TWILIGHT TIME – Tim Nau shared a moment with his mother, Olive, late in her life. Olive and Dan Nau made sure their four sons all got college educations.

CHAPTER 16

Two Major Events Shaped Our Parents' Lives

By TIM NAU

Our family moved to Fairless Hills in December 1952 from the Pittsburgh suburb of Munhall. Our father, Dan Nau, worked at a huge United States Steel mill that was located next door in Homestead. Our mother, Olive, and Dad had lived in Pittsburgh all their lives. Dad was born in 1915 and Mom was born in 1918. They had lived through The Great Depression and World War II. Their first son, Dan, was born at the beginning of WW II, and I was born in 1945, around the end of the war. Terry was born in 1947, and Larry in 1950.

Living through those two major events in American history had a major impact on our parents, and we saw glimpses of this as we grew older. Dad regretted that his essential worker status in the steel industry prevented him from serving in the war. Because of the Depression he had to quit school after eighth grade to work and help his family out financially. Mom was a superior student in high school but, like many women of her time, she wasn't in a financial situation to go to college. Both of our parents saw the importance of their children having a good education. They saw moving to Fairless Hills as a good opportunity for them but, more importantly, as a better opportunity for their children.

It must have been a scary thing for Mom and Dad to move 300 miles away from their family and friends, but many people from all over the state were moving to this area where a new mill was being built, which would eventually employ over 8,000 people at its peak.

I was in the middle of second grade when we moved, and I have some vivid memories of what Fairless Hills was like at that time. Schools were being built in Fairless Hills, but I finished second grade in a house along Trenton Road that bordered what would become the Fairless Hills Golf Course. By third grade Oxford Valley Elementary School was finished and we started the 1953-54 school year there.

Fairless Hills was about half-built then and it seemed everything on the lower side of Trenton Road was plowed over and muddy at that time of year. There were no houses built yet below Trenton Road. Students went to high school in Fallsington. Elementary and junior high schools were being built at a rapid pace in Levittown, Fairless Hills, Lower Makefield and Yardley. Many of the teachers we had were also new to the area.

Most of our teachers, being in their twenties, related very well to their students and made school fun. I remember my fifth and sixth grade teacher, Miss Novick, especially well. During lunch period she would come out with us and pitch softball as we played other classes at our school. Miss Novick was loved by her students. A good friend of mine in those classes, Tom Klein, and I continued to visit her until we were in our thirties. She made that much of an impression on us.

Lower Bucks County proved to be a great community for young families. Many of the parents had friends and family members who moved to the area from Pittsburgh and other parts of the state. Since all the kids were new to the area, everyone was eager to make friends. I have friends that I met in elementary school who remain in my life to this day, and it has almost been 70 years since we first met.

In that era parents didn't have to worry as much about the safety issues as they do now. During the school year we would get up, have breakfast as a family and go off to school. When we got home we would have a snack, then go out and play with friends. Around 6 p.m. we would come home for supper, then play until dark. We even tried to fit in some homework when we could!

The summers were great. With no school, after breakfast we just played all day. We had an old farm near us and we would go over there and eat apples, strawberries and other kinds of fruit. Within a short time after we arrived in Fairless, a playground was built next to our homes. After we woke up each day, we would go there and play baseball in the spring and summer, and football in the fall. We got kids together through word of mouth or by arranging times to meet over the house phone.

Our community, led by parents who were still fairly young themselves, had many community activities. When we were old enough for Little League, each spring the players would march in their uniforms from where Olds Boulevard met Austin Drive all the way to the end of Austin Drive where the field was located. It was over a one-mile walk and many parents lined the streets to encourage us. Parents who worked as volunteers built what turned out to be one of the nicest Little League fields in Pennsylvania for us.

The Fairless Hills Swimming Pool was built within a few years and became another fun place to hang out. Each year parents would organize a "Field Day" for the families where they planned all kinds of competitive races, prepared food for everyone, and held a dance at the end of the day for their sons and daughters.

Another thing I remember was getting together with a few neighborhood friends and riding our bikes for a mile and a half to the Fairless Hills Shopping Center to spend a nickel to buy a coke that was served in a white cone type of cup. You just don't see soda served that way anymore. (Or kids riding their bikes that far for a quick snack!)

As I mentioned earlier, my father regretted that he had to work as an essential worker rather than join the military and participate in the war effort, but he was so proud that three of his sons served in the Army and Air Force during the Vietnam War era. Education was another thing that was extremely important to our parents; and with their support and help, all four boys graduated from college.

As I am writing this, it makes me think how much things have changed over the years. Computers and innovations like Facebook have changed how our children and grandchildren spend their time. The Covid-19 virus forced us to avoid gathering in groups for almost all of 2020 and well into 2021. It has changed young peoples' socialization with its impact on schools and their opportunities to get together socially. It makes one wonder what lasting effects that will have on today's young people.

Tom Brokaw wrote "The Greatest Generation" about things our parents experienced in their lives, including World War II and the Great Depression. We experienced Vietnam and the political unrest of the 1960s which seems to be happening again in this current time period. But, as a nation, we have overcome many difficult times in the past, and I believe our children and grandchildren will do that, too. It says a lot about our country and the people who live here. I know I feel so fortunate to have grown up in our era, having two wonderful parents, terrific brothers, being lucky enough to have married my wonderful wife, Joyce, and blessed with two sons, Chris and Dan. The friends I have been fortunate enough to have all these years have added so much to my life.

I feel my friends and family and I appreciate the fact that we were so fortunate to have grown up when we did in this wonderful part of Bucks County.

FAIRLESS HILLS POOL – Jim Wysor served as a lifeguard at this popular summer hangout for several of his teenage years.

CHAPTER 17

*Swimming Pool
One of the Top Attractions*

By JIM WYSOR

My parents, Bill and Virginia Wysor, moved me and my two older brothers, Tom and Jack, from the Shadyside neighborhood in Pittsburgh to 205 Blough Court, Fairless Hills in November of 1953. I was six years old and in first grade. My dad was a chemical engineer working for Duquesne Steel in Pittsburgh. I suspect my parents were taking a risk moving their family from one end of Pennsylvania to the other, but this move was also a chance to provide a better life for all of our family.

Fairless Hills was a community of modest ranch homes built exclusively for steel workers. It was named after the President of United States Steel, a man named Benjamin Fairless. It is said he briefly lived in one of the first Fairless Hills homes, located at the corner of Oxford Valley Road and Trenton Road. It looked like all of the other homes except that it was constructed entirely from steel instead of wood.

I was initially enrolled at Oxford Valley Elementary School. I had to ride a bus to school which was a new and somewhat scary experience. I only attended Oxford Valley until April of '54 when all of the kids from the "H" section of Fairless Hills were transferred to Fairless View Elementary School, a new school that had been under construction when we first arrived in town. No more busing, as this school was only a couple of blocks from my house. Fairless View had an immense grass area surrounding the school which doubled as a place for our outdoor gym classes and for recess. On weekends and during the summer, it was a place for sandlot baseball and football. This is what we did when we weren't playing organized sports. It was also the place of choice where the neighborhood gang would gather and flip baseball cards, play stickball and at night, play flashlight tag.

Organized sports were initially limited to Fairless Hills Little League and in the fall, midget football. I played both sports and both of my teams were sponsored by Danherst Corporation, the company that built Fairless Hills. What many of us will remember about this company is the big yellow barn, the farmhouse and the out buildings that housed Danherst Corp. It was situated on a big hill just off Olds Boulevard and across the street from a field that would become the site of the Fairless Hills Babe Ruth league and the American Legion baseball team. My Babe Ruth team was sponsored by the Fairlanes bowling alley. Some of my teammates and opponents were my brother Tom, Jimmy Barnes, Bob Keen, Butch (John) Coutts, Ronnie Buckley, Jim Ghrist and Alan Maxwell (all PHS graduates). The one significant player I remember from my American Legion days was a catcher by the name of Rich Logue. He was probably one of the better baseball players in Lower Bucks County. He had an arm like a rifle and was a powerful hitter.

A story about growing up in Fairless Hills in the 50's and 60's would be incomplete without mentioning the FH swimming pool. This was a large swimming complex, reportedly one of the largest in the country at the time. The pool was 50 meters long by 25 yards wide with a 15 square yard diving well that had two diving boards, one a three-meter and the other a one-meter. I remember finally working up my nerve to jump off the "high" board. From the end of the diving board, it looked like it was at least 50 feet to the water! There was an expansive deck surrounding the pool and a separate baby pool, concession area and a shaded area.

As young kids, and later as teenagers, we spent a significant portion of our summers at the pool. This swimming pool was unique among pools in that it was constructed entirely of steel. We lived in a US Steel community, so it should come as no surprise that our pool was made from steel. I worked in the concession stand in 1965 with my high school classmate, Denise Queen. On really hot days, Denise could be found in the walk-in cooler, sitting on a milk can reading a book. I became a lifeguard the following year and worked there summers through my senior year in college. We had great group of lifeguards including Dick Spickler, Sandy Dunn, Jay Sozanski, Pete Farley, and his sister, Regina, and Don Becker, (who was an outstanding running back for Bishop Egan). The Fairless Hills pool is still in operation today.

Every August, just outside the fenced in pool, Fairless Hills Field Days were held. I don't recall who sponsored this event but it was a day of races, games and concessions. I remember running the 50-yard dash, the sack race and the three-legged race and if you won you got these cool trophies as well as free tickets for the concessions. At dusk, an amazing fireworks display on Lake Caroline concluded the day's events! We had a show much like today's firework displays, but there was also a ground display. What I remember most were the pinwheels and two cowboys shooting at one another using Roman Candles as their weapons. The evening ended with the American flag displayed in fireworks.

My Fairless Hills home was a small three-bedroom ranch built on a concrete slab like all of the homes in our community. What made my home special was a creek that ran past the back of our property. During the summers the creek became built-in entertainment for the Blough Court Gang. There was fishing, catching frogs, crayfish and tadpoles. We seined for minnows and occasionally would catch a water snake in our net.

Across the creek was a weedy, swampy area of 100 or more acres. We trapped muskrats, built secret forts and just had the best of times until in 1955 machinery arrived and cleared our paradise. In its place, a nine-hole golf course was built. It opened on May 29, 1957. Directly across the creek from my back yard was the middle of the fifth hole, a par three. That was in the days before it was fashionable to own a house on a golf course! Go figure!

My dad was an excellent golfer so you can imagine his delight. He went on to win two club championships, as did our next door neighbor, Jackie Meyers. He and my dad were two of the best players at that club through the 50's and 60's. Jack caddied for my dad for his two club championships and vice versa. I was introduced to golf at the age of nine or ten along with my brother Tom. Summertime then became split between golf, baseball and the pool. Most of the kids on my street raked for golf balls in the ponds and creek on the course. This consisted of taking a garden rake, tines up, and dragging it across the bottom of the pond or creek. When a golf ball bumped the tines, you simply reached into the water to pluck out a ball. If it was new ball and had no "cuts" in the covering, we could sell it for a quarter. Quarter balls were the best. After that the price dropped. Golf balls with a cut in the cover were only good for a nickel or a dime.

On days when I wasn't playing baseball, golf or swimming at the pool, I was testing my entrepreneurial skills with a lemonade concession on the tee box of the fifth hole. My dad helped me convert an old wagon into a lemonade stand. It had a two-gallon thermos jug, filled with lemonade my mom prepared. I paid her 30 cents to cover the sugar and lemonade for each jug. My dad made a "cash register" from a cigar box, with dividers to hold the various denominations of coins. My parents fronted me two dollars in change which I had to pay back. That taught me the difference between gross and net profits!

The beverage was dispensed into cone shaped cups, which sat in a plastic holder, reminiscent of how our cokes were served in the soda fountain at the drugstore. We built a cover so my lemonade was always shaded. On the back of the cover (the side golfers saw when they came from the fourth green) was a sign my dad made for me:

Jim's Canteen
A Par in Every Cup

Of course, in addition to ice cold lemonade, at 10 cents per cup, were some of their golf balls, for sale, that they had probably hit into the creek the previous day!

Looking back, I realize how fortunate I was to grow up in Fairless Hills. I have wonderful memories of a childhood well spent.

CHAPTER 18

Life's Lessons Fostered Independence

By BARBARA COOK

I can still remember how excited my eight-year-old self was on June 15, 1955, the day we moved to Fairless Hills. I was mesmerized by the uniformity of the houses, one right next to another, built in exact replication except for every third one which was a sideways facing version. They were so identical that at night, the color of the houses were made indistinguishable by the darkness, consequently leading to a few accidental "break-ins."

I remember the morning my dad told the story of how he unsuccessfully struggled to get his key in our neighbor's house the night before. Of course I thought it was hilarious, while my mother was mortified. Seeing a loaf of smushed bread lying in the street had become a familiar sight. The bread sometimes was placed on the back of a car by the bread delivery man, but unnoticed by the driver (very often my father) until it was too late. I can still see my mother frantically chasing my dad down the street in a futile attempt to rescue our bread!

During our first summer, the Danherst Corporation was feverishly building its last section of homes on the other side of Olds Blvd. The incessant sound of daily hammering during the construction was deafening, but no worries, those houses were completed within a week or two. At that time, our street was a total sea of mud, devoid of any vegetation, which further infuriated my mother. Adding to her despair, was that the one condition she had insisted upon for having to move there (apparently against her will), was that they purchase the only house on the street with two huge trees in the front yard. But as her luck would have it, my mother who cried daily about having to live in a so-called "matchbox house" would soon discover the trees were dead and would have to be removed.

My father, from Brooklyn and my mother from Montclair, New Jersey met while working in NYC. They both grew up advantaged, went to college in New York City, got apartments and lived a fun life. After marrying in their late twenties, my father was transferred to Chicago where my sister and I were born. Their good life continued until they moved back East. Now, here they were in Fairless Hills and my mother was miserable. Within the first year, she got a job as a secretary at the Pennsbury administrative offices. My dad was in sales and traveled most of every week. Judy and I became the original latch key kids, uncommon in a post war community of stay at home moms.

We lived on Chatham Road which backed onto a huge open area, separating our street from Olds Blvd. The best thing about that space was that it made a great baseball field and eventually I met enough kids to play softball with after dinner. Just behind our house and to the right of the open space was a wooded area where I spent many hours of quiet contentment exploring or creating forts from fallen branches or limbs. Chatham Road was the borderline that divided the community's student body into two elementary schools—Oxford Valley and Fairless View. Unlike most of the other roads in Fairless Hills, no kids my age lived on our street.

Although I had won the science fair one year, which probably should have been the highlight of my young life, I was most excited about and felt my greatest accomplishment was to have been elected the kickball captain of my class. For a girl, especially for me, that was unforgettable! I loved playing sports, but there weren't many other opportunities for girls.

The teacher I remembered the most was a male and I had him for two years. He was strict, demanding and short tempered, but he loved sports and included girls in class vs class kickball and softball tournaments. That aspect of being in his class made it totally worthwhile for me. Lake Caroline was a short distance from Oxford Valley and one year we had a gym teacher who let us ice skate there during gym class.

I remember a small airfield nearby from which family friends flew us in their Piper Cub to their home for Thanksgiving. It was both exciting and terrifying at the same time! Adding to the anxiety of being in an airplane piloted by my father's inebriated friend was overhearing a conversation about being low on fuel.

Every week we had the opportunity to dance and socialize at canteen in the school gym. Although we were still in elementary school, the ambiance transported us to our teens. My first party experience and introduction to the game "spin the bottle" was at Vicky Hadden's house on Austin Drive. For some reason I assumed it was a Halloween party, but it wasn't and to my horror I was the only one in costume! Luckily, my over protective mom was still parked outside and I was able to escape unnoticed and reappear appropriately dressed a short time later.

Because my father had been in a serious car accident, times became financially challenging for our family. Some years they didn't have the funds to join the pool, but when they did, I spent the days waiting my turn to jump off the diving boards over and over again.

It wasn't until I went to William Penn Jr. High where Fairless Hills students joined those from Levittown and Yardley that I met some of my best friends. Although, I was especially excited for gym class to begin, I soon realized there were some clear disadvantages. Gym could have been an opportunity to play sports, but I soon discovered that field hockey was too scary and basketball was too aggressive for me. I did love gymnastics and still remember the exuberance of climbing the rope to the ceiling of the gymnasium. Required gang showers and unstylish gym suits were a real treat too! One year I was selected to be a squad leader and used my rebellious nature to revise the job description of that role. I would collect all the personal numbers of girls who didn't want to shower and cross off those numbers, giving them credit for taking a shower. I remember feeling very satisfied about my benevolent contribution to their well-being.

I can't remember who I became friends with first, all I know is that till this day we are still friends and for that, I am grateful. I met both Sarah Wilson and Sue Courtney in French class. We were all very excited to be taking French. It was definitely part of my plan to become a fashion designer and to live in Paris. The method of teaching language was through the memorization of dialogs. We learned the first one, Bonjour Jean and the second one, La Bibliotheque, but then we quickly regressed. Everything was funny! We laughed way too much and made fun of our teacher who constantly sprayed us as she pronounced words in French with exaggerated enunciation. Although neither of us failed, our lack of progress was soon discovered in the language lab, where via headsets our teacher could listen to us struggle. The truth was out, we knew next to nothing which made us laugh even more.

Sarah and I quickly became partners in crime. Because both my parents worked, she would walk to my house in the morning from her house in Thornridge and hide in the storage shed in my carport until my parents left. Once she heard the cars pull away, out she popped! We'd spend the days practicing our smoking skills so we could look cool later. It was quite the effort! We would smoke, feel nauseous and dizzy, lie down for a while, then repeat the process. We practiced our dance moves by watching American Bandstand and thought of ways to improve our appearance. It was then that we decided Sarah should cut her hair! The girl who could literally sit on her hair was convinced by me to go for the Connie Stevens look. That meant the top half of her hair would be cut short and teased up to create a rather high voluminous puff which would somehow blend into her ponytail. And I was the one who would do it! Why she agreed is still puzzling, but fortunately it was successful and became her signature look for years. We also would discuss our wardrobe for the week which meant we pooled our clothes and rotated them between the two of us. A common question would be on which day would we get to wear the coveted bandstand skirt or the angel blouse. There were always kids to hang out with and Sarah and I spent our formative years walking all over Levittown and Fairless Hills from one shopping center to another, from Sun Ray in Levittown to Landy's and Fairlanes, the bowling alley in Fairless Hills. Then at night, twisted in the cords of our home phones, we discussed our adventures for hours.

Campaigning for the 1960 election, John F. Kennedy stopped at the Levittown Shop-A-Rama. Everyone came to see this popular presidential candidate. Children of the Cold War Era, we routinely practiced air raid drills in school, cowering under our desks for protection. Soon after Kennedy's election, the Cuban Missile Crisis occurred creating fear of Russian missiles that could be sent from nearby Cuba. Several families in Levittown dug bomb shelters in their back yards in preparation of the attack we all felt was inevitable. A little disturbed by the whole scenario and the ill preparedness of my family, I just accepted the grim possibility of imminent death.

Although friends earlier, Sue Courtney and I became closer later in high school. We also adopted the same routines — skipping school, which by then had progressed to catching a bus and going to Trenton for the day, riding around endlessly in cars at night with no destination in mind, but inevitably ending up in a diner, smoking, drinking coffee and eating toasted cinnamon buns. Sue and I had also become friends with Carolyn Hilferty, Janet Spor and Joyce Vancheri. During that time, Linda Farmer had moved in across the street from me and we quickly became friends. I loved her family, their West Virginia accents and welcoming ways. I would have moved in with them if I had been invited. Motown had become pretty popular and Linda was really good at portraying Diana Ross and recreating the dance moves of the Supremes. Of course, the dances at Hugh Carcella Hall and the Edgely Fire Hall had become our go to places as well as the occasional pajama party where you wouldn't dare fall asleep for fear of waking up with toothpaste and toilet paper stuck to your hair.

Unfortunately, by the tenth grade, I was told that college would not be financially feasible and that I had to take the business course route. I was not happy, that had never been my plan. I did not want to be a secretary nor did I want to get married yet. However, those were the expectations and I knew I had no choice. I felt pressure to move out after graduation and by my boyfriend who knew he would end up in Viet Nam if we didn't get married.

The summer before I graduated, I got a job at the Steel Mill as a short order cook in the main canteen. It was an amazing opportunity for me. I had made enough money to finally upgrade my wardrobe, get a ridiculous haircut, and pay for senior pictures, yearbook and prom dress. It was years later when I realized I probably could have paid for college if I had only known at the time.

Graduation was uneventful, I got married a month later and worked as a secretary for Nationwide Insurance Company, a job I got through the work experience program at Pennsbury. As fate would have it, years later Sarah, Sue and I continued our education at Bucks County Community College. Eventually, I transferred to Holy Family University and got a degree in Elementary Education and a Masters in Education Administration. So after many years of expert school skipping experience, making fun of my teachers and uncontrollable silliness, I became a school teacher in the Bristol Township School District. I also remarried and raised four happy, successful daughters. I wouldn't characterize growing up in Fairless Hills as the Happy Days I think others might, but it afforded me the opportunity to learn life's lessons in an environment that fostered independence while forming bonds with lifelong friends.

LITTLE LEAGUE STAR – Rich Dobos, second player from right in top row, competed for the dominant Yardley Optimists team in the Pennsbury Little League.

CHAPTER 19

Rich Dobos Recalls Mother's Tears Upon Arrival

By RICH DOBOS

Like many kids of my age I was a transplant from Western Pennsylvania. We lived in Homestead until my father took a job at the new "Fairless Works" steel mill located across the state in Morrisville. It was a great opportunity for my parents, but when I look back it had to be difficult. Leaving everything they knew as well as most of their relatives and friends, to an unknown future, much like the pioneers of the Old West without the Indians and dangerous travel conditions.

One of the memories, which must have been somewhat traumatic for me to remember, was that of my mom sitting on the porch steps sobbing and missing her mom, dad and brother as well as having to make new friendships. (Her dad passed away within about a year and her mom moved in with us for the remainder of her life.) Moving to Fallsington was really a convenience for dad, as it was only minutes down Tyburn Road to the plant. Buying the house was a real no-brainer as they were able to live there for the entire first year without paying a dime. It was a new development just outside of the "Historic Town of Fallsington." There were two such developments — Taylor Tract and Penns Development, where we lived.

I was only five when we moved here so my new friends were all from the immediate development. Two of my closer friends were Cliff Bray and Jay Crawford. Cliff's dad was part owner of Bray Brothers' Construction, which played a big role in the development of our area. Jay Crawford's father, like mine, worked at the mill. There were a number of boys and girls in the neighborhood with similar backgrounds. We would all play together whether it was baseball, football or other kid games like "Hide-and-Seek" or "Kick the Can." We filled many fun hours that as a young boy made it rather easy to forget about where I left, and to begin growing into where I had landed.

I started my education at Fallsington Elementary School in the First Grade (skipped kindergarten.) This is where my life began to grow. First meeting kids on the bus from the other side of Tyburn Road (Taylor Tract) as well as kids from Lower Makefield and Morrisville. What an experience!! There were kids my age like Ray Suntich, Ron Bowman, Tim and Melanie Warhol, and

Tom Shelly — just to name a few from the bus. Then kids from Fallsington proper. Kids like Butch Mattozzi (whose dad was a Falls Cop at the time,) Paul Christman, plus Kathy and LaVerne Kellett, whose parents owned Kellett's Market in town.

As I got a bit older around 11 or 12 I began to go up to the school to play baseball in the summer and football in fall and winter. Since it was such a small town there was a real age difference playing sports. I was one of the youngest. Older guys like Tom and Ron Nau, my brother John, and Bud Roberts led the way. I had to work really hard to learn, and play at a higher level so I would be picked on a team.

Some guys from nearby Vermillion Hills and Thornridge in Levittown would come to play as well. I would leave home early AM, pop in for lunch and right back out until the "street lights" came on. That's when I had to be home. Those lights turning on was my curfew, if you will. Great time to be a kid, didn't worry about anything. I played Little League Baseball at Pennsbury and Midget Football at Fallsington where I met guys like Bob Burkhart, Doug Powell, Brian Doster, and the Steiner brothers, to name a few. Great fun and experiences. Later in life I would meet my Little League baseball coach, Mr. Johnson, at one of my first jobs, Trenton Trust bank, where he was Executive VP and I was a Systems Analyst. Small world!

Summertime activities were really great. We had the Falls Recreation Department where we spent our mornings playing baseball. The great thing about rec was the organization. We would play teams from other school rec programs. Buses took us to other schools, or they would come to Fallsington. It was great competition and you got to meet kids from all over who just wanted to play ball.

In the evenings, and on Saturdays we would go to the Fallsington Free Library where they showed movies complete with popcorn and candy. Other nights we would just hang out and shoot the bull, maybe at Kellett's Store, or on the porch of the library. Proprietors would complain and at some point the cops would come and move us along. The Falls Police Station was right in town so as kids we got to know almost all of the officers (many of whom were our neighbors.) Since we couldn't hang around local businesses, they moved us and would let us hang in the parking lot behind the Police Station. We could do any damn thing we wanted and never had a problem.

In the winter there were a few great places to ice skate for us kids. The woods had creeks and swamp lands that would freeze and many of us would meet to skate, build small camp fires, and just enjoy being kids. What a great time and place to be a kid!!

As I got a bit older I did things like muskrat trapping (and sell the fur to Sears for a couple of bucks) and with the woods in my back yard, I started to hunt. Dad got me a 22 rifle and taught me how to handle it properly. We joined the Gun Club down by Curtis Lake (about a mile away) and learned to shoot. After spending some time in the woods shooting squirrels and rabbits I got my first shotgun.

There were a couple of farms, Taylor's and Else's, that would let us hunt. With dad working shifts I would hunt with a man named Dave Sterling. He was a house builder who had done most of the local homes and loved to hunt. We would hunt pheasant with a couple of others, kids my age as well as adults. I'll never forget his old dog Brick, a Springer Spaniel, and a great hunting dog. He would lead the way, jump a couple of pheasants as we followed, all the while herding them into a corner of the farm. Here is where the fun began. He would methodically jump pheasants one at a time, it was like a shooting frenzy . . . dinner would be great that night!

Seventh grade is when the real growth began as my grade of kids began attending William Penn Junior High, above three miles away in the adjacent town, Fairless Hills. I began to meet kids from all over Levittown and Fairless Hills. Everything changed! Now we went from a single class-room with one teacher, to seven class periods and seven different teachers and classrooms. I also realize that some of my friends from Fallsington Elementary that lived in Yardley and Lower Make-field were not here but at Charles Boehm because of the geographic location. The district was basically split in half with Route 1 being the dividing line. I began meeting people from Fairless Hills, and various sections of Levittown that I barely knew existed. My world was truly expanding.

Junior high school also brought some social growth with "Canteen," a Friday night dance that for the first time created an environment with boys and girls interacting on a more "personal" level. After Canteen many of the kids would walk to the Fairless Hills Shopping Center where the local "Malt Shop" Landy's became our hangout. There was another weekend dance that took place at the "Hugh Carcella Hall," home of the steel union of which most of our fathers were members. With an expanding circle of friends, I was introduced to one of the things I enjoyed most in summer, the Fairless Hills Pool. So many of us would spend the entire day into the evening at the pool before heading home. There also was always a summer Carnival sponsored by the Fire Company complete with fireworks to end the week-long event. In the winter I would now trade the small creeks and swamp land in Fallsington for Lake Caroline where everyone would come to skate, build bonfires for warmth, and just enjoy being a kid.

Grades seven through 10 were all pretty similar, playing football and baseball thru 10th grade after which I kind of lost interest in the discipline required to continue to the varsity level, and began just enjoying life as a kid. I had met a lot of kids like Jon Stroop, Russ Snyder and Dan Forester who would become lifelong friends. To this day we still play golf a couple of times each week, as well as enjoying the company of our wives at many social events.

Moving into high school we were reunited with the kids I had once known in elementary school. Pennsbury High at that time was located on Makefield Road in Yardley, about five miles from home. At this level, we become one. It also brought the much anticipated "Driver's License" which really expanded our access to places like Fairlanes Bowling Alley (a major hangout for locals; I eventually took a serious interest in the game), Red Barn, Gino's, Washington Crossing and so many other places to meet guys and girls from all over Lower Bucks County.

There were so many people I would meet and become friends with that to list them all would be impossible. There were however a few close ones that I would be remiss not to mention. Guys like Charley Stevenson, Jody Gambelluca, Carl Easterling, Dan Hackler, Steve Amoroso and Jim Neeld, all great guys, and great friends. You grow apart over the years after high school, but when brought back together at gatherings like the ones we have at "The Boot," it's like we never missed a beat and had been together all along.

Finally, the day we all have been waiting for . . . GRADUATION!! Everyone was excited to begin their life as adults. Many would go on to college, too many unfortunately were drafted into the military and some went off to Vietnam, others followed in their father's footsteps and went to work at the steel mill. As for myself I had no idea what I wanted to do with my life. I spent three weeks at the mill, realizing quickly that it wasn't the life for me. I spent some time going from job to job without any future, until a neighbor who worked in the "Data Processing" industry piqued my interest in the very new field of computers. I went to a school and learned how to program computers and soon found myself in a career so new that jobs were plentiful and opportunity knew no bounds. Once again Fallsington had played a big part in my future. If it wasn't for that neighbor, who knows where I would have landed.

As the years passed by I had met and married my wife of 50 years, Gail. I believe if not for her I might not have survived. Gail kept me grounded as much as possible. We had a daughter, Kimberly, who I tried to give a childhood as great as mine in rural America. We bought what was to be our first home in Fairless Hills, and just never left.

Kimberly became a pretty good athlete, playing softball, winning at the state and national level, then went to college at the University of South Florida and is doing well for herself. I found my way into the automated "Ticketing Industry" and was fortunate to have led the design and development of "Select-A-Seat" which was the forerunner to the current Ticketmaster. My greatest memory, however, was my overall responsibility for all admissions to the 1980 Winter Olympics. Later in life I would become a consultant working with local as well as international corporations before retirement.

When I look back after writing this, I am so taken by what an amazing childhood my parents had given me and what a wonderful place it was to grow up. I wish I had known this outcome back when my mom was sitting on the steps sobbing, or at least have told her later in life what a great thing they did when they moved to Fallsington!!

STILL CLOSE – Barbara Welch Merryman and Ginger Lane Bortz have been best friends ever since their high school years.

CHAPTER 20

Ginger And Barb Remain 'BFFs'

By GINGER LANE BORTZ

Goodbye, Poughkeepsie, New York! Hello Levittown, Pennsylvania! In 1955, my single mom, Edith, remarried, giving my sister, Pat and I a stepfather. Together we all moved from our quad home to a single-family house in the Elderberry section of Levittown. My stepdad, Bill, was a meat cutter for Penn Fruit grocery store. Mom was a stay-at-home mother for the first few years before working as a sales woman at JC Penney in the Levittown Shopping Center.

We moved onto Everturn Lane, which was mostly made up of boy neighbors around my age. Bob Timby lived next door and Jim Nemceff lived directly across the street. John Friemann lived on Elderberry Drive, located behind Jim Nemceff. We all attended Penn Valley Elementary School, picking up different people along our walk to school.

Our younger years found us outside until the street lights came on. Summers were filled with being outside, riding bikes, stick ball and many hours at the pool. In the evening, we would all get our jars with holes punched in the lid and collect lightning bugs, seeing who could collect the most. At the end of the night, we would release them, watching them blink off into the night sky.

As I got older, I rode the bus to Medill Bair. It's there that I met and started hanging out with a lot of friends from the North Park section of Levittown. Since my street backed up to North Park, it made it convenient to walk to their houses. Linda Dykes was one of my good friends. Her mom would always have Coke in glass bottles and Charles Chips as snacks. To this day, I still have my Charles Chip can from when they were delivered right to my house. Betsy Marozzi, Carolyn Hilferty and Carolyne Keefer were just some of the North Park girls that I became good friends with.

While at Medill Bair, I spent most of my free time playing basketball, field hockey and running track. I played roving guard in basketball. In track, I ran the 50-yard dash and anchored the 440 relay. Center forward was my position for field hockey. To this day, I can still hear, "Ground, stick, ground, stick, ground, stick, ball!" being chanted by our team.

My friendships only continued to grow when I attended Pennsbury High School in Yardley. Barbara Welch and Sandy Dunn were just two of my lasting friendships. Barbara and I were in each other's wedding and have remained best friends for over 58 years.

It was in high school that I realized I had another passion to add to my sports schedule . . . Canteen on Saturday night! It was truly what I looked most forward to each and every week. The girls from North Park and I would carpool. Once at the dance, the girls stood on one side of the floor and the boys on the other. When a slow song was played, we waited, hoping that special guy would come over and ask you to dance. The Bristol Stomp, a line dance, or a good jitterbug song would bring everyone out to the dance floor. Tom DiIorio was one of the great dancers in our class.

Those Saturday night Canteens paved my love for dance. I found myself rushing home after school to watch American Bandstand with Dick Clark on television. I learned all the steps to the jitterbug by holding onto my refrigerator handle and watching the dancers on Bandstand. I dreamed of being one of those dancers on Bandstand. That dream came true. I ended up going on American Bandstand twice! After all my years of watching, I was now there and dancing in person.

Getting to Bandstand was a big feat for me. My parents were very strict and I never expected them to let me go. A friend of mine that was a year older had her Mom drive us to Philadelphia. There we stood in line and prayed we were picked to go inside. Bandstand had their regular dancers and only a few extras were allowed in. I was ecstatic when we were chosen to go inside. Here I was standing at Bandstand, trying to take it all in. I was not watching it on TV, I was actually here!

There were bleachers on one side, separated by a podium where Dick Clark stood. The cameras were located at the opposite end. The extras were shown to the bleachers. Some of the regulars were sitting on the front row of the bleachers. Others were standing in small groups right on the dance floor. Once the music started, everyone was on the dance floor. Of course all of the extras were towards the back of the studio and away from the cameras. Dance away I did! To my surprise, one of the regulars who was known as "Rubber Legs" came up and started dancing with me. I had hit it big! I was dancing on American Bandstand!

Now after all these years, I am lucky to say I have remained friends with both girls and guys from our class of 1965. Meeting up at the "The Boot" for the last few years has not only strengthened old friendships but added new ones to my life!

'Philly Girl' Turned Princess

By BARBARA WELCH MERRYMAN

My family moved 20 miles up the highway from Philadelphia to Levittown in 1957. We had been living under the elevated train track in the Kensington section of Philly. We had a marble step in front of our house so we must have been the wealthy ones! My Mom eventually met my Dad, a British Marine whose ship was docked at the Philadelphia Navy Yard.

Dad got a job in Philly as a janitor after leaving the service. He eventually became a machine shop foreman and bam ... we were rich!

In 1957, Mom and Dad purchased a Jubilee-style home in the Vermillion Hills section of Levittown for $11,000. We drove up every Saturday to see the progress of the house. It even came with grass!!! Dad brought the builders beer every weekend so that they would do a better job on the roof!

My first school assignment in the Pennsbury District sent me to Fallsington Elementary. One of my first childhood friends was Diane Struck. What a hoot! We ice-skated on the creek, and at Lake Caroline. We roller-skated at the recreation hall at St. Joseph the Worker church on New Falls Road. We also attended dances at the church hall.

Diane died not long after our 50th high school reunion. She left us way too early. I miss her smile! We tried to hang with the popular football player, Ken Medlin, but even Diane with all her charm couldn't wedge our way into his crowd. We hung at the LPRA Pool in Magnolia Hill.

I attended William Penn and Medill Bair, then the old high school in Lower Makefield.

Ginger Lane became my BFF my senior year. She and her guy Marty Lengyel set me up on a blind date with Dick Merryman that year. He was three years older and had a hot 1955 Chevy! I was hooked! He joined the Navy and we married his last year in. I was a proud Navy wife. This year, we'll be married 53 years!

The rest is history!

CHAPTER 21

Sweet Memories of Our Youthful Years

By RUTH HENDRY

In June 1954, our family moved from the first home I remember, a two-story duplex on Greenwood Avenue in Trenton, across the Delaware River to Knoll Drive in Lower Makefield Township. My early memories from Trenton include walking to school for kindergarten and first grade, and getting hit on the back of my head by a swing on the playground. I remember my Mom cleaning the black dust off our windows from the nearby Ajax Rubber factory. I remember our small back yard that led to the alley and Jerry Fort's house. It was my parents' 18th move since their marriage in 1936 and the first house they bought. It was my ninth move.

Our house was the sample home for Pinebrook Farms, a development of 52 single-family homes, including our pink stucco ranch. It was bordered on the east by Hall's Orchard and Raab's Farm to the west. Our houses had been part of the Raab Farm property. It was easy to see we had moved to the country. Our backyard property line was marked off with a standard barbed wire farm fence. Roosters woke us in the morning and cows stopped by the fence to graze. I was flabbergasted the first time I heard a cow moo! Mr. Raab, would drop fresh corn over the fence for our family to enjoy. Mrs. Raab would call us on our party line, to tell us to keep our cat, Scotty, inside while they mowed the field.

The kids in our neighborhood spent countless hours building dams in Buck Creek at the end of Knoll Drive. Some years the creek would be easy to get into and in other years we'd slide down a steep incline to get to the water. On the other side of the creek was Scammell's Woods. It was a pine forest, with thick beds of red-brown pine needles, ideal for forts and adventures of all kinds. It would be several years before I met all the Scammell kids at school. We only saw our neighbors in the woods.

Behind the houses on Brook Lane, there was a field that was part of Hall's Orchard. It served as a baseball diamond, a go-cart track and the site of the neighborhood picnic egg toss. One time when I was waiting for a turn at bat, a boy in the class of 1964 asked me if my favorite pink shirt with a white collar was an Egyptian tee shirt. I said, "No." He then asked, "Then why are there two pyramids on the front of it."

RUTH HENDRY ... in her schoolgirl days

We would drive to Yardley, or Morrisville to go shopping. Len Murray's Five and Dime, Andy's store, Cramer's bakery, Phil's drug store, and Seplow's shoes were all part of my growing up experience when we visited nearby Yardley. I remember buying my first Elvis Presley magazine with Sue Smith at Phil's. One of my earliest memories of downtown Yardley is of the White Swan Inn, currently the Yardley Inn. As our family drove by one afternoon, we saw what a hunt had yielded: two dead deer and a dead bear hanging from the front of the porch of the White Swan. The Yardley Community Center was the site of Pancake Breakfasts and Canteen, a Friday night youth dance, where we danced to Elvis, and did the Stroll. I thought we had moved to the most remote corner of the world between the deer, the bear and cows in our backyard!

Our neighborhood was about half a mile from the intersection of Dolington Road and Main Street, just past Prospect Farm, built in 1682. For the first few years, the Starr bus line had hourly bus service to our street, but it wasn't long before the route stopped at Dolington and Main. We took the bus to Trenton to see movies at the Stacy and Mayfair theatres, to study at the Trenton library, and to swim at the Trenton YWCA. We didn't need to worry about bringing a bathing suit, since everyone had to wear one of the Y's truly terrible cotton knit suits, egad! All the latest fashions were available for a school dance at Yard's, Dunham's, or Arnold Constable's.

I remember August 20, 1955, when the Hurricane Diane flood sent a house smashing into the Yardley-Wilburtha Bridge. The flood waters came all the way to the canal and the Acme. A motorboat went through the Studebaker dealer's showroom window. The Army Corps of Engineers built a temporary Bailey bridge to link with the remaining bridge structure to allow traffic back to New Jersey.

Walking to school was now out of the question because there were no sidewalks. My brother, John and I spent years riding to school on yellow buses. As more people moved to the area, Pennsbury built additions and new schools to accommodate all the students. I went to three elementary schools and three high schools without ever moving from Knoll Drive. I was in Mrs. Carver's second grade class at Makefield Elementary School. Beth Haines, Sue Bennington and Heidi Brunner were among my classmates. Their moms were my Brownie Troop leaders. During that year's polio epidemic one of our classmates, Billy Long, contracted polio. Every-one in our class had to get hemoglobin shots, since the Salk vaccine was just invented and not widely distributed yet! I thought hemoglobin was the most difficult word to say or spell.

Just as I was getting to know my new friends at Makefield school, my brother and I were assigned to Yardley Elementary, the school at the top of the hill. Barbara Hubal, Suzanne Waterson and Sue Smith were some of my new classmates. Mrs. Ruth McCutcheon was my third-grade teacher. I loved that we both had the same first name because she was cool! The highest grade she gave in her class was an A+ with sparkles. When our class got rowdy, Mrs. McCutcheon would say, "First comes thunder and then comes lightning, and you don't want to see lightning!" We all would quiet down immediately. Mr. Budgy was my fourth grade teacher and my first male teacher. Mr. Robideux was my fifth grade teacher.

We brought our lunch each day because Yardley Elementary didn't have a cafeteria. We received milk and crackers for a mid-morning snack and we bought ice cream sandwiches for dessert. Once Yardley got a cafeteria, ice cream sandwiches disappeared! We were in the original part of the school with large windows. You needed a pole to open and close them. Many hours were spent wiping down the black boards and cleaning yellow chalk dust from erasers. It was time to say goodbye to Yardley and change schools again!

I was in the first sixth grade class in Quarry Hill Elementary. We wrote our names in the cornerstone. Mr. Robideux was our teacher again. We were the last classroom in the building and there were a lot of windows. One day, Calvin Day showed his gymnastics prowess and did a forward roll out the window onto the lawn! We had a cafetorium that served as our cafeteria and auditorium. I remember dancing to the song, *Beep-Beep, Little Nash Rambler* on days without recess. We were so grownup with our poodle skirts, bobby socks and saddle shoes. The year-end class project was a week at French Creek State Park. We planned all the meals, calculated costs, planned all the activities and studied the local history. It was the best part of sixth grade.

During the summers, the Yardley-Makefield recreation program had morning activities at Yardley and Quarry Hill. In the afternoon, we traveled to Bowman's Hill to collect tadpoles and climb the Tower, or to a pool to swim. The first year we took the bus to the Post Road Pool in Morrisville. In subsequent years, the program was held at the Aqua Club in New Hope. It would be a couple of years before pools closer to home were built. John and I both remember riding our bikes to the Newtown Pool on Yardley-Newtown Road!

In the winter, we'd go ice skating on Lake Afton, or the lake at Washington Crossing Park. We would go sledding on Whiskey Hill (Jervue Avenue, just on the other side of Hall's Orchard.) We could walk to Lake Afton along Buck Creek, to the bleachery, or down the canal path to town. Eventually, I rode my bike to Yardley and would visit with Barbara Hubal.

My classmates spent a lot of time at the Yardley Library, the ultimate tiny building before it was a trend! It was filled to the rafters with books. John and I used the library's copy of the World Book Encyclopedia for our homework.

In seventh grade, everyone at Pennsbury went to William Penn on South Olds Boulevard in Fairless Hills. It was great because we got to meet new kids from Levittown and Fairless Hills. Sadly, our class was split again in eighth grade as students north of Route 1 were assigned to Charles Boehm, and kids who lived south of Route 1 were the first students at Medill Bair. I have fond memories of dancing in the gym lobby during lunch, and Boehm's field day, Gymkhana. Like many girls, I dreamed of being a cheer leader. My dream came true for two remarkable days in 10th grade, when I was selected as Orange Team cheerleader.

Finally, in our junior year we were all back together as one class at Pennsbury High. It was great to be with kids from Bair, on the same teams, no longer rivals. Sadly, we experienced the assassination of President Kennedy late on a Friday afternoon in 11th grade. I remember that horrible November 1963 day in Mrs. Foreman's physics class, when Mr. Stringer announced that President Kennedy had been shot. It was the start of a weekend of tragedy we will always remember.

Bonnie Secor, Liza Hamill and I went everywhere together. There was the infamous Halloween Party at Tom Hanna's house on Makefield Road, where Bonnie and Liza were dressed as devils. Alan Maxwell, and Bob Keiger were angels! Everyone from the party went trick or treating at the Reedman's House. Then we all drove to Miss Tindall's house in Morrisville to trick or treat there. She was not amused and called the police. So much for that adventure.

For our Senior Prom, we transformed PHS into *3 Coins in a Fountain*, a Roman extravaganza prom theme.

I also remember in my senior year serving as a student guide, escorting rising sixth graders on a tour of the building since we were the last class to graduate from PHS on Makefield Road. I can remember thinking how little the kids were, and how mature I was.

As we graduated from PHS, no one had any idea of the tragic toll the distant country of Vietnam would have on our lives, especially those who served in the armed forces. Or the tragic assassination of Martin Luther King and other civil rights leaders, and Robert F. Kennedy. Or the impact of "the Pill" on women's lives, and the women's liberation movement. Our young adult lives were forged in tumultuous times, which prepared us for what we endure today.

I lived at 8 Knoll Drive, in Lower Makefield, for 50 years. My son Rob was born in 1971, at the 7th Army Hospital in Heidelberg, Germany, where my husband was stationed in the Army. My daughter, Lisa, was born in St. Mary Hospital in Langhorne, on April 29, 1975, the day Saigon fell, almost 10 years after our graduation from Pennsbury. My children remember playing in Buck Creek, attending the same schools that I did and having some of the same teachers. Rob went to the

Rose Bowl in Pasadena, and to China and Japan with the PHS Marching Band. I was there, too. Lisa was on the swim, track and cross-country teams, and was Sports Night Queen.

We share memories that span generations. Hall's Orchard, Raab's Farm and Scammell's Woods live only in my mind. Memories growing up in Pennsbury are now savored and shared with PHS alums at the Boot and reunions as we celebrate those bygone days.

1967 **2017**

Richard & Sandra

50 ANNIVERSARY

OLD DAYS – Sandy Dunn married her husband, Dick Spickler, when he was in the Army in 1967. The inset photo shows them 50 years later.

CHAPTER 22

Sandy Dunn Is a Fairless Hills Girl

By SANDY DUNN SPICKLER

October 1952 . . .

The Dunn family made the cross-state move from McKeesport, PA to Fairless Hills — a new community being developed as a result of the steel industry locating a new mill along the Delaware River.

I was just shy of my fifth birthday when we relocated. We left a BIG house on Sole Street in McKeesport to live in a three-bedroom ranch house in this new town. I so remember the house we left. A big yard, fruit trees and chickens in the coop out back. A porch to sit on in the evening and lots of large rooms. I still remember my older brother crawling out on the porch roof through my bedroom window so Mom and Dad wouldn't know he was going out.

We arrived in Fairless Hills as a family of six; Mom, Dad, my older brother Ronnie, me, my sister Cheryl and my little brother, Rick. The three-bedroom house was brand new and the perfect size for our little family. Who would have known then that two more sisters would come along!

Our house was so new that we did not even have sidewalks. Yes, they were formed out but the concrete was not poured nor were the streets. We had street lights that didn't work and all the houses looked exactly the same. As a family, we stayed with friends of my parents until our household goods arrived. We waited and we waited. The truck was long overdue. My Dad decided that we should take a ride in the car and see the new neighborhood. As we drove up one street in our section and down another about four streets behind ours we came upon a moving van unloading furniture into a house. My Mom became very excited and told my Dad to stop, they were unloading OUR furniture into some else's house! I can still remember the look on the moving man's face when my Dad approached and told them to pack it back up and take it to the correct house.

There was a large open field across the street from my house and soon an elementary school was being built there. Prior to this new school, I attended Oxford Valley Elementary School and made many friends. And a few years after they completed the school, work began on the community golf course. While the golf course was under construction, all the neighborhood kids would play on the trees that the bulldozers had knocked down to make the golf course. Then came the swimming pool. What a wonder that was. The largest all steel pool in the country. My older brother became a lifeguard there and we all took swimming lessons. A family could join the pool for the entire summer for just $6! What a bargain and of course, we spent all summer there when not going to the recreational programs the schools offered.

My closest friends lived on my street and the streets of my section. Jim Wysor lived down in Blough Court right on the golf course. Barbara Grigas was one of my very first friends; she lived three houses away from mine. Evelyn Cherepko lived a few streets back along with Joyce McClure, Carolyn Domarski and Vincent Basanavage. Mary Jane Buchanan lived up the hill across Trenton Road and many times I would walk to her house to play or just hang out. John (Butchy) Coutts and his sister Betty lived in my neighborhood and Betty and I became great friends.

I can't even begin to say how great it was growing up in those days. At night the kids would play until the street lights came on; a signal that it was time to go home. We swam at the pool, ice skated on the frozen ponds of the golf course and collected golf balls to sell back to the guys playing on the course. Of course, who could forget the O'Boyle's ice cream truck? You would hear that bell a few streets away, run in the house and ask for money to buy your favorite treat or pull the money from our piggy banks.

I was a member of the Fairless Flippers Swim Team along with many of my friends and kids from Fairless Hills. We had home swim meets every Tuesday at our pool and away meets on Thursdays. I had so many friends on the swim team. I first met my husband on the swim team and then as a co-worker at the pool. Yes, I worked at the pool; first in the concession stand and then as a lifeguard. Summertime and the livin' was easy!

What wonderful memories we gained from working at the pool. Working in the concession stand was an easy job but oh so very hot. No air conditioning and lots of sweat. I remember how one day it was so very hot that Denise Queen decided to sit in the giant cooler to get some relief. She was sitting on a container of ice cream mix when our boss walked in! Then there was the time someone left the frozen custard machine running as the custard spilled all over the floor. What a mess! A life of leisure for kids and work for dads. Not many of us had moms who worked.

Those were the good old days. Summer fun, school with your friends, and lots of things to do. My, how the times have changed. I have been very fortunate to stay in touch with many of my friends from my childhood. Some who have found me through Facebook or through another friend. I sincerely cherish all those friendships as well as the times we all spent together.

As we all reached that magic age where we graduated from high school and moved on with our lives, some have moved away. Many still live in the area. I love our hometown and Bucks County. We have the ability to travel up and down the East Coast, which is a megalopolis that has grown considerably since I first arrived in Fairless Hills. I remember Oxford Valley Road as a simple two-lane road and now it is a heavily-trafficked area as people commute back and forth to work. Route 1 was two lanes and now four. The Yardley and Lower Makefield areas were just farms when we first arrived and now many farms are gone and new housing developments have taken their place.

Oh, how my hometown has changed; but the one thing that never changes is the wonderful friendships that were afforded to me in moving to Fairless Hills. Thank goodness for the "Boot" as we often gather there to be with our near and dear friends.

CENTER OF ATTENTION – Ed McGurk played Santa Claus at a Pennsbury holiday dance event as Steve Battershell and Gay Ormsby looked on.

CHAPTER 23

'Jersey Girl' Crosses the Delaware River

By GAY ORMSBY SELGER

My parents, Ralph and Betty Ormsby, grew up together in Salem, New Jersey. They both joined the Navy during WWII. My mother was a Wave stationed in Seattle and my father joined the Seabees. He was stationed in the South Pacific and later the submarine service.

At the end of the war they returned to Salem and my father got a job as a telephone installer with the New Jersey Bell Telephone Company. His employment there would be instrumental in our journey to Levittown.

I was born in Salem Hospital on a hot, July day in 1947 as my father and grandfather sat across the street on the curb. My father built our first house in Pennsville, six miles away. I began school there and had finished second grade when our lives completely changed.

My father was promoted to a management position at Bell Telephone and we would be moving away. His job was in Trenton and at night he would drive around Lower Bucks County looking at homes where the three of us could relocate.

I remember coming to Levittown and walking through all the sample homes on Route 13. As a seven-year-old I thought all the sample furniture came with the house. My parents picked a home on Village Lane in the section of Vermillion Hills. At the rear of the property was a forest of trees, all the way to Newportville Road. I remember my father saying all of those trees were one of the reasons he picked this particular house. On one of our visits to see our new home's progress the forest was gone — clear cut all the way to the road. A shopping center with an A&P would eventually occupy that space.

We moved after school was finished in June and I turned eight years old in July. Our street was full of kids and you only had to walk outside to find a playmate. I quickly met Jean Cowie, Karen and Alan Slawter and Barbara Hewitt. We played jump rope, hop scotch, rode bikes and roller skated around the block. We all went to Fallsington Elementary School through sixth grade.

During the summer I had been used to going to a lake only on the weekend. In Levittown the pool was open seven days a week starting at noon. In our first year, pool tags for an entire family cost $6. Once you were 10 years old, you were permitted to go by yourself. What freedom to ride your bike to Magnolia Pool for the entire day!

In seventh grade, we started attending William Penn Junior High School. Linda Dykes became my first new pal. We have remained life-long friends. At this time, Lona Carlisle, Kathy Rick, Sue Markley, Sally Kopstein and Jo Kowski came into my life. We often went to the movies or bowling on Friday nights. We needed a parent to take us and pick us up. My dad always preferred "to take."

In ninth and 10th grades, we attended Medill Bair where I joined Future Nurses Club. Sally Kopstein's mother was our school nurse and the club advisor. Out of that club, Sue Markley and I both became nurses with long careers. I remember a Christmas Dance in the cafeteria. Ed McGurk was dressed as Santa Claus and you could have a Polaroid picture taken as you sat on his lap. I joined the hockey team and Mrs. Phillips was our coach. Years later I would work with Mrs. Phillips' son at Carl Sandburg Middle School in the nearby Neshaminy School District. One day he was sick and I was unable to reach his wife so I called his parents. Mr. and Mrs. Phillips came in and I jumped 30 years back in time. Mr. Phillips had also been my history teacher at Medill Bair. A strange day full of memories.

At Pennsbury High School we rejoined the kids from the other side of Route 1. I had 12th grade English with Miss Tindall and Mr. Corbett. Each day one-fifth of the class was missing as they were in "small group." I spent some classes sitting next to Terry Nau or Elliott Oppenheim. Alphabetically, Ormsby was always with those boys.

I spent a summer working as a nurse's aide at Lower Bucks Hospital. My father was adamant he was not paying for a nursing education if I did not like being in a hospital. That job did not deter me. I attended Wagner College on Staten Island and graduated with a Bachelor's Degree in Nursing. I taught nursing at Mercer Hospital in Trenton, was a staff nurse in a hospital and my last position was 24 years as a school nurse for Neshaminy School District.

I met my husband Russ in college and we will be married 51 years this summer. He had a 40-year career as an educator/counselor in the Hopewell Valley School District.

After living in a few places, Russ and I moved to Levittown and our children Kevin and Ashley grew up there. We have four grandchildren. Two of them are Neshaminy Redskins and I am proud to say two are Pennsbury Falcons!

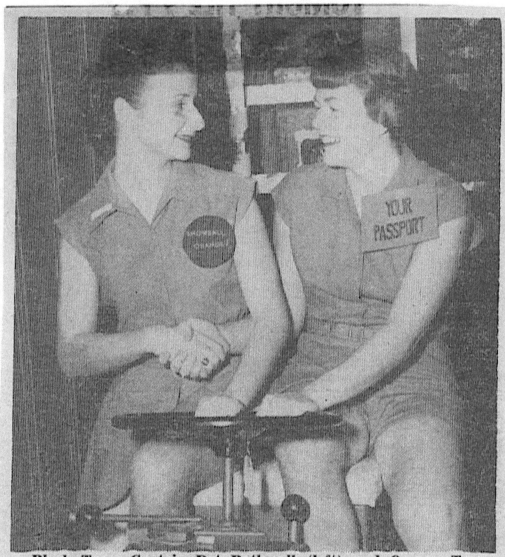

Black Team Captain Dot Rathmell (left) and Orange Team Captain Joan Marcotte exchange best wishes before last week-end's Sports Night competition between the two teams at Pennsbury High School. The Black Team captured the two-night event, 24-21.

CHAPTER 24

Joan Marcotte Used Title IX to Good Effect

By TERRY NAU

A s a young girl, Joan Marcotte learned quickly how teachers can play an impactful role in their students' lives.

"The first person to influence me was Becky Hoffman," Marcotte recalled early in 2021. "She was the first-ever gym teacher for me. I can remember sitting in class in the seventh grade at Oxford Valley, watching Mrs. Hoffman teach, and thinking, 'How can I do that when I grow up?'"

The Marcotte family had come to Lower Bucks County from Gary, Indiana in the early 1950s.

"My parents were Rauland (Raull) and Agnes," Joan said. "They had five daughters – Peggy, Joan, Marie, Cindy and Jackie. Rauland had been employed by US Steel in Gary and heard of the new steel mill being built in Morrisville. He made the move while our Mom stayed back in Gary with us girls. My mother, Jackie and Cindy joined our Dad a few months later and they picked out a house in Fairless Hills.

"The other four girls stayed in school in Gary until the Christmas vacation. Then our maternal grandmother put us on a train in Gary and off we went to our new home. In January 1954, the Marcotte girls started in the Pennsbury School District. Peggy in eighth grade, me in seventh grade, Marie in fifth grade and Cindy in kindergarten. Jackie was not yet of school age."

Marie, who was 10 years old at the time of the big move, still vividly remembers the train trip from Gary.

"It was a very long train ride but I remember it well," she said in an email. "I was a little nervous that my parents would be at the station but they were there. It was December of 1953 as we piled into the car and headed to our new home. When we pulled into Fairless Hills, everything seemed so new – the roads, homes and even the street lights. It was all very exciting and I thought we were rich!"

Not long after, Raul and Agnes divorced. Joan, Marie and Cindy stayed in Fairless Hills with their father while Peggie and Jackie went back to Gary with their mother.

"The only thing about the divorce is that we older girls had a choice if we wanted to stay with our Dad in Fairless Hills or go with our Mom back to Indiana," Joan said. "I made my choice mainly because Pennsbury had sports for girls and that is what I saw in my future school years. The high schools in Gary did not have interscholastic sports for girls at that time. Sports were that important to me."

Joan soon found a group of friends in Fairless Hills.

"My best friends were Janice Klein, Carol Fitzgerald and Gloria Hudock. We played a lot of sports together and I did a lot of bowling at the Fairlanes alley with other friends in our neighborhood," Joan recalled. "We also hung out at the Union Supply Drug store and drank milk shakes. Later on, I would work in the luncheonette at the drug store while in high school and when I came home from college.

"Another hangout was the Fairless Hills swimming pool," Joan added. "We spent the best part of our summers swimming and hanging out with our friends. The pool was the focal point of our summers."

Joan had shown some talent for sports but this was back in the day when girls' sports barely existed. She competed in three sports in high school – field hockey, basketball and softball.

"I do look back and wish we had the opportunities then that girls do now," she said. "However, I am thrilled to know that my generation had something to do with the progress woman's sports have made."

Marcotte found another teacher who served as a role model in high school.

"Ginny Napolitano also influenced me," Joan said. "As my physical education teacher and my varsity coach in field hockey and basketball, she was my inspiration and gave me the push I needed to pursue my dream of becoming a physical education teacher. As a side note, women's coaches did not get paid in those days. They were expected to take on a coaching job as part of their teaching duties."

Counting softball in the spring, Marcotte played three varsity sports for three seasons, serving as captain of those three teams in her 12th grade season. She won the Lower Bucks County scoring title for field hockey in her senior year, 1958. The physical education department voted Joan and Ray Hayworth as winners of the "Babe Ruth" award that eventually came to be known as the "Falcon Award" after the school mascot.

Joan went off to college, earned her degree, and took her first teaching job in her original hometown of Gary. In her second year, an opening came up at Pennsbury and Joan began teaching at her old high school for the 1964-65 school year. She moved over to Medill Bair for several years before settling down as a phys ed teacher and coach at Pennwood Middle School. She became the swimming teacher at Pennwood, and taught there until the swimming program was closed in 1992.

"In 1992-93, I was asked to implement a physical education program for Special Needs students for grades K through 12," Marcotte added.

Marcotte also coached varsity softball from 1969-81. Her 1978 squad finished second in the state, losing to State College in the championship game. Joan anxiously watched as the implementation of Title IX began to very gradually improve the plight of women's athletics at the high school level. Perhaps not fast enough for Joan and the other female coaches and teachers.

"While coaching the varsity softball team, I submitted a request for a pitching machine in my budget perhaps two or three years after Title IX was passed and it kept getting cut from the budget because 'there was no money.' All along, the baseball team had a pitching machine. That went on until Pennsbury finally installed a Title IX compliance officer to make sure the law was followed. The year after this position was created, I put my request in for a pitching machine and again it was denied because 'there was no money.' This time, I felt I had some clout. I filed a grievance under Title IX. The athletic director came to my classroom (the Pennwood pool) and promised me that if I dropped the grievance, I would get the pitching machine the next year. I said no, I wanted to pursue it. The following week, I got a visit from the Superintendent of the Pennsbury schools and he also promised me that if I dropped the grievance I would have the pitching machine the next year. I politely told him no, too. Both of them had told me the male coaches would not be happy about this because it would take away from their budget. But when the budget was approved in February, we had a pitching machine for softball. I was so happy to know that Title IX works that I went to my athletic director and asked if I could have an assistant coach. The boys' baseball team always had one. He said no, maybe next year. So I filed another grievance. I got my assistant coach that year and the following year, every girls' team, varsity, junior varsity and middle school had assistant coaches.

"Fast forward to my retirement in June 1998, my athletic director came to my retirement party and told the audience 'Joan taught me about Title IX.' That made me very proud."

In 2001, Joan Marcotte was inducted into the Pennsbury High Hall of Fame. In 2017, she was inducted into Pennsylvania Sports Hall of Fame, Bucks County Chapter. Earlier, in 1990, she had been inducted into the Trenton, N.J. Softball Hall of Fame.

MARCOTTE SISTERS – All grown up are, left to right: Cindy, Joan, Peggie, Jackie and Marie.

CHAPTER 25

The Marcottes and Mazenkos Had Some Fun!

By CINDY MARCOTTE MAZENKO

As with many of us, our family moved to Lower Bucks from somewhere else. In our case, it was from Gary, Indiana. My father was a steel worker in Gary who heard about the new United States Steel plant being developed in Morrisville, Pennsylvania. It was a great opportunity. With the steel mill came new homes and communities. There were an abundance of employment opportunities for construction workers.

I can remember touring the model homes on Route 1 in Fairless Hills. We set up residence on Waltham Road, near the Fairless View elementary school. My first friends from that time were the Mamie twins. Many of my neighborhood friends spent 90 percent of our summers at the Fairless Hills and Levittown swimming pools until we became old enough to work part-time jobs.

Some weekends my Dad would take us to the Levittown Shopping Center and we would get a soda at the Dime store. Also, the Towne Theater was a busy spot on weekend. It was a shame that it was torn down after we grew up.

Does anyone remember Doctor Suter? That was back in a time when doctors actually made house calls.

For fun, we used to go ice skating on the ponds at the Fairless Hills golf course and on Lake Caroline. I'd go home with frozen toes, but it was worth it.

Later, we moved to Parkway Drive. Before they built Wistar Woods, there was an empty lot referred to as "The Circle" where some teens would go to park at night. Memories, anyone?

Some of my best high school friends were Lorraine Goodwin, Kathy Klein, Denise Queen, Betsy Marozzi and Dolores Bak. We were lucky to be in schools where we had so many opportunities to participate in sports. Friday night football games and canteen were highlights of the week. I participated in gymnastics and cheerleading. They were my favorite activities. The Bairlympiad and Sports Night were also very special. I loved school!

I'm sure there are many good memories I just can't recall. That's why class reunions mean so much to me. They help jog my memory.

ANNUAL AFFAIR – The Mazenko family held family reunions for 53 straight years until Covid-19 forced them to sit out 2020. Top row: Mary Helen, Linda, Bob, Terry, Tom, Chuck, JoJo. Front row: Bill, Tim, Rudy, Bubs, and Jim. Absent: Peg Mazenko.

Mazenko Family Stuck Together

By TOM MAZENKO

Here we go! Way back in the 1950s, a tribe of Mazenkos came storming in to Lower Bucks County, led by Joseph and Thelma Mazenko. Only knowing the coal mines of Western PA, what a shock it was to see one house right after another. They all looked the same! We settled in the Goldenridge section of Levittown and then moved to Bath Road in Bristol before moving our family of 15 into Fairless Hills, over in the H Section, on Stanford Road.

My greatest memories are from our days in Fairless Hills. We lived in a modest house with three bedrooms and one bath. Our parents had 13 children (and two more who died young) but four of them were old enough and were already out on their own. There were nine children living in the Fairless Hills house. I want to mention all of my brothers and sisters because they were the greatest clan in the world. You can see them in the family reunion photo that runs with this story.

We were cramped into that house like little ants, but we were happy. We slept three or four to a bed and once you got into bed, you couldn't get out! We were poor but didn't really know it at the time. My mother was always doing laundry. And I think she baked 25 loaves of bread every week.

We had a lot of friends to hang out with, including John Quatrocchi, Jimmy Barnes, the Wysor brothers (Jim and Tom), Carey Vonada, John Coutts and so many others. If people could only realize how many amazing families and friends we had in our towns. My growing up years were priceless and unforgettable. We played sports all the time – baseball, basketball and football. Whatever was in season, that's what we played. There was a big field behind the church off of Wistar Road where we mostly played football and baseball.

When I went to the Fairless pool, there was a girl I fell in love with and to this day, Cindy Marcotte Mazenko, is the love of my life. We raised two wonderful people (Chad and Sheri) and have a beautiful granddaughter, Paige.

We have a "Mazenko Family Reunion" every year on the first Saturday in August. So far, 53 reunions and counting. Roughly 125 or 130 people attend. One highlight is the auction that helps fund the event. It's usually a three-day affair (Friday through Sunday). I've never missed a family reunion until last year, when everyone's lives were changed by that damn pandemic.

My Dad was a heavy equipment operator and a number of his sons followed in his footsteps. I had three brothers join the Navy, three join the Army and I was an Air Force guy. I've lost five brothers since 2010 and miss them every day, but what great memories I have.

Cindy's sisters (Peggy, Joan, Marie and Jackie) are great friends and a wonderful support system for Cindy and I. I feel so good and proud of my family and friends.

I played three varsity sports for Pennsbury – soccer, basketball and baseball. During the summer, we went to the Fairless pool every day. And we played either Babe Ruth of American Legion baseball.

We always had something to do when I was young. If kids of today could live in our shoes for just a short time, they would realize what family and friends can do to enrich their lives and influence their adult lives, too. The values and trust we put in each other is something we all seemed to live by in our hometowns.

GROWING FAST – Carolyne Keefer and her brother Bob posed with their parents during the early 1960s.

CHAPTER 26

Living the Life in Lower Bucks!

By CAROLYNE KEEFER JONES

You would have thought we were moving to a palatial mansion when my Dad announced we were moving from the projects in Lacey Park to the sprawling suburbs of North Park, Levittown in August of 1953! It was pure excitement to watch our new house being built on a slab of cement in just a day! Levitt set in motion the assembly line approach for building houses. Each set of workers had a specific job to perform which enabled each house to be completed in the record time of 15 minutes! At the time, as a service to WWII vets for their service, no down payment was required for buying a house. Imagine that today! While construction workers were assembling our house, landscapers on tractors were feverishly lowering the rotary drills to dig holes for new trees and bushes. Later we would welcome, as well as curse, the fruit bearing peach tree as our mother insisted we form an assembly line to produce jars and jars of peach jelly! Where else could you have milk delivered to your door or have the Bond bread man bring his tray of delectable goodies right to your house!

Many men came to Levittown and Fairless Hills to work in the steel mill or the other alternative, Kaiser, where my Dad was employed as a supervisor. After working one year at Kaiser while completing his B.S. degree in Education at Temple, he moved on to become teacher, principal and maintenance man in a one-room school in the New Jersey pines at Chatsworth. After a year of living in the basement of the isolated schoolhouse, he secured a teaching position with Bristol Township to be closer to home. I might add a note of interest here since the name Joe Mormello resonates with many living in Lower Bucks. Dad had the pleasure of having Joe in his class the year he taught at Oxford Valley Elementary. Their friendship lasted throughout the years. Joe was to become a chiropractor who influenced and inspired my brother, Bob, to pursue the same career path. Bob, (Pennsbury class of '70) after graduating from Palmer Chiropractic, moved to Florida where he set up shop, thanks to Joe Mormello!

Most mothers were stay-at-home domestic engineers but there were a few exceptions, my mother for one. She was a professional model and had the looks to go with the title. I've been told

131

the guys would use me as an excuse just to get a glimpse or gasp at my mother's good looks! Glad I could help them out!

Waiting for Penn Valley Elementary to be completed, the youngsters of North Park were shipped to Fallsington Elementary to begin their early education. North Park was becoming a virtual ant colony of kids who walked to school and quite a few also walked home for lunch. Many lifelong friendships were formed at Penn Valley. We hopscotched from Penn Valley to Oxford Valley for 6th grade, William Penn for 7th and 8th grade, (where I might add that puppy love relationships were born, including my own with Carl Jones. I would later become friends with his sister, Pam Dopson, on Facebook after I learned of Carl's early unfortunate passing in 2006). Then it was on to Medill Bair for 9th and 10th, and finally Pennsbury High for 11th and 12th to become part of a graduating class of 742 (although that number may be disputed!) It was at Medill Bair that we discovered a social outlet on Friday nights known as canteen, where we could let loose dancing the night away! I waited in anticipation for the "jitterbug" contest with my steady partner, Charley Stevenson. We didn't win but we sure had fun! It was tradition that after canteen, bunches of us would walk through the woods to Landy's where you never knew if the occasional fight might break out over some relationship issue. What other reason would incite a fight?!

It was also while I was a student at Medill Bair that I was reminded by Bob May that he escorted me to the 9th grade dance and the only time he escorted me anywhere, until 50 years later when we would run into each other at my 50th high school reunion and the rest is history! (Bob crashed it with his best buddy, Russ Kaufman. Their names would be synonymous with "double trouble!")

By 9th and 10th grade, relationships were forming and I was no exception, having met Frankie Paulsworth at the St. Michael's fair. Frankie was my boyfriend for the next three years and my first true love. We would later meet up after 50-plus years and I must say he was an "older" version of his "younger" self and that is a compliment! Other than romantic relationships, girlfriends became best friends known as BFF in today's lingo. Two of my BFF's are Marlene MacDowell, now living in Tampa, Florida, and Rhonda Shire, who resides in Medford, New Jersey. Although we are living far from one another, we are still in touch and see each other occasionally. The 50th high school reunion reconnected many past and future friendships, continuing at the Boot, initiated by our leader, Ron Meyers, who is the glue that keeps us stuck together! The "chicks" from the class of '65 still get together for lunch every few months, organized by our leader, Barb Merryman, who is the glue that keeps the girls together! Look for pictures on Facebook!

Who doesn't remember riding the big yellow bus to school? In those days that was the only mode of transportation for cars weren't allowed and most of us couldn't afford them anyway. I remember Jack was our bus driver and was as sweet as they come as he waited patiently for us to run and catch the bus. I occasionally would babysit for his children. Frankie would often wait for me after school in his green truck that he used for his landscaping business, saving me the long ride home in the "Cheezemobile!" Funny, the things you remember!

And now back to earlier days growing up in North Park. Although our houses were suitable for the family initially, expansion was inevitable, and so additions became necessary to accommodate growing families. My folks added up and out, with a dining room and family room on the ground level, and two bedrooms, one of which was mine, on the upper level, including a room to house my

Dad's massive HO train collection. And of course a bathroom was necessary for a growing teen! Many memorable parties were held in that family room!

North Park was a cornucopia of kids migrating from all parts of Pennsylvania and beyond so there was no shortage of friends. Some that I remember who lived close by were Marsha, Linda, Sandy, Patty and Betsy and to this day we are still in touch. Guess you could say it's the tie that binds! North Park had everything a kid could want: sidewalks for hopscotch; streetlights for staying out after dark; ballfields; playgrounds; and an Olympic-size swimming pool with a high diving board. And of course plenty of kids to play with; all ages, shapes and sizes! It was a utopian paradise of activities!

Thank goodness for the Levittown Shopping Center, because that's where we'd go when we played hooky from school. Now that I think about it, it's a wonder we didn't get caught! The shopping center was the first of its kind, all open with a variety of stores, most of which are now extinct, and the upscale (at least for that time) anchor department store, Pomeroy's, where I later worked. Who doesn't remember Lobel's, the go-to store for your Brownie and Girl Scout uniforms. Or the affordable Lerner's, with an inventory of everything from lingerie to prom dresses. Then there was Woolworth's famous lunch counter with red swivel stools, where you could order the traditional lunch grub. When you finished stuffing your belly, many aisles of five and dime items were up for grabs and easy on your wallet! If you couldn't find something at Woolworth's, there was always Kresge's or W.T. Grant to pick up the slack. Who remembers grocery shopping at Penn Fruit or Food Fair? Levitt sure was ahead of his time, and so Levittown continued to grow and grow and grow with many more sections being built to accommodate migrating families!

CHEERFUL GIRLS – The junior high cheerleading squad at Medill Bair in the early 1960s included, front row, left to right: Cindy Marcotte, Roberta Eisenstein, Linda Strang, Bonnie Antuzzi, Lorraine Goodwin. Back row: Chris Gudusky, Sandy Thompson, Denise Queen, Kathy Klein, Janie Griffiths, Coach Coral Koffke.

CHAPTER 27

Janie Griffiths Found Her Values 'Upstate'

By TERRY NAU

Long before her family moved to Fairless Hills in 1955, Janie Griffiths' value system had been installed during her formative years in "upstate" Pennsylvania.

"My parents, David and Thelma Griffiths, were from the Pottsville area, coal country, a little place that was called Newtown at the time," Janie recalled. "They changed the town's name to 'Zerbe' when I was young because of the Newtown that already existed in Bucks County. We lived about nine miles outside of Pottsville. Thelma did not like living in a small coal town. Earlier, when my father went off to fight in World War II, mom got an apartment in Philadelphia. She just loved the area outside of the city."

Janie came along in 1947 and lived her first eight years in a coal town.

"We got indoor plumbing for the first time when I was four years old," she said, laughing at the memory. "I learned my work ethic when I was very young, just by watching my parents. My dad owned a few small coal mines that he took care of himself. He would cut the trees down and work the mines without much help. His side of the family was Irish and mother's side was German. I can remember when all of my aunts would come to our house almost every Tuesday. They would bake up pies and cakes and cook for everyone. My father had some rules. There would be no crying. We should 'make hay while the sun shines.' That was one of his sayings that we heard often. Never lie, never steal. Be loyal and do good deeds whenever you could. Try to help out people who have less than you do."

Dave Griffiths began calling his daughter "Calamity Jane" at a young age.

"I was always getting into trouble," Janie said. "If any boys picked on my friends, I would punch them in the nose. One time my mother sewed me a new dress and before long I had jumped into a pile of coal and ruined the dress. When I was four, I went up to the bathroom and cut off all my hair. I guess I was a bit of a devil. That's when dad started calling me 'Calamity Jane.' "

In 1955, Thelma Griffiths finally got her wish. The family picked up and moved to Fairless Hills.

"We were the only part of the upstate family that moved out," Janie said. "My dad became a welder in the steel mill. We moved to Eldridge Road and I made some good friends right away – Mary Jane Buchanan, Glenda Himes, Merrily Evans and Cindy Marcotte. We played kickball, hopscotch, we rode our bikes behind the mosquito trucks … did you do that? We played baseball up at the end of the street. I slid into home plate one time and almost sliced a finger off on a bottle sticking out of the ground. I loved being on the swim team and water ballet team with Cindy and Denise Queen and probably other friends I can't remember."

"I was very much a tomboy," Janie admitted. "I was taller than everyone else. By high school, I was around 5-foot-10. All the boys seemed like shrimps to me. We grew them bigger upstate! All my friends were short except for Denise Queen."

Her real name was Jayne but everyone in school seemed to call her "Janie." The tall, smiling girl with curly brown hair tried every sport in school, including gymnastics, basketball, softball, swimming and field hockey.

"I also became a cheerleader," she said. "I don't know why. Maybe because I could do a cartwheel and a split."

Janie said she loved attending school and enjoyed all of her friends. Her family was not rich but Janie rarely lacked for anything.

"Dad had a good job and mother went to work at Reedman's," she said. "Thelma eventually became a controller in the Rambler department. Remember the Rambler? Well, my folks were making pretty good money because they both worked. Mom used to buy us clothes whenever we needed them. Once she bought me a cashmere coat. I gave it to a friend of mine. Mother wanted to kill me and made me get it back. I just always felt bad for the kids who didn't have as much as we did."

One thing Janie hated about school were the occasional bullies she encountered.

"Remember Raymond Gould?" she asked. "He was a very little kid with glasses. If he sneezed in class, he would put his hands up to his face and all the kids would look at him and some laughed. One time at a school dance, when the boys had to walk all the way across the floor to ask a girl to dance, Raymond walked over and asked me to dance. Everyone was looking. Of course I accepted. Absolutely! Those are the memories I have from school. That is one of the best ones, dancing with Ray Gould."

After she graduated, Janie found more calamity when she became pregnant.

"My parents never told me how NOT to get pregnant," Janie said with laughter in her voice. "I got married and we had the baby. When I was 19, I opened my own beauty shop in Yardley. We were the first salon to cut men's hair. The salon was called M'Lady's. But my babysitter had to move away and that ended my salon because I had to be the babysitter at home. I started teaching hair dressing at Lawrence Academy from 6 to 10 in the evening. We had two children and then we got divorced."

Janie moved back in to care for her father when he became sick in the early 1990s.

"I sold my house on New Hope Road in Wycombe and came back home to care for dad," she said. "I became interested in horses. That is still a passion of mine. I love horses. I began by mucking out a little stable on the road behind Reedman's. Over the years, I have owned a bunch of horses and showed them in a lot of shows. I still do announcing for horse shows but I stopped riding the horses when I turned 70."

Calamity Janie is still going strong. Don't worry about her. She is "upstate" tough.

WATCH THAT GUY! – Tom Scheffer once asked both Lorraine Goodwin, above, and Merrily Evans to the same dance when they were in grade school. Here he is just focused on Lorraine in ninth grade.

CHAPTER 28

From Farmland to Busy Suburbs in a Blink!

By LORRAINE GOODWIN

Under my name in the Pennsbury High Class of School 1965 yearbook, the home address is listed as 210 Center Avenue, Fairless Hills. But this is a bit misleading. When my parents, Tom and Marie Goodwin, sister Lois and I moved from a row home on Dallas Street in Northeast Philadelphia in 1948, there was no Fairless Hills. We were surrounded by farmland. The area we moved into was known then as Oxford Valley and we were moving to the "country."

We bought a sweet little two-bedroom house on a large lot with tall trees and lush green juniper shrubbery surrounding the foundation. We bought some chickens to fill the coops in our backyard and cooked hot dogs on the brick fireplace. We had grapevines filled with juicy concord grapes that we picked for our mother to use in the jelly she made and then sealed for later.

The farmland beyond our backyard bordered our property line and went as far as the eye could see. Our tiny dead-end street had only 10 houses and was bordered on one end by the then two-lane Oxford Valley Road, and on the other end by a field with some large apple trees that extended to the shoulder of the two-lane main highway, Route 1. Our mailing address was RD#2 Langhorne, that being the closest town with a post office. With no street name or house numbers we would all walk to the end of the street to pick up our mail from the large mail boxes placed there.

At the corner of Oxford Valley Road and Route 1 (where Pep Boys now stands) was a little country store where we would buy our groceries and other items. My mother would call in her order for the week and the grocer, Stan Lutz, would deliver to our house that afternoon.

The farm directly behind our house bordered our property line. Our neighbor, Walter Hill, was a pilot who did the "crop dusting" of that field in a small prop plane that was most likely hangared at the Old Star Airport across from the Langhorne Speedway on Route 1. We became very accustomed to his familiar routine and the roaring sounds of the low flying plane beyond our backyard.

My Dad began working as a milkman at Greenwood Dairies on Route 1. His alarm was always set for 2 a.m. He would begin his long work day by loading his truck with large blocks of ice and all the dairy products for his customers. After delivery he would return all the empty glass bottles back to the dairy.

His regular delivery route was the Council Rock/Newtown area. Some years later we had a very big snowstorm and since our little street was never plowed, he decided to walk the two miles to the dairy. That night he told us about the snow piles and huge drifts 8-10 feet high on both sides of the farm-lined roads. The next day he drove us up to see the sights and it was like driving through a long snow tunnel. That fascinated him and is a great memory that remains with me to this day.

By the time I was four years old, big changes were coming to Oxford Valley. Most of the farms off Route 1, Trenton Rd and parts of Oxford Valley Road had been sold off to the Danherst Corporation which would build Fairless Hills. During a burst of activity from 1951-54, heavy trucks, bulldozers and their work crews plowed over the old farmland and started building the simple, one-story prefab homes all the way to Trenton Road and beyond on both sides of Oxford Valley Road. On warm summer nights, our family would wander over to see the progress of the newly-built homes on Austin Drive.

About this time, my sister Lois had started kindergarten at the Fallsington Library, which was actually across the street from the school. Her first grade class was in the school itself, and by second grade the sample Fairless Hills' houses that had been built on Trenton Road became classrooms. I started kindergarten that same year in those sample houses.

Some of my Oxford Valley classmates were Barry Linington, Jackie Broadnix and Michael Ruski from Fallsington. By now, we were given a street sign and house number, mine being 210 Center Ave, Fairless Hills. Just to complicate life, Danherst installed an eight-foot tall cyclone fence topped by barbed wire to mark the boundary between Fairless Hills and the old Oxford Valley line.

Next came the giant water tower behind our neighbor's house. Luckily their huge sycamore trees formed a canopy of leafy branches to hide the tower's tall legs during most of the year.

Soon my little world would be expanding with many new faces. Once the Oxford Valley elementary school was completed, I attended first grade there. At some point during that year we were all transferred to the newly-completed Fairless View School. I loved my first-grade teacher, Miss Barbara Lex, and enjoyed school from then on through high school and college.

Mr. Williams was a favorite teacher at Fairless View as well as Mr. Rathgeber and Mr. Houser. One of my earliest and best school friends was Merrily Evans, who lived only two streets away on Andover Road. Since her house was a walkable distance from my own, we enjoyed a long friendship in and outside of school. Crazy memories from Fairless View School included the "duck and cover" air raid drills either under our desk or out in the hallway. And all the talk of needing to build bomb shelters in your basement or outside of your home. I only saw many of my friends during school hours, outside of school group activities or the occasional birthday party. Some friends were Eileen Miller, Ginger Fisher, Cindy Marcotte, Sandy Dunn and Janie Griffiths. There was also Jimmy Ghrist, Bill Richardson, Danny Forester, Fred Beck, Billy Ericson and my Center Ave neighbor, Lee Johnson.

And who could forget our cherub-faced friend Tommy Scheffer, who became friends with both

Merrily and myself and decided to invite us both to a cub scout event as his dates? We were only about 8 or 9 at the time and Tommy then apparently had some trepidation about the logistics of his arrangement, but his mother found out and made him take us both. But who can blame Tommy for being a playboy at such a young age? We remained friends throughout our school years and even went to the ninth grade dance together. But I guess he learned his lesson, and this time it was just the two of us!

Showing its dedication to the evolving suburban lifestyle, Danherst built a Little League complex just beyond the cyclone fence in our backyard. Over the years, weeknights and on weekends, the teams would play ball (seemingly non-stop) and the stands were filled with cheering parents and friends. Our job was to retrieve the foul balls that were hit over the concession stand and over the fence into our yard. There was always lots of activity at the ballpark.

When the Fairless Hills swimming pool opened, most of my school friends spent their summer days there. But since the families on our side of the cyclone fence were not considered residents, we couldn't join the pool club. Merrily's mother made a big fuss about this situation, and after that we were able to go as visitors and guests of the Evans family. But if my memory serves me correctly, the temperature had to be at least 80 degrees to go to the pool (as per Mrs. Evans' rule).

My sister and I had limited playmates on Center Ave since there was only one other girl, Cathie Hill, and six boys (four of the boys were much older). But at the end of our street and across Oxford Valley Road lived Bev Briegel, who would become a close and longtime friend. We would walk to her house or she to ours almost daily after school and on weekends. In Bev's basement was a row of antique school desks where we would love to play school and check out books in our play library. We loved jumping rope, playing hopscotch and roller skating as fun pastimes. In our backyard, there was a small detached building we called "The Little House." It was the perfect spot for our playtime activities. We loved playing with our many dolls, like Tiny Tears, Ricky Jr, Toni Dolls, Saucy Walker, Ginny Dolls and Madame Alexander. We would also spend hours playing with our paper dolls or board games like Monopoly and Clue. Fun memories and we still remain close friends all these years later.

Our black-and-white television got a good workout in the 50's and 60's. We never wanted to miss those Saturday morning or weekday afternoon shows. Some of my favorites were Howdy Doody, Ramar of the Jungle, The Lone Ranger, Sally Starr, The Mickey Mouse Club, I Love Lucy, The Cisco Kid, Superman, Lassie and Rin Tin Tin. Winky Dink was a fun show where a piece of vinyl plastic held by static electricity stuck to our tv screen. We would connect the dots on the magic screen to decode messages with our Winky Dink crayons.

In second grade, I was in a Brownie troop with some of my friends, and then we moved on to the Girl Scouts. One of those years, my mother volunteered to be "the cookie chairman" for our troop. This meant all of the cookie box orders taken by our members would be delivered to our house. Once delivered, they would be picked up by the girls to be distributed to their customers. We ended up having about 300 boxes of cookies piled to the ceiling in our tiny dining room.

After sixth grade, we went off to William Penn for seventh and eighth grade and had new experiences like changing classes, personal lockers, and meeting more new friends from Levittown,

Yardley and the Morrisville areas. Some of the new faces were Joe Baron, Tucker Schwartz, Carol Bethke, Kathy Klein and Roberta Eisenstein. Kathy and I still remain close to this day.

At Medill Bair, along with Cindy, Carol and Kathy, we had the added fun of meeting new teammates on the hockey and basketball teams and cheerleading squad like Bonnie Antuzzi and Denise Queen. There were also boys like John Friemann and Joe Hodgson. I still remember Joe driving the big white Lincoln Continental with the doors that opened from the middle the summer after tenth grade. Bairlympiad capped off those two years with fun times for all.

Looking back, I have to say my favorite school memories were at Pennsbury High School for 11th and 12th grades. I was able to rekindle some friendships from our middle years at William Penn and also meet many new friends at the high school. A few new faces in our now combined schools were John Davis in Mr. Lambert's Algebra class and "little" Bob Smith in French III with the always animated Mr. Cobb. It was amazing how large our graduating class had become.

As a cheerleader, the beginning of the school year was the start of our cheering duties for the weekend football games. We had the excitement of the pep rallies prior to the game and the fun of cheering at the big event either home or away. I loved football season and the fun times after each game. Of course, one of the biggest games was with our rival Neshaminy where crowds filled the bleachers. Then came cheering for all the varsity basketball games. The gym was always filled with cheering fans as the teams raced up and down the court. Always a fun night at those games.

Our biggest sports-related event was Sports Nite in the spring. The behind the scenes preparations for those two nights were overwhelming, but so rewarding. Meeting at homes to paint the large team murals for the walls of the gymnasium was a nice social get-together in a casual setting. My weekends usually consisted of fun activities with John Tanner and some double dates with Dennis Beuchler and Heidi Kosa or with Kenny Homa and Donna Servis. The senior prom was a very special all-night event to remember. The decorations, the dancing, the hypnotist and the breakfast to follow. I have such great memories of the prom. Finally, graduation was the culmination of all those wonderful years preparing for our futures.

I had a great start in life at good old PHS. And I am so thankful for the wonderful memories. I'm happy with the way my life turned out. We grew up in a fairly innocent time and I followed a good path. The fact-finding exercise into the past for this book has made me feel justified in saving those old scrapbooks with brittle pages and yellowed, crumbling newspaper articles and pictures for over 60 years. I knew they would come in handy someday!

Finally, I would like to end with a tribute to my parents, Tom and Marie Goodwin. My dad had a very hard life. His mother died when he was two years old. His father was 56 at the time and could not care for his two sons. He placed them both in foster homes. My dad dropped out of school in eighth grade and went out on his own. He often slept in the garage of a school friend's house and did odd jobs until he was 18. It was in a factory job that he met my mother some years later.

I will always remember my father never used an adding machine at the office after work to tally the day's sales. He just did it all in his head. It is sad when you think of all the fathers from our generation who dropped out of school early to help their families survive during the Depression. They did not have the opportunities that their children had two or three decades later. Like playing team sports in high school, the way Lois and I did. I do know that my parents were both very proud that they could buy their own house and raise their two daughters inside that comfortable home at 210 Center Avenue. They lived there until 1997, 50 years after I was born!

Marie Goodwin typified the wife and mother of the era. She supported her hard-working husband and cared for the needs of her children in the manner of television moms like June Cleaver or Margaret Anderson. She wore the uniform of the stay-at-home moms of the day, a "housedress" and bibbed apron.

She began her mornings packing our lunch boxes, then serving us a hearty breakfast before we headed out the door. Each afternoon we knew she would be waiting at the door as we walked down the street from the bus to our home. Dinner would soon be prepared and we were in for some delicious comfort food made from scratch. Desserts were usually homemade pudding like rice, chocolate or farina. Sometimes we had ice cream and cookies or her famous Hot Milk Sponge Cake.

Every Sunday after church, we would look forward to a meal that was most likely her specialty of roast of beef and browned potatoes. Dessert was usually a homemade pie, especially if my grandparents were visiting, as they did on most Sundays.

Nothing was too much trouble for my mother when it came to her family. She sacrificed so many of her needs to make sure Lois and I had a wonderful childhood, and in that she succeeded.

* * *

(After graduating from Millersville State College and completing post-graduate work at Trenton State, Lorraine became a second grade teacher for the Pennsbury schools. She married in 1972 and raised four children while living most of her adult life in the state of Washington. She has since returned to the east coast and lives at the Jersey shore. Three of her four children and five grandchildren still live in Washington State and her sixth grandchild lives not far away in Morrisville, PA with her daughter and son in law. Like most grandmothers, Lorraine has had to rely on FaceTime and other technology to keep up with her children and grandchildren. That being especially true now during the pandemic and the ongoing travel restrictions.)

BASKETBALL STARS – Medill Bair's 10th grade basketball team got together for a photograph back in 1963. Team members include, first row, left to right: Ginger Lane, Vicky Hadden, Merrily Evans, Kathy Klein, Lorraine Goodwin, Denise Queen, Karen Worsman. Second row: Nora Fee, Kathy Jonas, Ellen Waggener, Eila Daugherty, Bonnie Antuzzi, Toni DeZolt, Mrs. Rebecca Hoffman, coach. Third row: Carolyn Domarski, Kathy Rick, Sue Ross, Jane Powanda, Sue Rishel, Beverly Vanderburg, Linda Dykes, Janette Toth.

CHAPTER 29

Sports Genes Run Through Klein Family

By KATHY KLEIN BETHKE

Our family got its interest and athletic talent from my father, Chuck Klein, who played football, basketball, baseball and track for the Langhorne/Middletown school in the 1930s that soon became known as Neshaminy High. Dad was inducted into the Neshaminy Hall of Fame in 1988.

My mom and dad lived in Bristol after their marriage in 1941. My brother Mike was born in 1942 and sister Patti came along in 1943. Dad worked at Rohm and Haas until World War II intervened. He was called into the service in 1944 and served in the Pacific Theater as the Allies began closing in on the island of Japan. Dad was promoted to Sergeant and received a Bronze Star, which is most often awarded for heroism in a combat zone.

My father returned home in 1946. I was born a year later and my sister Penny followed me into the world in 1951. Because of the GI Bill, my parents were able to purchase a home in the North Park section of Levittown, moving there in September 1953.

Mom and dad purchased a ranch-style home that cost $9,400. It came with only two bedrooms and one bath, not much space for a family of six people. The home had an unfinished upstairs which my father and uncles finished, adding two bedrooms and a half-bath as soon as they could. So it was a little cramped in our home, to say the least. We were in the same boat as many other large families that had moved into Levittown and Fairless Hills homes during the 1950s.

My older sister and brother were very upset at moving away from their friends in Bristol when they were just nine and 10 years old, respectively. Pat later told me that her friends from Bristol visited her at Magnolia Pool and she was embarrassed because they were a very rough group. We were probably fortunate to have moved into the quieter town of Levittown.

I attended Fallsington Elementary for first grade because our neighborhood school, Penn Valley, hadn't been completed yet. My best friend at the time lived across the street from me. Her name was Karen Brazel. I switched over to Penn Valley for second through fifth grades but Karen went on to Catholic school.

It was great to be able to walk to school and visit friends that lived in the surrounding sections of Levittown. In fourth and fifth grade, we had dances called "canteen" which were a lot of fun. My first boyfriend was John Friemann and Karen hooked up with Bobby Stoddart. John and I won the slow-dance contest and for a prize they would open the Coca Cola machine and give us free cokes, in a glass bottle.

Looking through my things, I also found a newspaper article from 1957 with a short story about Sharon Griffith's 10th birthday party. Yes, the newspaper publicized birthday parties in those early days of Levittown! The list of names attending included Linda Dykes, Nancy Smith, Bob Stoddart, John Friemann and David Fretts. John and I won the jitterbug contest . . . too funny!

In sixth grade, we were bused over to Oxford Valley Elementary in Fairless Hills because Penn Valley had become too crowded with students. Levittown was growing too quickly for the schools to keep up.

My fifth sibling, Chris, was born in 1958, making us a family of seven.

There were plenty of outdoor activities for us kids to engage in. We played hide-and-seek in the evening. We roller skated with metal skates that required a key. We rode bikes everywhere, went to Magnolia Pool almost every day in the summer and some nights we went to the Pinewood pool with my Dad.

We could walk to the Towne Theater in the Levittown Shopping Center and watch a movie for 25 cents and get a snack for 10 cents. We could even shop at Woolworths. My dad took us to Greenwood Dairies on Route 1 in Langhorne for their huge cones overflowing with our favorite ice cream. In the winter, we could skate on Lake Caroline in Fairless Hills.

During the summer, Penn Valley Elementary offered crafts, kick ball and field trips. Every year, they would take us to Connie Mack Stadium in Philadelphia to see the Phillies play. My favorite players were Richie Ashburn and Robin Roberts.

Once I entered seventh grade, Pennsbury combined students from Fairless Hills, Levittown, Lower Makefield and Yardley into William Penn Junior High on Trenton Road, about a mile or two from North Park. This is where I made many new friends, including Lorraine Goodwin and Carol Bethke. Lorraine and I remain close friends today and have traveled to Europe and Mackinaw Island together. Carol is my sister-in-law. I met her brother Fred, Class of 1962, through her. Fred and I have celebrated 53 years together with two sons and four grandchildren.

We switched over to the new Medill Bair school for ninth and 10th grades. I had a great time in those years, playing field hockey and basketball. We had a Bair Leaders Club which was a group to lead classes and to assist in directing the physical fitness program that President Kennedy had created after his election in 1960. I became a cheerleader and also participated in the BairLympiad. Our cheerleading squad supported the soccer, football and basketball teams. Members included Chris Gudusky, Sandy Thompson, Denise Queen, Jayne Griffiths, Cindy Marcotte, Roberta Eisenstein, Linda Strang, Bonnie Antuzzi, Lorraine Goodwin and myself. But in 10th grade, cheerleading was dropped. Instead we focused on BairLympiad. I served as captain of the Orange Cheerleading squad for that event. The theme that year was North against the South. Cindy Marcotte and Bob Burkhart were captains for the Orange team. Denise Queen and Doug Powell captained the Black team. The Orange prevailed!

We changed schools again for 11th and 12th grade, taking the bus to Yardley where Pennsbury High School was then located. I played varsity softball and basketball during my final two years of school. Girls basketball was a lot different in those days. We only played half-court. That changed, not sure if in 11th or 12th grade, but the coaches added a roving forward and guard situation. The rovers could cross over into the other court. Seems so archaic now, considering all the advances in girls' basketball since Title IX became law of the land in 1972.

All of the Klein children played sports. My brother Mike, who graduated in 1960, lettered in three sports – baseball, football and wrestling. Patti, Class of 1961, was a cheerleader and also played basketball. Since Pennsbury's colors were orange and black, we used to decorate our father's old black car with orange paint and the cheerleaders would ride in the car during a parade before every home game.

Penny, who graduated from Pennsbury in 1969, played field hockey, basketball and captained the Black team during Sports Night. She was inducted into the Pennsbury Hall of Fame in 2006.

Chris, Class of 1976, played football and wrestled. He is in the Pennsbury Wrestling Hall of Fame and went on to play football at the United States Naval Academy before graduating in 1980. Chris became a Navy pilot and did flight training at Pensacola Air Base in Florida. He served on the Independence, an aircraft carrier, and flew an A7 jet. He is now a Captain with American Airlines.

I have watched and participated in sports almost my entire life. It was fun to watch my brothers and sisters, nieces, nephews, great nieces and nephews, children and now my grandchildren play sports. Fred and I still love to go to games to see our grandchildren participate.

LIFELONG PARTNERS – Ed Quill met his wife Virginia, also a Pennsbury High graduate, a couple years after high school while on a blind date.

CHAPTER 30
Ed Quill Recalls Wonderful Life

By TERRY NAU

"My father was a milkman," Ed Quill revealed. "Some of my favorite memories of growing up were the times when he would take me on his route early in the morning. I think I got my work ethic from my father."

Ed was one of five children who grew up on Woolston Drive, a busy road that Pennsbury school buses would travel on their way to the high school in Yardley. William H. Quill and his wife Barbra kept their eyes on the children, Bill Jr., Edward, Jim, Ann and Geoffrey. They also fostered three children.

"What encouraged my parents to provide a home for the three lovely kids was they had raised the children's father as a foster child. My Mom and Dad always had a place in their hearts for people who were less fortunate. We absolutely treated them as part of our family and we have somewhat stayed in touch. We considered them our cousins," Quill said.

The Quill children had to be careful when they stepped out of their driveway.

"You know where Tyburn Road fed into Route 1?" he said. "When you went under the tunnel on the way to Pennsbury High and turned right, that was Woolston Drive. We didn't have as many houses there as you would see in Fairless Hills or Levittown. There were not as many kids to play with. My neighbors included Ken Homa, Dennis Beuchler, David Poole and Ricky Bilger. Ricky introduced me to Mike Chalifoux, who lived a couple miles up Route 1. Mike would tell me stories about the work he had to do on his family's farm. I was pretty grateful we didn't have to work that hard!"

Ed's family arrived in Lower Bucks in the early 1900s.

"They originally settled in Newark, Delaware," he said. "Then they migrated to Lower Bucks County. My father's family settled into the Woodside/Edgewood section, just outside of Yardley. His whole family worked for Hancock Nursery, who were rose peddlers. I was born in 1946 and in 1951 we moved over to Woolston Drive. We had a great time as kids. Our parents told us to come home before it got dark, before the street lights came on. But I don't think my mom ever worried about us. We were good kids."

Quill played recreational sports with the Pennsbury Athletic League in Lower Makefield. His neighbor, Kenny Homa, became a star football player who went on play at Duke University.

Ed was more interested in automobiles.

"I decided to attend Technical School over on New Falls Road because I was a mechanical nut," he said. "I loved everything about automobiles. This was during a time when teachers were telling us we should all go to college. Tech School gave me a chance to learn about things I was interested in. The only problem was Tech students had to attend Medill Bair instead of Charles Boehm, where most of my friends went to school. Our school schedule would have us spend two weeks at Bair and two weeks at Tech School. I had my Lower Makefield and Yardley friends and the kids from Medill Bair who were from Levittown and Fairless Hills. That experience taught me how to get along with everyone."

Tech School drew students from surrounding schools, too.

"We had students from Bensalem, Neshaminy and Woodrow Wilson," Quill recalled. "That could be a problem when our football teams had big rivalry games to play. But again, I got to know more people. What I learned from my Tech School experience is how dirty my hands got as an auto mechanic. I didn't want to go through life that way."

Ed Quill eventually landed in the newspaper business, working as a circulation manager and in marketing for the Trentonian and Trenton Times during a long career.

"The lessons I learned about problem-solving in Tech School helped me in my job," he said. "As I gained more experience in life, I realized that Tech School taught me valuable lessons in skills that are necessary. One of my brothers had a doctorate degree from college but he couldn't change a flat tire. From my position, I think the kids of today don't learn enough of the basic skills we need to get through life. So I have never regretted going to Tech School. We were in on the foundation of Tech schools. I think the educators were learning as they went along, just as we were."

Ed is the lone survivor among his brothers and sisters, which makes him sad. His wife Virginia passed away in January. They had two girls, Jennifer and Kimberly. Ed is retired now and lives in Bluffton, S.C.

"Ginny and I are both Pennsbury alumni," Quill said, thinking of his late wife. "She was the Class of 1967 and I was Class of 1965. Even though we attended school together, I wasn't fortunate enough to meet Ginny during high school. I do remember seeing her ride the bus to school with her friend, Lisa Ide. I was fortunate enough to meet Ginny in 1968 while she was attending Rider College. We actually met on a blind date. That poor girl must have been blind, figuratively speaking!"

"We got married in 1970 and in 2020 celebrated 50 years of marriage. As we both went through life dealing with all the problems that come with raising a family and earning a living, we both came to the conclusion that we were blessed. Life is a gift and we should all be grateful for what we have been granted."

Looking back, Ed appreciates the wisdom that comes from leading a full life.

"As we approached retirement, it was nice for Ginny and I to look back at all the memories we shared. Now that Ginny is gone, my faith has kept me strong. The secret, I think, is always to remain grateful. Make a list of everything for which you are grateful, even if it's just opening your eyes every morning."

Among all of his life memories, childhood stories have never lost their luster.

"I look back on those days when we were young and realize that was just a perfect time to grow up," Ed Quill said. "I've truly been blessed in my life."

TEMPORARY BRIDGE – The U.S. Army installed a Bailey Bridge over the Delaware River in Yardley after the Flood of 1955. The temporary bridge remained in place for six years.

CHAPTER 31

The Wrath of Connie and Diane

By PATTI SHEEHY

How One Family Survived the Flood of 1955

Two names are indelibly etched in my childhood memory: Connie and Diane. They were a couple of characters—loud, violent, and destructive. Their rage yielded untold harm and suffering. They came uninvited, and they didn't take "no" for an answer.

Being late to the party and making a dramatic entrance, Diane got most of the blame. She dazzled people with her derring-do, pulverizing homes, upending trees, and turning the tranquil Delaware into a wild torrent of chaos and debris. But Connie had prepared the way; she was no innocent bystander.

The sister hurricanes formed in August 1955 and arrived in the Delaware Valley a week apart. It had been a hot, dry summer and the soil was hard and parched. The drought broke on August 7 when a heavy storm dumped a hefty 2.9 inches of rain on the area. But that was just the beginning. Hurricane Connie made her debut on August 12, delivering five inches of rain within 24 hours. At first the ground was able to absorb the assault, but Connie was relentless, dropping water like a fire hose.

When Diane arrived on August 17 the soil was unable to absorb the added water, causing the Delaware to breach its banks. Water gushed into the river from upstream tributaries, submerging roads and ravishing homes and businesses. All told, the area had been pummeled with 12 inches of rain in fewer than 10 days.

My family owned a house on River Road in Yardley, halfway between the Yardley Inn and the then unbuilt Scudders Falls Bridge. I was nine, my brother Bill was eight, my sister Jane was five, and my mother was seven months pregnant. A collie named Mitzie completed our family.

My parents' tenth wedding anniversary was on August 18, and they had invited my grandparents and my Aunt Helen, a Sister of Charity, to help them celebrate. My grandparents lived in Connecticut and were staying the week; my aunt was enjoying a respite from her professorial duties at the College of St. Elizabeth.

My parents had tickets to St. John Terrell's Lambertville Music Circus the evening of August 19 and left me to babysit my siblings. I expected them home around midnight. It's trivial to say it was a dark and stormy night, but it was. Wind whipped the trees and rain pounded the roof like a herd of wildebeest. My parents returned around 9:30 p.m., soaked to the skin. The show had been cancelled due to poor acoustics and fear that the tent would collapse under the weight of the water.

The next morning the rain ceased falling, but the river kept rising. While the pavement was dry in front of our house, water was over the road in both directions and was lapping our back-yard garage. People waded through the water in rubber hip boots. We were trapped.

Neighbors gathered outside to talk. The consensus was that our house was on high ground, and since it had never been flooded before, we would be spared. My father wasn't so sure. Yardstick and notebook in hand, he periodically measured the rise of the river against the riverbank stairs.

The water was advancing at an alarming rate. From our front lawn we watched sheds, out-houses and massive trees float downstream. Later that morning a bungalow, perched on its side, demolished half of the Yardley-Wilburtha Bridge. Afterwards, the U.S. Army Corp of Engineers replaced the missing bridge section with a "temporary" Bailey bridge that remained until the Scudders Falls Bridge opened in 1961.

Grim-faced, Dad walked into the house and announced that we had to move our belongings to the second floor. My middle-aged aunt wrapped her arms around the console TV; Bill helped with tables; I lugged lamps, books and dinnerware. My father and grandfather handled larger pieces of furniture. Not all was saved.

The next order of business was to secure a boat. Fortunately, my brother recalled that our next-door neighbor stored a canoe in the rafters of her garage. Ecstatic, my father offered to take Mrs. Piper to safety if she would lend us her canoe to evacuate the family. Wading through water up to his armpits, he liberated the canoe from storage. He and Grampa paddled Mrs. Piper a half mile to the Towpath Bridge where a volunteer fireman escorted her to safety. Now they needed to do the same for all of us.

Upon his return, Dad announced the evacuation plan. The canoe could only hold two people in addition to my dad and grandfather. Mom and Jane would go first. Then Bill and me, etc. Aunt Helen announced that the plan should adhere to Roman Catholic Canon Law. Visibly annoyed, my father stated that he, and he alone, would decide the order of departure. My mother worried aloud about the difficulty of paddling against the current. Dad shrugged and calmed our fears.

After Mom and Jane departed, the rest of us waited on the back porch. By then the waters of the Delaware River had joined the Delaware Canal, which ran behind our house. The muddy water was rushing up the driveway and spilling into our cellar. My stomach lurched at the sound of water invading our house.

After what seemed like an eternity, my father and grandfather returned for my brother and me. We stepped into the canoe amid swirling water. The canoe tipped to one side and my father righted it. We floated over the clothesline and watched in awe as wildlife struggled to survive. A black snake slithered by.

Three more trips were required: one for my Aunt Helen who was transported alone due to her weight, one for my grandmother and Mitzie, and a very foolish trip to bring my pregnant mother back home to use the bathroom.

Friends housed us for a week before we headed to Connecticut to stay with relatives. My father remained behind to work on the house, which contained a foot of mud and had been flooded with five feet of water. We lived there happily for ten more years.

Looking back, I'm amazed at how calmly and competently my parents handled the situation. At the time, my mother was 29 and my father was 34. Since no one died, the flood was viewed not as a tragedy but as an adventure worthy of decades of storytelling.

I have no idea what happened to the canoe.

* * *

Patti Sheehy grew up in Yardley and graduated from Pennsbury High School and Rider College. She is the author of two books: The Boy Who Said No *and* Stalked. *She resides with her husband in Haddon Heights, New Jersey.*

FOREVER HOME – In 1947, George Milne stood with wife Eleanor, daughter Nancy and son Dennis on the front yard of their first and only family home.

CHAPTER 32

George Milne Saw His Dream Come True

By NANCY MILNE

In 1947 my parents, Eleanor and George Milne, as well as my brother Dennis and I moved into the first and only house they would ever own. The ownership of one home lived in for close to a lifetime was not unusual in those days as people didn't relocate like people do today.

Our house was located on Glenolden Road in Makefield Township. The land had once been an apple orchard and for a number of years those trees gave us many sweet red apples to enjoy and strong branches to climb. These were two of the many fun outdoor activities we were fortunate enough to enjoy in our younger years.

Our house was the first of many homes built in this quiet idyllic area located between the Delaware River and the Delaware Canal. The builder was a man named Charles Blauthe, who my father had met at Trenton Country Club where he was the Head Golf Professional. My dad, like many of his time, came from a hard-working family that never would have dreamed of owning their own home. When Mr. Blauthe took my dad to see a home he was building, my father fell in love with it and purchased it on the spot. When he told my mother she of course was quite surprised and not sure. After he took her to see it, she wasn't thrilled but she could never tell him, as he was so very proud to be able to give his family a home of their own. She lived there for 51 years, my dad for 36, and my brother and I were raised there.

Our little neighborhood grew into a perfect size that was not real small, but small enough to still be a close knit community with a lot of children. It was not uncommon for our parents to tell us to be home before dark and they never worried about where we were or who we were with. One of our biggest and most enjoyable events was our Fourth of July picnic and parade. All the kids in the neighborhood would decorate their bikes with red, white and blue streamers and we would ride all over the neighborhood for everyone to see.

Meanwhile our mothers prepared delicious food to be shared at the family picnic which was held at the end of our street in a small patch of common ground. We also would go into the nearby farmer's field that wasn't being farmed anymore and pick fresh raspberries and blackberries.

Halloween was another big event in the neighborhood that was preceded by "Trick or Treat" the night before Halloween. We would get together with all our friends and go from house to house ringing door bells and throwing corn. Most of the neighbors were very considerate and just went along with the prank. However, there was one neighbor that lived two doors down from us that didn't appreciate it, so one year he threw water on us from an upstairs window. Obviously, some kids got wet and had to go home and change but all in all it was just a fun time. This was also the neighbor that never gave candy, but rather a penny or a nickel! Back then people usually made their own Halloween costumes rather than buying them. One year I was a deck of cards. My mother cut a hole in a sheet for my head and two more holes for my arms. She attached playing cards all over the sheet and we made a hat out of cards. If you wanted to receive a treat on Halloween most neighbors required you to come into their home so they could guess who you were and then you received the candy. Those early years for us certainly were a time unlike any other we would probably ever experience again.

When growing up in the 1950's it was not unusual to have your pet dogs with you and your friends while you played all over the neighborhood. Dogs had to have licenses, but they didn't have to stay on your property or be chained up. While we lived on Glenolden Rd., we had quite a few dogs over a period of probably thirty years, which was even after Denny and I each had married and moved out.

Although it was an idyllic time, we still had moments that were sad and difficult. Our first English Setter, Patsy was stolen from us and our second setter named Jill we had to give away. She was very protective of Dennis and I and one day when he was playing cowboys and Indians a neighborhood boy picked up a stick and went towards my brother. Jill instinctively thought the boy was going to hit him so she put her paws on his back. He ran home crying and screaming even though he didn't have a mark on him. His parents made such a fuss we had to give Jill away. When the constable came to take Jill away, Dennis and I were bawling our eyes out and feeling like our world had come to an end. However, one day shortly thereafter, we were having our usual Monday (Dad's day off) family car ride through the country and guess what! We saw Jill and her new owner out in the field. Jill looked healthy and happy.

Of course, you are wondering how we knew it was Jill. She had a crook at the end of her tail and we knew she had been given to a nearby farmer. Although we were sad at first and did shed some tears, we felt fortunate to know she was just fine. In those days the majority of the land in Makefield Township was farmland. Like a lot of places, that has changed and now there is an abundance of houses. When I was young we girls played dolls, hop scotch and jump rope all day long. Boys and girls rode their bikes, played hide and seek and kick the can often until dark. Oh how we hated to have to go in the house on Sunday nights for a bath and school the next day.

I went to the Pennsbury School District from kindergarten through high school and it was a wonderful learning experience as well as a safe, enjoyable and rewarding time. Yes, for the most part I did like school. In kindergarten I met many of the students that I would know well into adulthood and two of those classmates would become my best and lifelong friends. One was a girl that did not live in my neighborhood but I could ride my bike to her house. Her name was Kate

(Huffy) Reddan, and the other was Jaci Harper. As Huffy and I grew older we wanted to do everything my brother and his friends did which included playing baseball and football.

Getting the boys to let us play was a hard sell, but eventually they let us and as I remember we were better than a number of the boys. We also would play "rock and roll" records in her basement and jitter bug. I remember the first record we danced to and that was "Rock around the Clock" by Bill Haley and the Comets. I also learned to jitter bug with a string tied around a door knob in our living room while I watching American Bandstand in Philadelphia with Dick Clark.

Huffy and I would ride our bikes up to Yardley along the tow path next to the Delaware canal. We would go to Cadwallader's Luncheonette on South Main Street and have a vanilla coke which was popular back then. We would also go to the five and dime where we could buy penny candy. Some of the favorites back then were candy cigarettes and little wax bottles filled with colored sugar water that came four in a pack. Then there were lots and lots of single pieces of any kind of candy you could imagine for just one penny each.

During the winter, kids would ice skate on the canal and play ice hockey. Needless to say it was a safe place to be and a safe way to get to Yardley to see friends and have fun.

While going to Makefield Elementary School in kindergarten through sixth grade I always rode the bus, but many children lived so close that they walked to school every day. I loved riding the bus with Huffy but sometimes I was a little jealous of the kids that walked, because they often came to school early and got to play on the playground.

There were many wonderful teachers in our school, but two stood out in my mind. My fifth grade teacher was Mr. Rathgeber who was my first male teacher. He was an excellent teacher that made learning easy and fun. He also introduced us to new things such as poetry. I never forgot him and how he was able to help every one of us to learn. I was fortunate to be able to speak to him a few times throughout the years so I could remind him how appreciative I was to have had him as my teacher.

The other memorable teacher was my sixth grade teacher named Mrs. Utz. She drove a big old black sedan that most people had already retired to the junk yard. One day she arrived at school with her passenger door missing. She had a mishap on the way and lost it, but it didn't stop her from making it to work that day. She also had an unusual way of handing out punishment to students that misbehaved in class. If you were that lucky person, you had to clean out her water basin. The basin was used to clean her false teeth in a few times a day. It meant carrying it full of dirty water down to the janitors' closet and cleaning it out. Needless to say no one wanted that dirty job, but later we all would laugh about it. We certainly never forgot Mrs. Utz.

My brother didn't have sixth grade at Makefield, but rather he went to the Edgewood school. Through the years I heard many funny stories about the building, but the one that stuck with me was about the holes in the floor. Apparently there were a number of actual holes as the school itself was quite old and in some disrepair. The kids on the upper floor could see down to the lower floor and loved dropping little things on other students and sometimes the teacher's desk. I am sure many of my friends from Yardley that I met in 7th grade know exactly what I am talking about and more. Sometimes shiny and new isn't always the best.

The flood of 1955 was a time I will never forget for a number of reasons. We had 27 inches of rain in 10 days due to Hurricane Connie and then Hurricane Diane. Our neighborhood became an island because Black Rock Road was the only way into and out of our neighborhood.

The Delaware River crested at 20.3 feet which overflowed River Road and part of Black Rock Road. At the same time the Delaware canal flowed out of its banks and came down Black Rock, stranding all of us. Of course all the children thought this was a new and exciting adventure until we realized we had no safe drinking water and the situation would require tetanus shots.

The army arrived in amphibious vehicles commonly called ducks and brought us fresh drinking water. Needless to say there was a lot of excitement, cheers and joy when they surged through all the water. Once we were able to drive out of the neighborhood and into Yardley we were shocked at all the devastation. The bridge into New Jersey was bent in the middle due to a house that floated down the Delaware. There were also parts of the bridge that were missing and hanging down.

All the buildings were wet up to their second stories and they were covered with mud and debris. Just south of the Yardley Bridge was a factory that manufactured stays and bands for men's shirt collars and they were hanging all over the trees. Probably the longest lasting impression I had of the whole event was the smell, a smell that I will never forget and hopefully will never smell again. Yardley was certainly a mess and it would require a lot of time, money and work to get it back to some kind of normalcy, but like people do, they banded together and brought Yardley back to life.

After elementary school I went to William Penn Junior High School in Fairless Hills where I met many new students and future friends. It was our first experience having a homeroom and changing classes. During the two years in that school the girls took Home Economics and the boys took Shop. We girls learned to sew, cook and bake while the boys learned how to make things out of wood and metal using tools.

We had gym class in a real gym which included gym uniforms, a locker room and taking showers. The latter was always a bone of contention with the girls, as many did not want to do that. At "Willie Penn," as we called it, we were introduced to canteen which took place every Friday night. Someone would play records for a few hours while some students danced (mostly girls) and some just watched. For me this was the real beginning of realizing there were many different kinds of people in my world and how amazing it was to experience that diversity. Now if my parents had known who I was talking to on the phone a lot they may have had a different perspective!

After William Penn, I attended Charles Boehm for 9th and 10th grade. It was located in Makefield Township so we were separated from a lot of the new friends we had just made, but we knew in two years we would be together again in the high school. The three most memorable events that happened those two years involved a snake, American Bandstand and sports. Our 9th grade biology teacher was Mr. Semancick and he loved all types of reptiles. Our room was full of snakes, lizards, frogs and turtles. When he was having an assembly for the entire school he asked if anyone would like to drape his six foot boa constrictor around their shoulders. I don't know what possessed me, but I said yes! The snake was warm, soft and well fed thank goodness or I may not have lived to tell this story.

In 10th grade Jaci Harper and I talked our parents into giving us an excuse to leave school early so we could go to American Bandstand in Philadelphia. Jaci drove us down and needless to say we were very excited to be on TV and see all the regulars. Well the regulars got to be right in the front of the cameras and we had to go to the back. This probably however was for the best, as we did enjoy the whole experience and no one at home saw us on TV, especially our teachers.

At Charles Boehm, sports were offered after school which was of great interest to me as I had grown up playing a number of sports and loved them all. In fact this was about the time I started to think about what I wanted to pursue after high school. My perception about careers for girls in those days was to be a nurse, a teacher, a secretary or a beautician; even though I was told I could be anything I wanted to be.

In 1962 we were all back together for our final two years in the school district at Pennsbury High School. It was during our junior year that most of us felt like we needed to decide on college, a career or getting married and having a family. I always knew I wanted to go to college and part of that decision was influenced by Mrs. Cora Clinton, the girl's health and physical education teacher and my field hockey coach. Mrs. Clinton was an amazing teacher and an excellent coach and I guess I wanted to be like her. I knew I wanted to teach Health and Physical Education and even more I wanted to be a coach. Ideally I wanted to coach field hockey and tennis.

Pennsbury offered the three usual varsity sports for girls at that time, which were Field Hockey, Basketball and Softball. So before there were ever any conversations about having equal sports for boys and girls, Jaci Harper and I decided to go out for the boys' tennis team. We both made it and lettered in our senior year. Little did we know what a controversial subject this would become many years later?

Probably the biggest event in our last year was Sports Nite. It was an idea conceived by the school superintendent William W. Ingraham in 1949. Its purpose was to help support student activities and the spring sports programs. The school was divided into two teams with each one represented by the school colors. One was the Orange Team and the other was the Black team. Both teams had overall captains male and female as well as class captains. I had the honor of being the girls' Black Team captain along with Harry Hamilton and Janet McTaggert was the Orange Team captain along with Sonny Vucin. Our Black class captains were Jaci Harper, Eileen Schimpf, Mary Beth Logan, Fran Crea, Sandy Stockert, Chet Dalgewicz, R. Peresta, Mike Danovich, Tom Hayes and Jeff Davis. While the Orange class captains were Bev Briegel, Bunny Menges, K. Steketes, Rosie Tait, M. Setting, Fred Philhower, Ken Medlin, Art Lendo, Rick Kelleher, G.Griffin and Dick Bartels.

All the girls and boys participated in the event either by being involved or cheering from the stands. The first night was girls' night and the boys were the second night. All the girls' and boys' gym classes put on a dance with costumes we made. There were also races and skill contests. Every single event was judged by the staff and given points, with one big winner declared at the end.

Needless to say the competition was intense for one year of bragging rights! The many talented art students got together and made amazing murals for all over the gym and the school. The cheerleaders made their own costumes and cheered for every single event. It was just a wonderful collaboration by students and teachers, as well as fun and awesome to watch.

After high school I did get my Bachelor Degree of Science at West Chester State in West Chester, Pa and I did go on to teach and coach both field hockey and tennis. I choose West Chester on the recommendation of another Pennsbury Falcon graduate named Roger Sanders. Thank you Roger as it was a wonderful four years during which I received an excellent education.

As I look back, especially during this pandemic, I realize how blessed my life has been. I was so fortunate to have grown up during the 50's and 60's in the United States of America with my wonderful family and friends.

The only thing left to say is "thank you Terry" for this opportunity to relive my growing up years with the good and the bad. I laughed, I cried and I became more thankful.

BIG BROTHER – Bob May, center, towers over his younger brothers at the beach.

CHAPTER 33

May Brothers Invade North Park

By CAROLYNE KEEFER JONES

Robert May Sr. packed up his tribe of four boys, ranging in age from two to seven years old, with another on the way, and looking for greener pastures found them in Levittown. North Park, to be exact. Bob, the patriarch of the family, left his wood-making job in Scranton to work at the Kaiser plant, assembling and manufacturing airplane parts.

The boys slept in a finished "attic" in their new home, two in each bedroom until Jeff came along and then a coin toss determined which set of boys would make room for a third. Not only did Robert Sr. convert the attic into two bedrooms, he was one of the first home owners to install an in-ground swimming pool in the backyard, making the May brothers the most popular kids in North Park!

The matriarch of the family was the lovely Ann Bray May. As the boys grew older, she escaped the household by working at Pomeroy's and later at Lenox China store. She needed the extra income to feed her brood. Mama May was an exceptional cook, famous for her Beef Stroganoff and Sunday suppers.

Bob Jr. was the eldest and tallest at seven years of age, and the most prone to get into mischief, notably with his best friend, Paul Schatzau, aka "Skeeter." When they weren't building forts at King's Farm, across Route 13 from North Park, they could be found making rafts out of scraps of wood and drifting down the canal in Falls Township. A reincarnation of Tom Sawyer and Huck Finn!

It takes a "gang" to bring these projects to fruition, so under the leadership of "Tom" and "Huck," their troops included: Jack Kitcherman, George Higgins, Jimmy Pennebaker, Bobby Brown, Al Brewster, Wayne Mettinger and Jim McWilliams, all of them from North Park.

Jim McWilliams would later be known for managing Reenie's, famous for its cheesesteaks and other over-sized sandwiches.

Athletically, most of these kids exercised their skills in Little League baseball in the summer and youth football in the fall. Stickball was a great game to play when you only had two or three kids available. All you needed was a broom, a tennis ball and a wall.

Bob May played running back in football, and first base or outfield in baseball.

North Park became an ant colony of kids and the May brothers certainly were prominent in this commune. After Bobby, there came Richard, two years younger, and known in high school for his good looks and adroit dancing skills. Richie appeared on the Jerry Blavat dance show. In his adulthood, he became a chiropractor, opened up a sports therapy center and worked for a neurosurgeon inserting implants. Just where remains to be known!

Following Richard came Eddie, three years younger than Bob. Eddie was the quiet brother. Somebody had to be the listener. He worked as an inventory manager in Texas. Gary was two years younger than Eddie and became a book distributor. Then he branched off into financial planning. Jeff was the baby of the May crew, a 1972 graduate of Pennsbury who later prospered as a veterinarian.

Bob Sr. took a job transfer that landed him in Texas in the 1970s. Jeff, Gary and Eddie went with their father. Bob and Richard were old enough and remained in Bucks County.

Back when Bob was in elementary school, he attended Penn Valley and became a teacher's pet to Mr. Williams and Ms. Draper. In those days, kids were allowed to go home for lunch. Mr. Williams gave Bob and Skeeter special dispensation to stop by his house to retrieve a radio so they could listen to the World Series during the afternoon.

Ms. Draper took Bob to his very first Philadelphia Phillies game, a memorable experience.

Not only did the teachers go out of their way to help students, the night custodian at Penn Valley would unlock the doors to let the kids in to play basketball on a real hardwood floor. Bob and Skeeter were schmoozers from early on in their lives.

A true lifelong friendship began for Bob when he went to sixth grade at Oxford Valley in nearby Fairless Hills. He met Russ Kaufman there. One might say that's when the trouble began to brew! They were inseparable. More about them later.

Some of Bob's favorite childhood memories occurred on the family dairy farm in Susquehanna County. It was on the farm that Bob learned how to milk cows, shoot and dress a deer, wield a knife and bow-and-arrow, ride a tractor, and perform almost every job imaginable. It was a great learning experience for a kid from the suburbs. This was always Bob's happy place and continues to this day, minus milking cows, but still riding his John Deere tractor, a newer, more improved version.

As Bob got older, he needed money for more expensive toys, so he worked delivering newspapers on his new Schwinn bike. One time, trying to aim a paper for a precise shot, he fell of his bike and broke his front teeth, and so began an expensive regimen of dental work.

While his five boys were growing up, Bob Sr. somehow managed to pursue a degree in Metallurgical Engineering from Drexel University in Philadelphia. With degree in hand, Bob Sr. secured a job with Exxon. The family moved to London for two years, where Eddie and Gary attended and graduated from private schools. They dressed in bell bottom pants and grew their hair long, under the Beatles' influence. Jeff returned to Bucks County in time to graduate from Pennsbury in 1972.

As Bob entered high school, he made new friendships with guys from Fairless Hills like Jack Dale. They hung out at the Fairlanes bowling alley in Fairless Hills and not always to bowl. Bob, along with Jack, Russ, Bob Davis and Paul Christman, also would play tag on the Fairless Hills water tower that rose 150 feet in the air. They camped out in railroad cars located on the tracks that ran through the Five Mile Woods, just off the old Route 1 highway. Occasionally, this crew would play hooky from school and experience a day of fun in Tullytown Cove, exploring an abandoned barge, swimming, fishing and cooking near the Penn Warner Lake.

One time, in search of more fun, the gang decided to throw shotgun shells into a roaring camp fire near the Lakeside storm drain. To avoid the pellets, they race into the storm drain's cement tunnels and emerged on the other end, right in the Lakeside neighborhood.

High school brought romance for Bob and Russ, who became involved with Donna Clausson and Linda Farmer, respectively. The two friends would both get married. Russ and Linda are still going strong after 53 years but Donna died from breast cancer at 42, leaving behind two children, Kim and Jeff, whom Bob raised into wonderful people.

Like many of his childhood friends, Bob ended up serving in the Vietnam War. He worked in the Signal Corps, attached to the 25th Infantry Division, at the Cu Chi Base Camp, 45 miles northwest of Saigon.

As he grows older, Bob looks back on his childhood with great wonder.

"Life presented many challenges when we were kids, along with exciting escapades, interesting adventures and friendships that have lasted a lifetime," he said. "I probably should have paid more attention in school, and less time on socializing, but overall, growing up in Levittown was a wonderful experience for me."

SUMMER FUN – Craig Eisenhart gets ready for a Little League game as his father, Henry, looks on along with grandmom Mary Eisenhart and sister Lynne.

CHAPTER 34

Levittown American Little League Memories Linger

By CRAIG EISENHART

M y family moved to Levittown in 1952. My father, J. Henry "Hank" Eisenhart, got a job teaching math at a newly-formed school system in Lower Bucks County called Pennsbury. Dad, who was raised in the Upper Bucks County borough of Perkasie, had been teaching at the Bordentown Military Institute. Bordentown was located 14 miles east of Levittown in central New Jersey. One of Dad's pupils at BMI had been future Army General Norman Schwarzkopf Jr.

Hank Eisenhart and his wife Edna were looking for a place to raise their family. I was four years old when we moved across the Delaware River into this new community being carved out of farmland in Lower Bucks County.

Our house address was 278 Magnolia Drive. Newportville Road (now named New Falls Road) was in our back yard. On the other side of the road was an abandoned asparagus farm, then woods, and then the Fairless Hills Shopping Center. My father's intention was to reside in Falls Township, which was part of the Pennsbury School District. But our street was located in Bristol Township. He had been told this area, all east of the Levittown Parkway, would be ceded to Falls Township, but that never happened.

Levittown was a rapidly growing community in 1952. Construction of the first homes only began in February of that year. Our family moved in during the early stages of home-building. One of my enduring memories was the mud. It was everywhere. A sure sign of the town's growth was my elementary school experience. I went to John Fitch for first and third grade but second grade was reserved for the new Thomas Jefferson School. Then I went to fourth through sixth grade at James Buchanan. Many of my friends went to Pennsbury schools but I attended the Bristol Township schools.

There were several constants to Levittown. When the Levitt brothers built this community, they set aside land for community services. Land for schools, churches and recreation was part of the blueprint in every section of the town. There were five community swimming pools surrounded by adjoining fields. Our pool was the Magnolia Hill pool. Every pool had a baby pool in addition to an Olympic-sized adult pool with diving boards. Tom DiIorio was the diving diva at Magnolia. All the pool facilities included a building that provided locker rooms and a snack bar. Out back was a basketball court surrounded by a chain-link fence. There was also a wall made of cement that we turned into a stickball facility. Our Little League field was right across the sidewalk.

All of our schools featured playgrounds, open grassy fields and baseball diamonds. It was paradise for young children. Levittown was an exceptional place to grow up in during the 1950s and 1960s. Young families from Philadelphia, Trenton and the surrounding areas moved in. Many families arrived from western Pennsylvania because United States Steel opened a huge mill on the Delaware River, not five miles from our home. My mother grew up in Arnold Palmer's hometown of Latrobe, not too far from Pittsburgh.

Organized leagues for young kids were common, with fathers often coaching their sons. My father had been an exceptional athlete, winning four letters at Sell-Perk (now Pennridge) High in football, basketball, baseball and tennis. At Juniata College in central Pennsylvania, Dad was named to the Pittsburgh Press's All-East basketball team, and he went straight from college to pitch for the Cincinnati Reds in the major leagues at the end of World War II.

Dad made himself available to me as a coach but never pushed me to participate in athletics. In our neighborhood, kids were always available to play stick ball, tackle football, ice skating, basketball and sled riding.

At age 8, I signed up to play in the Pony League, the division for 8- and 9-year-olds in the Levittown American Little League. I actually made the all-star team. We played one game, my first chance to play on the "real" Little League field next to Magnolia Hill pool.

In my second year, I played for the "Angel Shops" team. Our sponsor's store was located on Newportville Road, not far from Levittown Lanes. We practiced and played at the Penn Valley Elementary School. Sam Gumbert was a teammate and his father served as our coach. We won the league championship.

In 1959, at age 10, I made the "major leagues," playing for the Halperin Real Estate team. Our uniforms were assigned by height, shortest to tallest. I was No. 13. We played league games at Magnolia Pool Field. Even though I was at the youngest age of the 10-12 league, I played occasionally and even started a few games. My eyes got big at the all-star game, watching John Quatrocchi, Jim Simpkins and our other older players. For a young kid like me, it was a thrill to watch and learn from them.

Most of the boys I played with attended Pennsbury schools. Despite being from Bristol Township and not attending school with them, there was never an issue. In the fall of 1959, I tried out and made the Kiwanis squad in the Pop Warner football league. I got to meet more Pennsbury students. Rollie Clark, Jim Hollis and I were the only "Bristol" boys on the team. Rollie was a little guy and had to put rocks in his pockets in order to pass the minimum weight threshold. Other players on our team were Joe Mormello (quarterback), Jim Grauel and Joe Fioravanti. Little did we know what 1960 would bring!

Levittown was growing so fast that in 1960, Levittown American split its players up. Some moved over to the Continental League. I hit my first over-the-fence home run, a grand slam. I finished second in the league in homers behind Joe Mormello and made the all-star team.

Even with our league splitting up, our all-star team was stacked. Joe Mormello could throw a fast ball more than 70 miles per hour over the 46-foot distance to home plate. Another pitcher, Julian Kalkstein, was nearly as fast and featured a high leg kick that confused hitters. Our team had everything we needed to succeed: fielding, hitting, pitching and coaching. We even had cheerleaders!

We practiced three times a day, and at game time it showed. We "ran the table," winning 13 games in a row as we captured the Little League World Championship. We outscored our opponents, 89-19. Mormello, Kalkstein and Tom (Tucker) Schwartz pitched well. Little Rollie Clark hit a home run in the state finals, the only game where we had to go to extra innings in order to prevail.

The town of Levittown erupted. From farm fields to world champions in less than 10 years! We had a big parade down Levittown Parkway. We were treated to banquets, gift certificates and trips to both Philadelphia Phillies and New York Yankees' games.

WBCB radio and Butch's Market organized a trip to Connie Mack Stadium, home of the Phillies, for a twi-night doubleheader. Our team took infield and outfield practice between games! Mormello got to throw a few from Little League distances. He was pumped. I'll never forget the gasp from the fans when Joe threw full-out. Fire!

My family moved to Lower Makefield a week after we won the world championship. Because I had started in Levittown American Little League, I was allowed to remain in the league for my final season. Gary Saft, Chet Gardner Jr. and I were the returning veterans. The 1961 team did not have the overpowering pitchers or as many hitters as its predecessor but we played unbelievable defense. We won our first 10 games, outscoring opponents, 70-9.

We returned to Williamsport as defending champions. In our first-round game, we ran into a really good pitcher. Our pitcher, Dennis Pesci, got hit by a pitch early on and couldn't continue. Sam Gumbert, my Angel Shop teammate, relieved. After six innings, the game remained scoreless. We didn't score in the top of the seventh and in the bottom of the seventh, our opponents ended things with a home run that cleared the fence by inches.

There were no parades, banquets or celebrations when we returned home. But we had extended Levittown American's playoff winning streak to 23 games before we lost, and that remains a record for the Little League World Series. We created a lot of memories and learned an enduring life lesson about hard work and practice paying off.

When we moved to Lower Makefield, our life changed. There were some similarities to my former existence. We still had plenty of kids to play ball with but now our games tended to be played in backyards. The landscape was more open in Lower Makefield. There were no street lights so night games were out. A good friend, Harry Scammell, had a quarry on his family's property, which was known officially as "Scammell's Corner." Some of us made a movie at the quarry. Kudos to Kevin Lendo, Karl Saks, Dick Black, Georgia Moreton and Harry. The movie won a Kodak prize. It was called, "Her Majesty's Secret Sewage Department."

Afton Pond in Yardley was a great place to fish and ice skate. Instead of a 5-minute bike ride that we were used to in Levittown, pedaling in my new environment often took 10-20 minutes to get places.

Lower Bucks County was still growing. Pennsbury had to build a larger high school to accommodate the growing student population. We moved into the school for our senior year in 1965-66, even though it wasn't quite finished. I was one of four kids hired in the summer of 1965 to pack up the old high school. John Yurechko and I worked into the fall on the job but the other two fellows quit. We had to move art supplies, typewriters, books, materials from the Chemistry lab and – the big one – books from the library. We packed them up at the old school and unpacked them at the new school, which was located perhaps eight miles away in Fairless Hills, a half-mile from our original family home in Magnolia Hill. Levittown American's Little League field was a long home run away from the school's parking lot.

I alone continued working through the winter and began to learn all the cubby holes in the new building. I even had keys. My knowledge of the building, and the access I had, helped us pull off our senior prank of putting a Nabisco sign on the roof of the new high school. Guess who put the sign up there?

My class graduated on June 7, 1966. I followed in my parents' footsteps and attended Juniata College. I failed the NCAA physical exam for athletes (and the Army physical, too). My father signed a release that allowed me to play baseball. I earned a letter but quit because my bad knee just wouldn't take it.

After college, I went to the University of Pittsburgh's School of Dental Medicine. In 1974, I started my own practice back in my college hometown of Huntingdon, PA. I practiced for 41 years before retiring in 2014. I served 17 years on the state dental association's Board of Trustees including one year as President. I am currently in my 34th season as a volunteer assistant baseball coach for Juniata College.

In 2019, I returned to Pennsbury when the school re-named its baseball field in honor of my high school coach, Victor Napolitano, who was a good friend of my father. They had played against each other in the minor leagues. And they taught school together for many years. Dad had passed away in 1987 and Mom died in 2008.

On the same day Pennsbury honored "Coach Nap," Levittown American Athletic Association held its Opening Day ceremonies. Joe Pesci, son of my Little League teammate, Dennis Pesci, is Pennsbury's head baseball coach. His father has served as an assistant coach. Bill Rednor, a high school classmate of mine, was announcing the festivities and the game on WBCB radio. All of this occurred within one-half mile of my former Magnolia Street home. I couldn't help thinking that Victor Napolitano Field had been an asparagus patch in 1952.

On that trip home, I drove all over Levittown, reminiscing about my childhood. Most Levittown homes have been remodeled beyond recognition. Magnolia Hill pool is gone. It is now a park filled with trees. My elementary schools were either decommissioned or gone. Yardley and Lower Makefield are more recognizable, if a bit more citified. Growing up in Lower Bucks was a gift from my parents, and it gave me the chance to achieve many things in my life. I guess you really can go home again.

YARDLEY TRADITION – Jim Spahn and his sister Judy often biked along the canal that runs parallel to the Delaware River.

CHAPTER 35

Growing Up in Yardley Borough

By JIM SPAHN

I was born in 1946 and lived in Yardley Borough, not just in the zip code which included Lower Makefield Township, Fallsington and parts of Morrisville but the borough itself. That meant smaller Pennsbury elementary schools for the borough students; small town local businesses and the people who owned or managed them, and just generally growing up in an area where everyone truly knew everyone else.

For the first six years of my life, we lived in a house on Edgewater Ave, literally a stone's throw away from the Delaware Canal with the Delaware River just two blocks behind our property. We had already moved away from there before the "Great Flood of "55," when on August 19th of that year all the homes between Edgewater Ave. and River Road were under water, due to the combined ill effects of Hurricanes Connie and Diane. But those first six years included lots of great childhood memories not the least of which was attending kindergarten — which was uniquely housed in one single room on the second floor of the Yardley Borough Fire Station!! Our teacher, Mrs. Beach, was always fondly remembered through the saying: "Mrs. Beach is a peach!"

At the end of my Kindergarten year in 1952, and because my father was a career soldier in the US Army, he was to be transferred to France. Though my mother had been born, raised and graduated high school from what was the original Yardley High School at the "top of the hill," she readily welcomed the opportunity for our family to live in France for those two years. Our family "set sail" on the Queen Elizabeth, a memorable experience in and of itself as I celebrated my 7th birthday on board the ship! For two years while in France, we lived in a house in Bordeaux and my older sister and I attended school on the Army base to which my father was assigned. I remember losing my yellow rain slicker while touring the Eiffel Tower and had always hoped to return to find it! When my father's tour was over in France, we then flew back to the United States accompanied by our new little sister Sharon, who had been born in a hospital in La Rochelle, France.

After that, Dad was then assigned for two more years to Ft. Gordon, GA and we accompanied him again and lived in Augusta. When he was next assigned to Ft. Devans, MA, my mother said "enough is enough" and in 1957 our family returned to our beloved hometown of Yardley while my father completed his tenure, coming home to us about once a month. That year, I began my fifth grade year at what was by then called Yardley Elementary School (the original Yardley High School) at the "top of the hill." Mr. Wise was our teacher, and so began again a life-long journey of small town memories and friendships.

We rented an apartment on top of "Kappys" in Yardley at the main intersection of town; it is now a Starbucks Coffee. We all walked to school as the rule was that if one lived within a mile one must walk. Well, most everyone DID live within a mile! In terrible weather, families who owned cars would drive the students to school. At the end of the day we would all line up to walk as a group back down the hill.

In those days, we shopped at Louis Seplow's department store on Main Street and Beener's Hardware store at the corner of Main Street and Afton Avenue. Since Bill Beener was part of the Yardley volunteer fire department, when a call came in from the department, he would go out to the intersection and work the red light to direct traffic, allowing the firetrucks to safely pass thru the intersection! We also shopped at Maloney's Sporting Goods store on Afton Avenue for our fishing gear, balls and cleats, etc. All are gone today except for Cramer's Bakery, the best little bakery in the heart of Yardley, never to be missed when back to visit.

After the apartment, we then moved and rented a house on Letchworth Avenue, still in the borough. The Green family was our neighbor and their daughter, Donna, and I became good friends walking to and from school. Mr. Green would drive us to school depending on the weather. It was at that same time that I also became good friends with a now lifelong friend, Ed Johnson. Ed lived on Main Street and we would all walk to and from school together. Ed and I were both in the same grade. His father, who was very active in organized baseball, coached our Little League team, sponsored by Fallsington Ford. Later Ed and I both played Babe Ruth ball for Mackensen Kennels with Mr. Glenn as our coach.

For sixth grade we went to Edgewood School located at Edgewood and Heacock Rd in Wood-side. The entire school consisted of just our two sections of sixth grade and had no cafeteria, so everyone had to bring their own lunch while our milk cartons were thankfully chilled in a refrigerator. Mr. Westcott was our teacher. There I met another lifelong friend, Art Lendo. Today, the old Edgewood School property is the site for the newly-erected Lower Makefield Veteran's Square Monument.

In seventh grade, my parents finally bought a house on Morgan Avenue (one block away from the river) and at that time we Yardley seventh and eighth grade students went on to attend the William Penn Junior High School in Fairless Hills. There, we met and made friends with students from Fairless Hills, Levittown, Lower Makefield, Morrisville, Fallsington and Yardley. At that time, a new lifelong friendship was forged with Gene Stacer from Fairless Hills.

Morgan Avenue was a great place to live. Across the street were Ron, Ricky and Candy Carver; Ron, Rich and Rob White lived down the street; Bruce and Tommy McDonald lived on Edgewater Avenue as well as good friends, Harry and Ray Barnes. Billy and Patti Sheehy lived on River Road but their back yard backed up to the area at the end of Morgan Avenue where there was an open field owned by the electric company. The electric generator took up one corner of the land but the rest of the field was ours to play baseball and football during the season. Ray Barnes was always a threat for a long ball home run. All of the "guys" were always playing some sort of sport for hours on end in that open field. Bill Austin, another lifelong friend, would also come down from Brook Lane to play sports in the field. We all enjoyed the Delaware River for boating and water skiing, and, occasionally we used a dock or two to play tag. The canal was used for skating and fishing as well as beautiful Lake Afton alongside the historic Yardley Library for skating. Footnote: Lake Afton and the library itself remain a source of beautiful paintings and photography. As if all this natural beauty and resources weren't enough, Pennsbury School District always offered basketball on Saturday mornings in season and day camps during the summer.

Ninth and tenth grade was at the newly constructed Charles Boehm Junior High School. Eleventh and twelfth grades were at Pennsbury High School which is now Pennwood Junior High School. When Newtown Park and Swim Club opened in 1960 in Newtown, many families became members. I spent my last four summers in high school at that pool. I subsequently became a lifeguard and then a pool manager at LPRA (Levittown Parks and Recreation Association). Again, fond memories and lifelong friendships were fostered.

POSTSCRIPT: Upon high school graduation in 1964, I attended Trenton Junior College for one year but when I received my draft notice, I decided to enlist. Valentine's Day 1966 I entered the Army and went to boot camp at Ft. Dix. After airborne and electronics training I ended up in Vietnam with the 173rd Airborne Brigade. Upon completion of my service time I returned to Yardley and attended Bucks County Community College under the G.I. Bill. That led to a BA from Lock Haven State College and then a M.Ed. from what was then Trenton State College. My wife and I even bought our first house on Fairway Drive, bordering the Yardley Golf and Country Club. Though I taught Phys Ed and coached high school swimming at Hatboro-Horsham, I soon found my way into the Hospitality Industry, working first for Pepsico and then Popeye's. Both of those jobs eventually resulted in our moving out of state. After many years in the corporate aspects of HR, and finally landing in Carmel, Indiana, I founded my own HR consulting & recruitment firm and worked for over 23 years before retiring. Carmel is a very nice place to live . . . but nothing can ever compare to Yardley!!

CHAPTER 36

We Can't Thank Our Parents, Coaches Enough!

By DON BENTIVOGLIO

There is so much I remember about growing up in Levittown and Bucks County that narrowing down my memories is difficult. Giving it some thought, I will focus on two: the Walt Disney School located between Lakeside and Pinewood and two "midget" football teams that practiced and played on the massive school grounds.

My parents moved to the Pinewood section of Levittown when I was in the fourth grade. Prior to that, we had lived in South Philadelphia and Drexel Hill. Like all relocations, it was a bit trying not to know anyone. Levittown was an unknown, never experienced. My first school was St. Michael the Archangel on Levittown Parkway, which I attended until my graduation in eighth grade. That was during the days when a single nun could control a class of 50-90 rambunctious kids all day long (we didn't change classes) with a sinister look, a periodic scream, and no hesitancy to use a yardstick or ruler (graduates of the Catholic school system will appreciate this remembrance). It was a good school, but unlike the public school system, we didn't have any of the "extras," such as a gym or gym class. Our sports activities revolved around teams and groups not associated with the school.

The Walt Disney school was (and still is) surrounded by a huge expanse of open grass area that lent itself to outdoor activities, such as a couple of basketball courts and a lot of grass to roam around on. Walking or driving our bikes across the field was our primary method of getting from Pinewood to St. Michaels or the Levittown Shopping Center, the place where many of us learned the basics of "hanging out" after school and on weekends. Unlike today, most of our parents didn't drive us each morning or pick us up each afternoon. Starting with first grade, we got to school pretty much on our own—riding a school bus, biking, or simply walking. Once our parents (usually Mom) provided our breakfasts, the rest of the school journey was generally up to us.

Next to Walt Disney was an old Air Force jet that we were able to explore by climbing through, walking on the wings, and often falling off. I remember the sharp pieces of metal protruding from various points inside the jet. If I got too close to those jagged pieces (which were difficult to avoid),

I would get cut. Back then, it seems skin damage was no big thing. A kid would walk home bleeding, Mom or Dad would ask why, and the event would be related. The parent may or may not have admonished, "You should be more careful," just before the cut was doused with iodine and the issue was over. There was never a thought of "who should I sue," "the school is responsible," or "we're going to sue the Air Force." We adventurers put a band aid on our cuts, sucked it up, and moved on (and probably climbed back on the jet the next day).

The school grounds were also a central point of social interaction because the Pinewood Pool abutted the acres of open field. The Levittown pools were significant to our adolescent growth because they were where we met girls in the summer, played basketball and baseball throughout the year, and perhaps even drank a few bottles of beer after dark in our later teens. I recall that joining the pool cost around $6 per year for a family membership.

Because of their size, the fields around Disney also supported a number of local "midget" football leagues and teams. The two teams that many graduates of PHS Classes 1964 and 1965 and I were associated with were Am-Vets and the Levittown Boys Club.

Starting around 1960 a gentleman by the name of Bill Morgan (who lived two streets away from me in Pinewood) along with several other fathers, including Paul Miller, Bob Neeld, Frank Schultz, and Tom DiIorio Sr., started and coached a "midget" football team known as Am-Vets. It was called "midget" because a player's maximum weight was 120 pounds. The team widened my early social network because, as a Catholic school kid, the only way I could meet kids from the public school system was either in my immediate neighborhood or on sports teams. The friendships I made at this early stage of my life carried me through high school and beyond.

Through the efforts of our coaches, Am-Vets became a good team; several seasons we went undefeated. Jack Mack was our quarterback and most of our scoring was done by Tom DiIorio, Dave Neeld, and Dwight Ritter. Looking back at an aged newspaper clipping from the *Levittown Times*, I see there was one game in which Tommy scored 5 TDs against a team known as the "Wildcats," with Jack Mack and Dwight Ritter scoring two. The same news clipping reported that Joe Mormello scored three TDs while playing in the same league for our primary rivals, the Kiwanis team. We even got to play a Bowl Game in Lake City, Florida, where another *Levittown Times* clipping recounted that *"Tom DiIorio thrilled the crowd of 2,200 by returning a punt 80 yards."* Dwight Ritter, Dave Neeld, Jack Mack, and I scored the other TDs. Winning was nice but in retrospect, it is hard to imagine a crowd of 2,200 small town spectators showing up to watch a group of 120-pound kids play football! It was quite an experience for us.

As we grew older, we also got bigger, so the 120-pound weight limit no longer applied. To keep the team together Mr. Morgan and his colleagues created the Levittown Boys Club which upped the maximum weight to 150 pounds. There never really was a "Boys Club" other than the football team. Team uniforms, equipment, registration fees, travel, etc. were all financed by selling raffle tickets door to door in our neighborhoods and donations from various sponsors and our parents. This well-coordinated effort involving families, coaches, and friends was led and held together by a tight group of highly dedicated adults.

These wonderful coaches, all of whom had "day jobs" and families to take care of, spent untold hours teaching us about teamwork and instructing us to practice hard, do our best, be good sports, and accept our inevitable losses. They didn't suffer fools easily and weren't afraid to slap a player on his helmet when he acted out. They scheduled every practice (many night practices on Walt Disney were lit up by the coach's cars lined up with their headlights on), arranged for team meetings, ordered and distributed team uniforms and equipment, and made travel arrangements for "away" games. Over the years, in addition to Lake City, FL, and nearby Trenton, NJ, our ambitious coaches also arranged "away" games in St. Augustine, FL and Stamford, CT. When we traveled to Florida and Connecticut, they made plans for us to stay at the home of a team member on the other team. For many of us these trips were our first time out of the Levittown zip codes.

To facilitate our away game travel, our coaches made arrangements for a train to make a special stop at the Levittown train station. They even booked a reserved car with overnight and dining accommodations. I now realize the organizational skills and dedication this planning entailed: every detail was accomplished over the phone with people whom our coaches never met—without the assistance of any electronic devices. We had no answering machines in those days so I can only imagine how many "call backs" were required to confirm our itineraries. If I remember correctly, my very next train trip was from Philadelphia to Fort Bragg, NC, for basic training.

Levittown and Bucks County have changed dramatically since those days, but the area was a wonderful place to grow up. In grade school and high school and on various sports teams, I made lifelong friendships. My current golfing buddies consist of six guys I met in either grade school or high school. We have been fortunate enough to stay in contact over the years despite not living in close proximity for extended periods of time.

I wish I could somehow go back to the team coaches and thank them personally for the herculean efforts they put in *after a full day's work* to arrange and supervise practices, to prepare for weekend games and to teach us the fundamentals of football and sportsmanship. In all they did for us, they modeled the meaning of hard work. Adults like this are truly the proverbial "unsung heroes" of our lives. Thank you all and thank you for making *Growing up in Levittown and Bucks County* the amazing experience it was!

CHAPTER 37

My Friendship with Unforgettable Alan Schultz

By HAL BLAISDELL

In the spring of 1956, we moved into our house in the Lakeside section of Levittown. Since I was new to the neighborhood, I wanted to make friends with someone near my age. Our next-door neighbor told me a boy my age lived in the house next to her and that I should go over and introduce myself. So off I went, a little timid, and knocked on the door. A huge man with an Italian cigar clenched tightly between his teeth answered. He was imposing, at least to my nine-year-old mind, and looked like Ernie Kovacs. It was my first contact with the Schultz family. I told the man my name, and that I had just moved in. I asked if he had a son my age, and he said yes, but I could not see him. He was getting over the measles, and I should come back in a few days.

I no sooner got to the sidewalk when I heard someone yell, "Hey, kid." I turned to see a kid about my age climbing out a bedroom window. He ran up to me and said, "My name is Alan, but most people call me Al and I think we can be friends. How old are you?" (Our birthdays are a few days apart, his the fourth of March, mine the seventh.) So begins the first of many events in which there was never a dull moment. In hindsight these stories are hilarious but at a time were of grave concern to our poor parents.

Many of these mini-sagas stand out in my mind, not dulled by age but kept alive in the retelling of these happy, comical memories. Fast forward to approximately 1960—"the shoe polish in the living room" story. We lived across the street from Pinewood Pool; we spent every day in the summer at "The Pool."

One sweltering afternoon, we were bored. We, actually Al, decided we should go back to his house and cool off in the air-conditioning, a rarity in those days in Levittown. Perhaps an hour after we got situated in the cool of the living room, Al decided he needed to shine his shoes. Al went to the storage room. (If you lived in a Levittowner, you know what I'm talking about) and returned with a bottle of black "Scuffcoat," a liquid, plastic shoeshine product that is guaranteed to cover anything. We learned later that this was probably true. He proceeded to sit down on the rug in the middle of the living room and apply the black liquid.

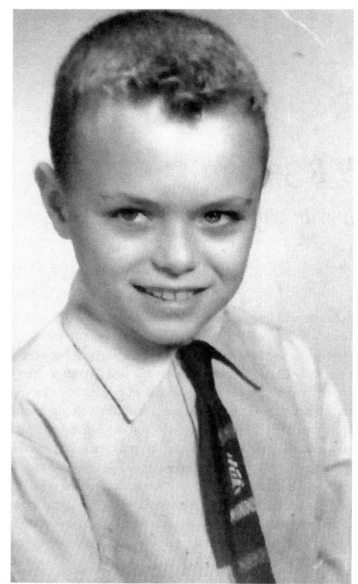

LOOKING BACK – Hal Blaisdell was only nine years old when his family moved to Levittown and he met his next-door neighbor, Alan Schultz.

I asked, "Ahhh, Al, don't you think we should be in the carport?"

"Nahhh, it's OK," said Alan, nonchalantly.

I knew what was going to happen but before I could utter a word, he bumped the open bottle with his foot, spilling it on the rug. A small pool of black liquid rapidly spread over the beige fabric. Both in panic mode, we grabbed towels and tried to wipe the polish up, only making the problem even more extensive. Years later, I learned we should have blotted the stain but at 13, who knew.

"The old man is gonna kill me; we gotta do something," said Alan.

Using our brilliant adolescent minds, we decided to wash the rug. In those days, most Levittown houses didn't have wall-to-wall carpet, but rather large area rugs. Taking the rug outside wasn't that difficult. We stacked the furniture anywhere we could find space and rolled up the rug to carry it out back. We thought we were smart by going out the back door, not drawing the neighbors' attention. We believed it was a masterstroke. It wasn't. We used a "Jet" of water from the garden hose and a stiff brush, scrubbing and scrubbing. After half an hour, we told ourselves that it looked "good." We then dried it, using most of the towels in the house. We then dragged the semi-dry, "clean" rug back inside. Now a stain in the middle of a carpet requires some crafty and well-thought-out placement. We turned the rug one hundred and eighty degrees. Since it was rectangular, we had only two options.

Al: "Think this will work, Hal?"

Hal: "I think it will work." (If his Dad is OK with a chair in the middle of the room, I mused, but kept that thought to myself.)

Al: "You gotta stay until after the old man comes home."

Hal: "OK, I'll stay."

I was a coward and started inching towards the door when the side door from the carport swung open. "He's coming." The "old man" entered under a full head of steam, glanced at the living room. I darted for the front door but realized I wasn't going to make it unnoticed. I heard what I'd heard thundering from his father's voice many times before, "A-L-A-N !!!" The volume was somewhere between a jet winding up for taking off and a rock concert.

The "old man" to me: "You're not going anywhere; stay here."

We then received a chewing out so fierce that I can remember it over 60 years later like it was yesterday. In the late '70s, Sherry and I were at the Schultz's home for dinner. Fran told me the next-door neighbor ratted us out. She watched us from her patio, thinking it was the funniest thing she had ever seen, so he knew what happened before he got home. Until that evening over a decade later, I had never figured out how he knew with just a glance into the room.

I think Al and I were about 15 years old when this "story of the weights" occurred. We ran from Lakeside to The Fairless Hills shopping Center and back every other day (I soon bailed out on that commitment) and lifted weights on the non-run days. His weights, stored in the carport or left in the grass, rusted over time. So one day Al decided the weight plates all needed to be painted. He went into the storage room for a black can of spray paint. The plates were placed on the driveway in the carport. He pushed the nozzle down, and nothing happened; he tried can number two, same results. At this point, he was so frustrated that he grabbed a hammer, intent on crushing the cans. Before I could say, "N-O-O-O," Al brought the hammer down squarely on the can. Just because a spray can isn't spraying doesn't mean there isn't pressure in the can or on the contents. The hammer impacted the can and it exploded, sending paint everywhere. Everything within six feet was covered in jet black paint—including the driver's side of his father's new shiny white Oldsmobile Cutlass. When the can exploded, it sounded like a gunshot, and just as suddenly, his father appeared in the doorway. The expression on his face was priceless. To this day, I can still picture it in my mind, a mixture of shock and disbelief. I was going to run, but I was laughing so hard I couldn't move. "A-

L-A-N!!!" Al spent a week compounding the car to remove the spray paint, and although I helped him work, I would crack up every time I thought about how it all happened.

Although many incidents from my years growing up in Levittown have faded from my memory, these are among the stories that will be forever in my mind and are recanted again and again.

* * *

(Sadly, my friend Alan Robert Schultz, USMC, was Killed In Action 11 August 1967, in Quang Tri Province Vietnam at age 20. I sometimes wonder what we would be doing today if he were still with us.)

STILL GOING STRONG – David Christian met his future wife, Peggy Todd, when they attended Bishop Egan High School together in the mid-1960s.

CHAPTER 38

David Christian Grew Up Faster Than Most

By DAVID A. CHRISTIAN

(EDITOR'S NOTE: One of the Vietnam War's most decorated soldiers grew up in Levittown during the 1950s and 1960s. David Christian's story is "different" than most of the others you will read in this book. It is retold here based on accounts from David's own book, "Victor Six.")

A lot of people still blink twice when they hear my story of being commissioned the youngest Army officer since the Civil War and leading men into combat in Vietnam as a teenager. The story makes more sense once you hear how my life sped by so quickly as a child.

I grew up a lot differently than most people. My mother was a very strong woman, even though she stood only 4 feet, 11 1/4 inches tall. She joined the Women's Army Corp (WAC) and moved up the ladder to work on General (Douglas) MacArthur's staff, writing and typing up press releases. She was with the General in the Philippines, and went with him to New Guinea and Australia. She returned to the Philippines with General MacArthur and met my father during this period. He was a typewriter repairman. MacArthur loved his publicity and probably considered fixing a typewriter more important than fixing a jeep.

My parents married after the war. They had originally lived in Gainesville, FL., where I was born, but my mom eventually decided it might be best to move back to her hometown, Croydon, not far from Philadelphia. My father had a problem with alcohol and mom thought a geographic change was necessary. Family life was up and down with my father doing construction at the US Steel Mill and my mother working at Kaiser's Fleetwing Aircraft in Bristol Borough. Dad continued to abuse alcohol and mom continued to find pint bottles to throw out. Dad drank. Mom prayed.

At five years of age I found myself, my brother Douglas and sister Dorothea in the back seat of a large black vintage model De Soto automobile. We were traveling the mud roads carved into the old farm fields of Lower Bucks County. We saw a sign saying "Azalea Lane." My mother exclaimed and my father turned the car up the road past what seemed to be worker ants carrying tools and wood.

"They should not be working today," said my father, inquisitively. "It's Sunday."

"There it is," shouted my mother, "number 68." This was our future house; a sign painted on a stick with our house number staring back at us. Everyone was excited in the car including our dog, Frances. There was just a slab of concrete and mud everywhere. There were no houses to be found.

Most people moving into these soon to be homes were Veterans. My parents were both Veterans. They put $100 down and were given a Veterans Administration mortgage. Many of our neighbors were Veterans of WWII and Korea. (Half the street ended up being Veterans from wars around the world. Before Levittown, we lived with aunts and uncles in nearby Croydon, if we were not renting a house.)

Every house lot had people roaming or just gawking out their car windows at what was to be their new home. All of them seemed to have the same characteristics. They appeared to be a young family just starting out in life; a father and mother and a trail of children seemed to be a prerequisite for buying.

My dad was an imposing man of 6 feet, 4 inches. A tall handsome man destroying himself with booze. One day, he went off to get the lawn mower fixed and never came home. My mother, Dorothy Christian, became the sole source of support when we were little, but she had just delivered her fourth child, Daniel. We had no money. I became the man of the house, trying to take care of things for my mom. In those days, the state did not give out food stamps. Families in need waited in line for surplus food. We would go over to Bristol and stand in line. Other kids would see us in what were called the 'poor lines' and they would tease us at school.

There were four children in the family – Douglas, David, Dorothea and Daniel. We were very close to each other, latch-key kids before the term became popular. I would do anything to help my mother. When I was 13, I hitchhiked to New York City, hoping to find work and send money home to help pay the mortgage.

I had done a lot of reading by candlelight as a kid, after everyone went to bed. New York City fascinated me. I read about New York and I would see shows on television that were set in New York. It wasn't more than 90 miles away and back then hitchhiking was permissible. With my mother's blessing, I set off for New York. I ended up in Manhattan, asking for jobs, but nobody would hire me. I went over to Brooklyn. Same thing. I lied about my age, told them I was 15 or 16, even 17. I rubbed the powder from concrete on my face to cover up my peach fuzz. Finally, one day I walked into a place in Brooklyn. The guy said he would hire me but if anyone asked, I should say I was part of their family. That was because unions were so strong in those days. This was 1961. If you don't say you are family, you get the owners in trouble. I got work as a carpenter's helper, at Flatbush and Atlantic Avenue. I worked as a laborer, hauling 2 x 4s back and forth, doing anything I could. I lived in the bowling alley that we were tearing out of a four-story building. I still remember the name of those alleys – State Lanes. The construction company also had a little hotel nearby where the crew could rent rooms for $15 a week. Just a small room. And a communal shower.

The streets were tough. You walked to the wrong corner and all of a sudden you were in a confrontation. Every group of kids had their own turf. After a couple of brief encounters I realized my place was with the older workers. They always headed to the bar after our shift ended. I would go with them and get served a pint of beer. I got paid $1.50 an hour, pretty good money in 1961. I worked a lot of hours. Kept $15 for subsistence and sent the rest home to my mother. Our mortgage was $67 a month. That wasn't a big mortgage but when you have no money, it's like a million dollars.

After four months, I returned home to Levittown and resumed school. I spent one year at Bishop Egan High School, where I first met my future wife, Peggy Todd, and finished up at Woodrow Wilson, where I graduated with honors. That's the linear version of my story. The real life version was more complicated.

In our family, when you turned 16, you were on your own. You had to get a job. I turned 16 in 11th grade. I asked my mother if I could stay in high school and graduate. She said if you get a job and make a man's wage, you can stay in school. I got a job in Tullytown, at a place called Optical Scanning. I became the foreman's supervisor on the night shift. I was going into my senior year of high school and the work experience of building and maintaining bowling alleys in my earlier years had given me a lot of confidence in myself. I learned that I had to push myself on people. The answer would always be no unless you asked. I got that from my mother. Mom always had to fight for things. She taught me to always "Speak up." You have to have a voice, and assert yourself. And, all through my life, I have spoken out against things that I thought were wrong.

Long story short, I graduated from Woodrow Wilson High in 1966, at the age of 17, and was in a hurry to get going with the next stage of my life. My mother and I talked about how the GI Bill would pay for college, if I first joined the military and put in the time. The family's military tradition also played a role. Family served in all the wars back to the Revolutionary War with England. My great-grandfather on my father's side had fought for the Confederacy and was a prisoner of war just over 100 years earlier. The Vietnam War was heating up in 1966. I could almost hear the drums of war from far away. "Greetings" from Uncle Sam and the war would soon take away the innocent part of my life. Our lives are like diamonds with many facets. Above, I shared parts of life that developed my work and compassion characteristics. But, the magic of being a child and growing up in Levittown developed my outgoing personality. My desire to explore the woods, "cricks," lakes, rivers and ponds that surrounded the "Boot" of Bucks County had to that point satisfied my sense of adventure.

I had the good fortune of going to both Catholic and public schools. I had friends from Yardley to Morrisville, Fairless Hills to Tullytown, Edgely, Bristol and Bensalem. We had community pools in Levittown and community churches. It was a planned community and for me it was perfect.

However, it all seemed to change for me. A few of my friends and I went off to serve our country. We came home from the Vietnam War to a different country. Most of my soldier friends found it difficult to settle back into their old lives. They moved to other towns because their communities had changed. The magic seemed to disappear. Many of the pools and schools were changing or closing. It hurt because many of the returning GI's that took their oath to serve their country at 401 North Broad Street in Philadelphia saw a different world and were not here for the changes — they were no longer part of their magical hometown.

No dances at Hugh Carcella Hall or Edgely Fire hall. We had Roll a Rama for skating, Gino's steaks, bowling alleys that have mostly disappeared. Shopping shifted from the Levittown Shopping Center and movie theaters to large enclosed shopping malls. My friends were nowhere in sight as I tried to find swimming parties at the Cove on the Delaware River. The friends that went off to college seemed to change. I spent years in Valley Forge General Hospital and the Philadelphia Navy Hospital, recovering from war wounds. The world had gone on without me.

I know that change is hard for many people but it can be especially difficult if you were not part of the change. Bucks County had its own Veterans and its own stories. But no one seemed to want to hear because even the neighbors changed. The generation of the 1950s and 1960s went off to college, war, jobs and the majority never returned. I miss that childhood magic.

* * *

POSTSCRIPT: When David Christian joined the Army at age 17, he applied for Officer's Candidate School in his first year in uniform. David received his commission as a Second Lieutenant at age 18, when most people his age were just getting out of high school. To this day, he is considered the "Youngest Commissioned Officer since the Civil War." Dave completed JFK Special Warfare and Paratrooper Schools. He landed in Vietnam at 19 and was assigned to the First Infantry Division, 75th Rangers. He took over as Executive Officer of a Long Range Reconnaissance outfit, known as "LRRPs," and also commanded RECON 1/26 who would discover 52 enemy camps over the next few months. (Commanding officers recognized Christian's performance in their Officer's Efficiency Report as equaled by very few, recommending him for promotion. They identified his Recon team as the most successful in the Battalion, always volunteering for the most hazardous missions. Because of the confidence his superiors had in him, his unit was allowed to operate independently in enemy controlled territories for days and weeks at a time. The report praised Lt. Christian's belief in his men and his success in dangerous missions that is seldom seen in an officer of his grade and age.)

Christian was wounded on seven different occasions: shot, stabbed and napalm-burned over 40 percent of his body in early 1969. He would earn combat awards for Valor, the Distinguished Service Cross; two Silver Stars and seven Purple Hearts. He recuperated from his wounds at Valley Forge Army Hospital and the Philadelphia Navy Hospital. Christian returned home to Lower Bucks County medically retired as a Captain. Frustrated by the treatment of Vietnam War veterans, he has worked hard for veterans' disability rights ever since. David lives in Upper Makefield Township alongside the Delaware River with his wife, Peggy, whom he met in high school. They have four children and six grandchildren.

As a civilian, Dave went on to work for four different Presidents and spent eight years as the senior advisor to the U.S. Senate on Foreign Relations, National Defense and Veterans Benefits.

Christian says, "I am always proud to state that my roots relate back to the town that encouraged me to follow my dreams — Levittown."

You can learn more of his adventures by visiting www.davechristian.com

CHAPTER 39

Barry Miner Has Been Around the World

By BARRY MINER

My entry into Bucks County and Fairless Hills started the summer after I finished third grade in northeast Philadelphia. My Dad's job at Leeds and Northrup moved from downtown Philly to Lansdale. In Philly, we lived in a row house across from a vacant lot, with the back of a movie theater to stare at from our front step and the backs of small stores on either side of the theater (Betty Lou's Ice Cream Shop, Castor Avenue Bar and Beer Distributor; a bakery, corner drug store, etc.).

BUSY KID – Barry Miner's life journey began in northeast Philadelphia and soon took him to Fairless Hills.

I loved my neighborhood in Philly, which was predominantly Jewish (I even went to Soloman Solis-Cohen Elementary School). I was lucky to have such good neighbors (the Pearlman's, Balthasar's, Bachmann's, Weinstein's, et al.; they took good care of me when needed, treated me to good food, and taught me a lot of good values). I often say I went to more bar mitzvahs than any other kid on the block! I loved my friends and our adventures together (like me and Tommy Ward secretly hiding on the canvas top of a beer truck, and riding around the city (at 10 years old!) for most of a day during beer deliveries). All the kids got together and turned the vacant lot across the street into a baseball field. My older brother Ron, who was a good ball player, and his friend Larry Flood from our church, led that project.

It was a Tom Sawyer/Huck Finn adventure every day, and we felt safe. (My Uncle Bill, a crusty WWII Vet, loved me and called me *"Huckleberry Barry"*). The First Methodist Church was in view, on the corner of Tyson's and Castor Avenues, and it was another place for recurring fun social events and outings. My first "girlfriend" was Reverend Harold Flood's daughter Joyce. My mother, Mabel, served as the church pianist and led the cherub and junior choirs, and ran Church charity "shows". She did the same after we moved to Fairless and became members of the Fairless Hills Methodist Church.

Moving to Fairless was, as it turned out, just another stop on the adventure trail; and a good one at that. At that age then, how could you not enjoy the opportunities available to kids? Lake Caroline (swimming, fishing, ice skating—done whether legal or not!), the Fairless Hills Swimming Pool where we spent most of the day (me getting sun burned badly, always. I am paying for it now). We had our Little League, a shopping center nearby with a bowling alley, the Eric Theater, and a few soda fountains that could, in the right light, have filled-in for Jimmy Stewart's soda fountain scenes in "It's a Wonderful Life." Then there was the Fairless Golf Course (going in the mucky ponds to retrieve and then sell lost golf balls was a great source of income for elementary school-aged kids). Speaking of which, you can't get much better than being introduced to a new school (Oxford Valley Elementary) than by having a great 4th grade teacher like Mrs. Reynolds (who incidentally had a beautiful daughter I immediately fell for, Cathy . . . a Pennsbury High School 1964 classmate of mine, as many of my friends back then later became; and we are still friends today; over 60 years later!).

Our home on Auburn Road was modest, about all we could afford. Through the years my Mom worked part-time at "Bargain City" to supplement family income, and me and my friends (usually sans allowances) always found ways to earn a few bucks, depending on the season, by shoveling snow for neighbors or mowing lawns. (As an aside, I have been living in Falls Church, Virginia for the past 25+ years and not once has a group of young kids come by to ask to shovel snow or mow our lawn! Go figure!).

We had quite an industrious pick-up kid's work crew back in the day — Mike Belletiere, Rick Croushore, Terry Bloomingdale, Doug Carder, Russ Gowton, Rick Guest, Fred Beck, Wayne Holman, Bob Henry, and several others. In the summer it was mow lawns early, then go to the pool and get "fried" or go to little league practice or a game. Our baseball team, the "A's," won the league championship two years in a row, mostly thanks to our star hitter, Jack Dale. A few of us made the league's All-Star team (certainly Jack, and lucky me at second base) and that was fun with more superb memories.

My elementary school years in Fairless were remarkably formative, though I value all the years in the broader Pennsbury School District area for a variety of reasons, noted below. I consider myself incredibly lucky to have landed where our family did in Fairless Hills, aside from what I mentioned before, how can any of us forget where we (the guys especially) "tried" to learn to dance at the "Canteen" dances on Friday nights at Oxford Valley Elementary (always chaperoned with parents and some teachers). Guys had to wear a sport coat and tie! Though incredibly young, we were and continued to be influenced by Dick Clark's American Bandstand broadcasts out of Philly . . . Fun, fun, fun 'til her daddy takes the T-bird away!

We had wonderful teachers and role models throughout the larger Falls Township community and into the expanded Pennsbury District within the County. Back then, it was unusual to find male teachers at the elementary school level, but I had three I can remember, and they were all great. You could not get away with much as a miscreant at school or, for that matter, anywhere you roamed. There was always some adult (without worrying about a lawsuit) who knew you from your neighborhood, from your participation in Scouts, from school (like teachers who would not hesitate for a microsecond to call your parents), from your neighbors who would either chastise you directly for any aberrant behavior or make sure your parents were told (they would also take care of you, feed you, and do whatever else was needed to assure your welfare), and from church leaders who you probably saw and interfaced with a lot.

The Fairless Hills Methodist Church on Trenton Road was more than just a church for many of us. It was another "classroom of life," and as I mentioned an active social setting. Many of those with whom I graduated from PHS (Russ Kaufmann, John Armagost, et.al.), were also long-time friends from the Church, and many were in my Mom's cherub and junior choirs (Mary Beth and Ruth Ann Logan, Carolyn Beers, Joyce McClure, Lois Baker, to name a few); they remember my Mom well. Mrs. Miller from the church apparently had a mission to teach me the value of volunteerism and "giving back"; she would pick me up every Saturday morning in her Nash Rambler and take me to Bucks County Hospital to do volunteer service (I was assigned to the X-Ray section). She also was a leading force behind our Church's mission to do volunteer work at a Methodist orphanage near Henderson, Kentucky, back deep in the Appalachians. Those were "character" building trips.

Through the Church, we got around Bucks County a lot, doing "Hymn Sings" at various churches in the area, sponsoring Penny Suppers, Youth Fellowship meetings, camping trips and outings with our Church sponsored Scout Groups (like camping and boating (and swimming, it wasn't illegal then!)) along the Delaware River or at Pennypack Creek. Picnics and outings at Washington's Crossing and other area parks were usually group events throughout the seasons, and trips to downtown Philly or Trenton with friends and their parents who would invite you along were frequent enough. And we can't forget we had two professional baseball teams close by: The Philadelphia Athletics and the Philadelphia Phillies! Eagles football and Warriors/76ers basketball. Too expensive for us to attend games but comforting to know we "might" and that they were doing so well!

After my elementary school years, the interfaces with the same people and groups and organizations continued at the Junior High School and High School levels. I loved playing sports but chose instead to start concentrating on music. By this time, my brother had enlisted in the Army and was assigned to Korea. That was a strange concept for me then, it later turned out to perhaps be an "omen" of my future. In any event, I could walk to William Penn Junior High and Medill Bair, but finally had to take the bus to Pennsbury High School on Makefield Road. Again, I was fortunate with the music opportunities available to me. I made Pennsylvania Regional and State Bands (qualifying on several instruments), which again allowed me to travel around PA and the Mid Atlantic area, and our award winning High School Stage Band, after playing on the Chubby Jackson Show in New York, at the Newport Jazz Festival in Rhode Island (first High School Stage Band to ever play there) numerous appearances at the St. John Terrill Music Circus in Lambertville (with Stan Kenton and Maynard Ferguson Orchestras, among others), and after several appearances on Philly TV stations, we were invited to appear on the Johnny Carson Show in New York City. Very cool for a bunch of High School kids! Locally in Bucks, John Byzek, Bruce Fye, Skip Green, Ted Edge, myself, and a few others started a "Jazz Combo," and we were the "entertainment" and "dance to" group at various places in New Hope, and at Rotary, VFW, and American Legion events in the County. We also played a lot of Bar Mitzvahs!

But music was not going to be my career, I was headed off to college, and even with some scholarship money, I had to choose a good, but not so expensive school that my parents could afford. So off to Columbus, Ohio and Capital University (with some extra courses done at Ohio State). Not the academic achiever I should have been in high school, I was rather nervous going off to college, especially after being informed that my freshman roommate was a National Merit Scholar. But a good education at PHS (and some stern guidance from Mr. Seacrist about my math aptitude), allowed me to test out of all freshman and sophomore required Math and English courses, while my roommate struggled with both! After getting my B.A., I started working for the Ohio Civil Rights Commission as an investigator, going to law school at night, and was headed into a law career. Then came a life-changing event that I took in the most positive way I could. I was drafted, sent to Fort Jackson, South Carolina for basic Army training, as a Private, then selected for Infantry Officer Candidate School at Fort Benning, Georgia, then Vietnamese Language School, reassigned to Russian Language School and Army Intelligence School in Arizona, after which I was sent off to Korea (three times), Europe, the Pacific, and was involved in support of operations in Grenada, Iraq and Afghanistan, Kuwait, and other places across the globe (retiring from the Army as a Colonel). I did manage to pick up a master's degree in Computer Science from George Washington University along the way and have taken several PhD related courses post-Masters, but my formal education is done! Since my military retirement I have served in the commercial Defense Industry and have undertaken a lot of volunteer work.

It has been an enjoyable and satisfying life (and I surely hope it continues!). I do owe a lot to the mentoring and guidance and the great "learning" environment I encountered over these 70+ years, especially at Pennsbury and from the community where I grew up. Instilled in me (and many others) early in life were the core values of "commitment, dedication to doing right, kindness and consideration, and sharing". I guess I have been working for over 80% of my life. I think that is lucky. I sincerely hope I am pursuing Mrs. Miller's guidance and that I am "giving back." I also hope I am contributing to honoring our PHS Alumni Veterans, which is a key reason I founded the PHS Wall of Honor Foundation in 2017 as a Pennsylvania and IRS 501(c) 3 charity and I try to help organize Veteran's presentations every year to PHS honors students (supported by my good PHS Alumni friends and classmates Jim Spahn, Terry Nau, Marge Wysor, Craig Fring, Terry Wallace, Dave Anderson, Don Bentivoglio, Rick Croushore, John Armagost, Ray Parker, Ed Johnson, and our liaison, Aly McBryar, at PHS). I try to stay directly involved with our great PHS 1964 classmates, and I think we do a good job of that. I thank my Classmate Art Lendo for starting the tradition of "Class Mini-Reunions" and we did well with that for about the last 20 years, trying to get a large group of our 1964 Classmates together every year. As more of us fully retire and move to warmer weather in the South, our opportunities to get together annually have waned a bit. But we still stay in touch! My wife Debra and I love to travel and have been many places around the world, including some with my PHS classmates! I now have three grown children and 10 grandchildren (6 on their own), and despite the creaky bones, sore knees, and shoulders, I love my life!

CHAPTER 40
There Were Few Rules in Old Days!

By BILL THOMAS

My family moved to Fairless Hills from Dravosburg, Pennsylvania in the summer of '52. My dad, like most of my friends' dads, worked at the mill. One of my pastimes that summer was to mosey from my yard on Austin Dr. down Fairfax to Andover so that I could watch the guys building the street. The workers would come over and entertain me and I enjoyed watching them work. I was five years old! Never be allowed today.

That September I started school. Oxford Valley Elementary must not have been finished yet as I took a bus somewhere. The first day on the bus I made my first friend, Hughie Wilson. Hughie and I were very good friends back then and I've often wondered how he made out over the years. Hope his life is going well.

I think it was second grade when I met Alan Maxwell and we became best buddies. We were usually in the same class in elementary school and I think it was second or third grade when Vicky Hadden actually skipped a year and landed in our class! That was a real shock to Alan and me since we didn't know that was even possible. I think all of us boys had an immediate crush on Vicky.

Another shock came in third or fourth grade when our friend, Dick Secrest, was killed while riding his bike. That was the first time we had had to deal with tragedy. We worked through the grieving process without a herd of grief counselors descending on the school. Amazing.

I would be remiss while writing of Oxford Valley Elementary without mentioning 1955 or '56 when we all got marched up to the gym for the first Salk vaccinations. I don't recall ever thinking about polio before that. All I know is I got the shots and my parents were happy about it. Today it would require special classes to prepare us for the coming vaccination and R&R to get over the trauma.

Hughie, Alan, George Dost, John Tracey and I used to spend a lot of time roaming around the creek (pronounced crick, thank you), Sterling's farm, the Five Mile and Girl Scout woods and riding our bikes everywhere. We played softball at Oxford Valley Elementary, ice-skated on Lake Caroline, rode bikes to the shopping center and the pool. Bikes were our keys to freedom. We rode everywhere and as long as we were home for dinner it was OK. In the summer we would then go back out to play until the street lights came on. Street lights were like an alarm clock back then, time for everyone to go home.

I guess it was about eighth grade that Rick Shaffer and I became buddies, still are. I always jokingly accused Rick and his older cousin Ralph (sadly, gone now) for teaching me to smoke cigarettes. Looking back, Rick and I did a hell of a lot of nothing but we enjoyed it and always kept each other laughing. Rick's cousin, Ralph Shaffer, was a year ahead of us so we absorbed a lot of Ralph's mature "knowledge" which he laughingly dispensed. We walked or thumbed everywhere then, pool, shopping center, movie, bowling alley. Bikes were no longer "cool." We were champing at the bit to drive a car.

When we turned 16, a lot of guys and girls got their driver's licenses (not me, my parents wouldn't let me due to my poor grades). Now we're havin' fun! Riding around trying to pick up girls with little success (probably get arrested today) or just riding around. My good friends Mike Wilson and Karen Worsman even let me drive their cars on occasion, with no license! Karen's father was a Falls Township police officer (and a great guy) at the time!

Fun, Fun, Fun.

Oh, I did get my license at 17 although the grades didn't improve.

After graduation I worked at Singer Brothers Men's store in the shopping center for a year. I had had enough school. Rick went off to college, Bill Lennon (another buddy) went to the Army. I mostly hung around with old friends — Ron Meyers, Jay Lynch (another good friend gone), Wayne Mettinger, Neil Bonner and the other guys that were just going to work and "hanging around," kind of waiting for our futures to unfold. Hanging around doesn't sound like much fun but I sure enjoyed it.

In Sept. 1965 the brand new Bucks County Community College opened. Another pal, Mickey Brown (gone now, too) and I enrolled for night classes. We went three nights, decided that was enough, had a couple beers and ended up at a Fairless Hills institution, The Hi Hat Diner. I really enjoyed that diner. Most nights ended there. Some nights there would be 10 or 15 of us hanging around, drinking coffee, smoking cigarettes and yakking til the wee hours. Fun!

Oh, I never returned to Bucks County Comm. College.

Now, fifty-some years later some of my favorite days are when Ron Meyers organizes a Boot get together. I really enjoy getting together with friends and acquaintances who are now old friends. Like the country song says, you can't make old friends.

If I were to relive my life I would choose Fairless Hills or Levittown in the '50's and 60's to begin it. No "Play Dates" or car pools to haul us around. Find your own people to play with and take your bike or walk if you need to go somewhere. Just be home when the street lights came on.

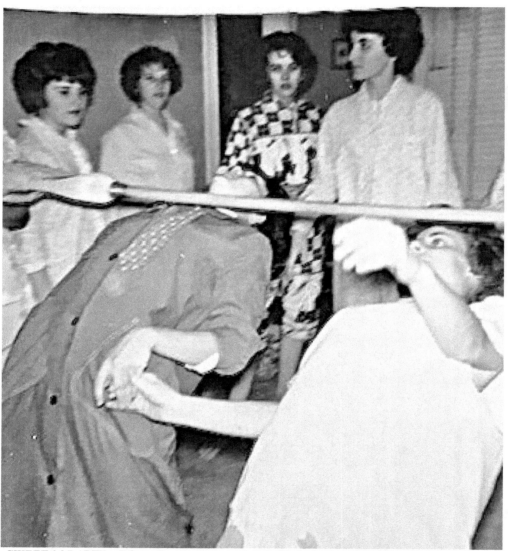

SWEET 16 PARTY – Eileen Gannon goes under the limbo bar on the right as Donna Tettemer waits her chance during a birthday party sleepover for Barbara Hubal.

CHAPTER 41

Yardley Residents Could Relax in a Safe Haven

By BARBARA HUBAL

I lived in Yardley, on South Main Street, with my mother and father, Aldona and Michael, my brother Michael, and my grandparents, Anna and George. My grandparents were immigrants from Czechoslovakia. My grandmother came to America when she was 17. Her voyage was paid for by a young man, who wanted a bride. When my grandmother arrived, and met the young man, she said she would not marry him. She worked cleaning homes and cooking, and paid the young man the money for her ticket. I don't know how old my grandfather was when he came to America. He settled in the Scranton area and worked in the coal mines. My grandparents met, and were married. They had five children.

We had a very large backyard, and my parents planted vegetable and flower gardens. My grandparents would work in those gardens almost every day. Weekends were weeding and taking care of the yard. My brother and I had our share of yard work to do. Whenever anyone stopped by the house, they went home with flowers and vegetables. At the end of summer, my Mom canned vegetables and made chow-chow, which was a combination of chopped cabbage, cauliflower, onions, green tomatoes, green and red sweet peppers, and the pickling spices. It took quite a while to prepare and to put in cans, but well worth it.

I also have memories of my grandmother baking bread for the holidays, and throughout the year making noodles and perogies. The food was wonderful.

The town of Yardley started out as a village, in 1862. The village was named Yardleyville. The village grew, with businesses and an increasing population. It was incorporated in 1895, and the name was changed to Yardley. If you want a detailed story of the town's growth and development, I recommend reading, "Images of America … Yardley," by Vince Profy. The book is filled with pictures and stories of the people who made up this wonderful little town.

During the 1950s, there were a lot of home delivery businesses. The following would come to your house and either be delivering or picking up something. There was the milk man. He came two times per week, leaving your milk and cream in an aluminum box. The soda/beer truck came once a month. We got one case of beer and one case of mixed soda. Blakely laundry would pick up Dad's shirts every week. The bread man, don't remember how many times he came to the house. Of course, can't forget the Charlie Chip man. Now that I think about it, it was like having a primitive Amazon Prime.

Now, let's skip forward to our town's schools. Yardley Elementary school stood at the top of West College Avenue. It was built in 1917. It taught students from first grade through high school. The class of 1948 was the last graduating class, and the Pennsbury school district was founded. The school continued with the elementary class until 1980, when the building was sold to Abrams Hebrew Academy.

Most of the students walked to school. There were 27 of us who attended Kindergarten classes together. At some point, there was a fire in the school, and we then attended school in the firehouse/municipal building. To go out for recess, we would use the fire escape that led into the small yard. There, our most wonderful teacher, Mrs. McGrath, would have us play the usual kid games of Ring around the Rosie, Leap Frog, and others that I just don't recall.

My close group of friends during the elementary years and into high school were Suzanne Waterson, Eileen Gannon, Bonnie Randal, Joan Maroney and Jill Whitehead. We would go to each other's homes and think of things we could do. Ride our bikes, play games, climb trees in the woods behind Layne's home (Eileen). One summer we were into putting on small plays, for ourselves. It was very funny. The one very cool thing was that Layne had a very creative grandfather, Mr. Caffey. He built a wooded roller coaster in the back yard. It was probably 30 feet long, with two bumps in it. We used to gather at Layne's front steps, waiting for the newspaper to read the comics and Dear Abby. During high school, in the winter, we would skate on Afton Lake. And today, that is still a busy lake when it freezes. There were weekly high school dances. Our parents would take turns driving us to the dance, and then pick us up, and travel over the Yardley Bridge to the Dog House for a burger. And let's not forget Dirty Bill's, on River Road. He grilled the best hot dogs on that old grill. I have met so many people over the years that would come over from New Jersey for one of those hot dogs.

When I was in 11th grade, the girls started to have sleep overs. For my 16th birthday, I was allowed to have a sleep over. I believe there were at least 18 girls. Dad went to his bedroom, and Mom was working the 3-11 shift at General Motors. We were dancing and doing the Limbo dance, and just having FUN. When Mom came home, she made us food to eat . . . probably some type of breakfast. There were girls all over the house, trying to find a place to sleep. Even in the bathtub.

Life was good growing up in Yardley. It was a safe haven. Most residents of South Main Street knew each other. You could leave your house unlocked, and the keys in the car. Such fond memories of home, school and friends. Thank you all for being my friend!

CHAPTER 42

Bill Wilson Grew Up
as a Reporter in Lower Bucks

By BILL WILSON

I did not grow up in Levittown but as a young man I covered it. You might say I grew up as a newspaper reporter in Lower Bucks County.

My parents, like most GIs (my Mom was Navy and Dad was Marines), were looking for housing after WWII as the Baby Boom and returning veterans created a housing shortage.

That shortage gave birth to Levittown.

As a child I lived in Northeast Philadelphia with my grandparents and later we moved to Phoenixville in Chester County where my grandfather was mayor.

Then in 1951, we moved to a row home in suburban Delaware County. Folcroft Borough was almost 40 miles from Levittown in Bucks County.

At the time my Dad was working at the Philadelphia Inquirer and eventually WFIL-TV (now WPVI) and our home was closer to the Inquirer and its new TV station.

I heard news reports about Levittown and its massive housing development. My grandparents would spend Saturdays at Butch's Auction in Trevose — that's all I knew of the area.

After the Air Force and Journalism School, I went to work as a reporter-photographer at a paper in Hagerstown, MD.

The job changed drastically due to major staff changes and I eventually wound up editing, reporting and taking pictures for the paper's Tri-State section.

In short, I became a utility fielder. I was planning to get married to a New Jersey newspaper-woman and a change was in order.

In the late spring 1967, I answered a blind ad for a job and got a letter back from the Bucks County Courier Times managing editor "Sandy" Oppenheimer.

After a phone call in which I called Sandy "Miss Oppenheimer," I thought my chances were doomed. But he invited me to an interview at 8400 Rt. 13 in Levittown.

Sandy, a colorful hard-nosed Brooklyn newspaperman, gave me a writing test and we chatted about my job. He liked that I was a utility fielder type guy.

I started in July of 1967.

For a while I commuted from Delaware County to Levittown. Not an easy drive as Interstate 95 was yet to be completed. My first impressions of the Bucks County Courier Times (BCCT): first, that Sandy would be a good teacher (he was); the paper seemed ultra-modern; the newsroom large; and it had a wire room (where I'd later work as wire editor) filled with chattering teletypes. A far cry from the cramped Victorian building in Hagerstown.

NEED YOUR PHOTO ID – Bill Wilson gets ready to take picture for his Courier Times press card.

It was a Saturday morning and I got a couple of papers to read. On Page One was the soap box derby race. A big event it turns out and Sandy told me that the paper's emphasis was on local. I thought it odd . . . but the BCCT was one of the first really local suburban papers.

Local news it was. Covering municipal meetings, Little League baseball, fires, Boy Scouts, social notes and everything in between that was "local."

After the interview, I drove around the various Levittown sections. I would soon become familiar with the sprawling green sections and interesting names. And I walked around the spacious shopping center and drove up the Levittown Parkway, which I thought was beautiful.

In July 1967, I began my job covering Bensalem Township, which was growing rapidly. I worked on Saturday as a desk assistant. I'd often take spot news pictures of fires and accidents.

By 1968, my new wife and I settled into a garden-style apartment on Rt. 413 across from one of the sections ... Forsythia Gate. My drive down Trenton Road to the Parkway was filled with vistas of perfect homes and manicured lawns. Once I found an apartment, the drive would be a great commute and a lovely place to live.

While I covered Bensalem's meteoric growth (Neshaminy Mall, Neshaminy Valley and a race track), living in the Levittown/Lower Bucks area was far cry from the city of Hagerstown and the old suburban landscapes of Delaware County.

For a decade the BCCT and Levittown were my home. The library was a spot I enjoyed. I lunched at the Sunray Drug Store at the Levittown Shop-A-Rama. Pomeroy's, the anchor store, was where I did Christmas shopping for many years.

For my wife and I the library became more than a place to check out books. In later years my wife, a civically and politically active woman, was involved in the expansion of the library and would continue until the time of her death to be active as Friends of the Levittown Library's President.

The many taverns, pizza joints, the Levittown Hobby Shop, The Towne Theater . . . all haunts fondly remembered. The Kenwood Tavern was a fave place to devour cheesesteaks and few beers with newspaper colleagues, some of whom became lifelong friends.

While Levittown over the years seemed to wax and wane, the chutzpah of the residents was always there. That chutzpah produced colorful characters, politics and many unique businesses.

One colorful character was Hal Lefcourt, a public relations guy who was a fixture at the paper. Story ideas about the LPRA, local synagogues and entertainment events were his shtick. And at Christmas, Hal was always good to leave a bottle of wine on each reporter's desk.

He was an old-time press agent also who could score press passes for all sorts of events. I even interviewed various Miss Americas and even Tiny Tim's wife and a memorable concert of Peter, Paul and Mary.

Foremost, Hal was THE champion for Levittown. He wore the moniker "Mr. Levittown" proudly.

Hal was also in local politics and years later when I worked for the late State Rep. Tony Melio and I took a legislative job in the Casey Administration in Harrisburg — Hal was there.

He became a good friend and colleague. We worked on the Delaware Canal Board together to save the historic waterway. He was there to usher in the new Levittown Library and worked to restore the aging Levittown Shopping center which was eclipsed by new Neshaminy and Oxford Valley malls. (I would cover the openings of both malls.)

Speaking of politics, Levittown yielded a Governor in Mark Schweiker and a Lt. Governor, James Cawley, both Republicans.

Three well-known writers come to mind who were Levittown denizens. Sol Weinstein was perhaps the best known Levittowner. The former Trentonian journalist penned a James Bond satire, Israel Bond. Sol became a prolific author, script writer and columnist. Stellar sports writer and columnist Maury Allen also worked in Levittown.

The third is Levittowner and Neshaminy High School grad Steven DeSouza. Generations after the other writers, Steve would become a well-known TV and Hollywood script doctor and producer.

He got his start producing a local film on the drug culture (marijuana). Set in Levittown "Arnold's Wrecking Co," his project won an Atlanta Film Festival award and had its local "premier" at The Towne Theater.

The star was the late Mike Renshaw, a Levittown transplant from Northeast Philadelphia and a BCCT colleague (a life-long friend who became editor of the BCCT.)

Some scenes were shot in Levittown. The Holiday Inn and the BCCT building were also set locations. I played a cop in the film. Other local figures were extras like me.

Reflecting on my 40-plus years in Levittown and Lower Bucks, I must say I thoroughly enjoyed the "little town" that was NOT a town. Most Levittowners know the "town" is actually comprised of parts of Middletown, Falls, Bristol Townships and Tullytown Borough.

I recall covering at our local shopping center the Easter Parade, political rallies and other promotional events prior to Lower Bucks being mall-ed.

The small stores, taverns, and barber shops were part of the normal rhythms of my life as I grew from a 20-something reporter to one of the paper's older editors. Levittown gave us a lot more than the song about "ticky-tacky boxes."

Now, I live in the mountains of Central Mexico. The historic town, a World Heritage City, reminds me in many ways of "New Hope in the Mountains."

One of Levittown's biggest failings in this journalist's observation is (was) the lack of public transportation.

Over the years in the newsroom — because I sat directly in front of Sandy — I got lots of good hard news stories (double murders, plane crashes, etc.) and it was working with Mike Renshaw that we became great friends and became team reporters.

"Send Wilson and Renshaw," often heard in the newsroom.

Mike and I would cover big school bus accidents, concerts, fires, presidential campaigns and the murder of the first police officer in Levittown -- Detective Sgt. George Stucky.

Later in our careers I'd become City Editor and Mike was editorial page editor and eventually became editor in chief.

In retrospect, my saddest moments were covering the deaths Levittown's Vietnam soldiers.

We'd get a wire story that a person died and with the wire copy in hand I'd knock on family's doors. I would respectfully ask for a photo and often wound up talking to a young widow.

It affected me, deeply. That was one of the reasons I eventually became a Quaker.

Years later I'd present a proclamation from The Governor on the dedication of Bristol Township's Vietnam War Memorial. Not long after the dedication I would pen a poem, "We Remember." For many years, a copy hung in the meeting room of the township building.

The sacrifices of those young men are remembered.

My stay at the BCCT was the highlight of my news career. I later worked for weekly and monthly business magazines, covered the United Nations, edited the Sunday newspaper both in the US and in Mexico. I also edited senior public relations positions in healthcare and transportation.

I left Levittown at the turn of the century. A new life in Mexico provides challenges but I will always remember Levittown as where I grew up as a professional and young man.

For me it was the best of times.

* * *

(Bill Wilson, who lives in the UNESCO World Heritage City of San Miguel de Allende, has covered nearly everything from sewer board meeting to the United Nations. He and his wife and their poodles live high in the mountains of central Mexico. They enjoy retirement but Wilson misses a good cheesesteak.)

CHAPTER 43

The Night of the Scary Sleep Out

By TOM WYSOR

Those of us who grew up in Fairless Hills and Levittown in the late 1950's were a lucky group. We had lots of woods to play in, organized sports to play and plenty of open areas in which to roam. We had few rules to follow except be home for dinner.

One of our favorite things in the summer was to sleep outside in each other's back yards. One summer we decided to sleep out in the Fairless View school yard. We all had to ask permission from our parents. The kids from Blough Court all got their parents' approval. The gang was Bob and John Keen, Jim Barnes, Tom and Jim Wysor and Carey Vonada. The only guy who could not get his parents' approval was John Potts, a real character.

As night began to fall we all met in the school yard with our sleeping bags and snacks. We walked across the back of the school yard to a spot next to the creek that ran from Lake Caroline to Olds Boulevard.

We got all our sleeping bags laid out and began to organize our snacks and tell stories. It was a perfectly clear night and we picked the darkest part of the yard. The stars were beautiful.

I was laying on my back just about asleep when a blur went by my face, then a second and third. I had woken up enough to hear splashing in the creek and the rustling of grass. I looked across the school yard to see all the guys I was out with running hard towards Jimmy Barnes's house. They were yelling.

As I rolled up on my elbows and stomach all I could see was the bottom of a long trench coat and a pair of boots. Before I realized it I was on my feet and running to catch my buddies. The next thing I heard was uproarious laughter I knew exactly what it was. I tried to stop the guys from running to Jimmy's house but it was too late. Jimmy's dad had heard the commotion and was coming to meet us. He took Jimmy into the house and told the rest of us to go home.

We went back to pick up our sleeping bags before we went home. That's when the rest of the group found out who had come out to scare us. I knew because of his laugh. John Potts. Because his mom would not let him sleep out with us he waited until she went to bed and climbed out of his bedroom window, walked to the school, crossed the creek and waited quietly until we were all quiet. He then splashed through the creek, sneaked up on us and you know the rest.

John Potts scared the hell out of us. He had the last laugh. This is just one of the great memories I have of growing up in Fairless Hills and the great friendships that we formed in our childhood.

Tom Wysor in his youth football uniform.

PART OF THE GANG – Bob Smith, Mike Tapper, John Witman and John Replogle could usually be found along North Main Street in Yardley, plotting their next adventure.

CHAPTER 44

Yardley's North Main Street Gang

By MIKE TAPPER (With memory help and editorial review from Bob Smith and Bud Haldeman)

"The characters, places and events described herein are entirely fictional, and any resemblance to individuals living or dead is purely coincidental, accidental or the result of faulty imagination."
-In God We Trust: All Others Pay Cash, *Jean Shepherd*

Three boys of Yardley, now in their 70's, sit together sipping Stag's Leap Chardonnay and an occasional very, very dry martini, stir and straight up with dirty ice, at a local gin mill and one says, do you remember so and so and such and such. Then another chimes in, what about the time when . . . the barkeep now is summoned for more snack peanuts. With that, it all began. The memories.

Yardley is a borough in Bucks County. The town is bordered by the Delaware River to the East and Lower Makefield Township to the North, South and West. This is the story of three young Yardley sidekicks in the 1950's marching that long yellow brick road of life. Yardley was a Mayberry clone before Andy Griffith even got on television. Our town had Chief Waterson playing Chief Andy Taylor, Assistant Chief Lee Carol as Barney Fife, a local version of Otis and numerous stay-at-home Moms as Aunt Bee. Opie—that's our three young lads—Bud, Bob and Mike.

To understand Yardley and the playground of our lads, one must picture the town before I-95, before Main Street became a super highway and before the developers turned the area into down home for New York and Philadelphia commuters. It was once a land of forests, fields, and farms. That was before suburban sprawl.

Like all small towns of the era, there was a main street, and of course Yardley had one. Running from north to south, the borough was cut in half by Main Street. It was then divided into North Main and South Main by Afton Avenue. Our lads resided on North Main and were known as the North Main Gang.

BICYCLES: As I take you back to yesteryear, one must understand the importance of the bicycle. The bike was the main means of transportation for The Gang—the means of getting to baseball fields, the Downtown area South of Afton, the golf course and many other parts of town. As one gang member recently put it, "we must have ridden 1,000 miles." They rode the kind of bike John Wayne and Clint Eastwood might ride—strong, durable, made from the finest steel that may have come from the local Bessemer Converter or from Bethlehem Steel or from the mills in Gary, IN. None of the skinny tire English racing bikes nor the jumping, twisting bikes of today. Just heavy duty Schwinn models. Fat tire models with all steel frames, fenders and spokes—steel not aluminum.

SOUTH OF AFTON: The home territory of The Gang was North of Afton, but there was the lure and treasures to be found South of Afton. On many occasions The Gang ventured south. The real draw was the sugar fix they needed. The Gang, like many others, had become addicted to glucose.

There were, however, attractions other than sucrose South of Afton: Bill Beener's Hardware Store, the supplier of BB's for the official Red Ryder two-hundred shot BB gun; gourmet dining overlooking the picturesque Delaware River at Dirty Bill's Hot Dogs; the elementary school for a baseball or dodge ball game; the Yardley Golf Course, finding lost golf balls and providing income by being a caddy and "carrying the bag;" the Yardley Continental – the working man's emporium for a shot and beer after a long day's work. The Continental was the local home for the town's version of Mayberry's Otis.

South of Main there was no attraction equal to Len & Pearl's Five & Ten. It was the holder of many sundry delights. Heavily sought after was the prized Duncan Champion YoYo. For The Gang, nothing would do but a Duncan. As Spring began to turn to Summer, Len and Pearl would bring the gems into stock and put them on display. They had other models but only the Duncan would suffice. As the summer began, Len and Pearl would bring a Duncan YoYo expert to town to work with the young folks on tricks: put the yo yo to sleep, walk the dog, around the world, cat in the cradle, etc.

Yoyo's were nice but the real lure of the Five & Ten was its ability to satisfy The Gang's sucrose addiction. To pacify the dextrose monster nothing better than penny candy, old fashioned penny candy. The Five & Ten had it—it was The Mecca for the 1 cent sweets: Mary Janes, licorice pipes, wax teeth and mustaches, Swedish fish, JuJu Babies, root beer barrels, licorice whips both red and black, Necco wafers, Bazooka Joe Gum, and so on and on and on. The Gang invested heavily in the candy to the extent that they helped send one of Len & Pearl's off springs to college. Dr. Jack Hewson, the community dentist, thanked The Gang and the penny candy stand for his business.

NORTH OF AFTON: So much for the South. It was North of Afton where the gang roamed and played. There was Monopoly, ping pong, badminton, horseshoes, and basketball on a packed mud court and other mundane activities. These the Gang did in their spare time. Just something to pass the hours in between the big stuff.

Bob took the lead and asked, do you remember: semi-monthly Cub Scout Meetings and Merit Badges; summer recreation camps with swimming, archery, and crafts; winter sledding on Cold

Spring Drive when the police would block the road off to car traffic for the sledders (can you imagine the outrage today if the plow trucks left a road untouched so it would become packed with ice and the police blocked it off for the kids to sled?). There was also sledding on the 17th hole of the Yardley Golf Course. There was riding those famous bikes down the center of North Main in the early evening, following the truck spraying for Mosquitoes. And then again, decorating the bikes with the red, white & blue to ride down North Main for the Memorial Day Parade.

THE CANAL: Now called The Delaware Canal but in those days it was "The Canal." A source of many hours of delight. In walking distance from The Gang's houses, the canal afforded ice skating which could go all the way to Morrisville. Ice hockey with makeshift nets. Trapping for muskrats. And best of all playing "ticky" on thin ice. Yes "ticky" . . . that great game of skating on thin ice which as it gave way would give a ticking sound. The game was to skate on the thin ice and try to escape before it broke thru, plunging a foot in the ice cold water—a "soaker."

Then there was fishing on The Canal. The Gang and many others were constantly in pursuit of an elusive giant catfish that supposedly roamed the waters. Did he hide at the locks or was he under the bridge? Made no difference. Nobody ever caught the great fish, settling instead for "sunnies" and an occasional small mouth bass. My guess is that even today, kids are still in pursuit of that great catfish.

Bud, the oldest of The Gang and the leader, took over. He called for another round and along with the drinks came more bar nuts and those mini pretzels that many bars still have—stale of course. Since we were the only ones in the establishment, the keeper of the inn sat and joined us to hear the tales of yesteryear. Bud was remembering the Great Flood of 1955 that was the end result of back-to-back hurricanes. The Delaware River could no longer stay within its banks and flooded to meet the flooding of the Delaware Canal. Yardley was under water to the extent that the National Guard was called in and the town had its 15 minutes of fame as it was on national television. The Gang did its community service and was heavily involved in the clean-up effort. Hip boots, water and mud, mud, mud.

Bud brought back memories of going to the movies and shopping in Trenton. (Remember when one went to Trenton for shopping?) He also relived the days of playing pinball at Cappy's Drug Store, having a Vanilla Coke at Phil Freeman's drug store, a flat top haircut at Archie's Barber Shop . . . the best of the best—Cramer's Bakery and those great donuts.

Bob was squirming on his barstool realizing that Bud was on a roll and hitting home with his memories. So Bob reached back and decided to go for it all with one big swing and got it. He called out HALL'S ORCHARD! Mike, Bud and the barkeep all froze. He just rang the bell, got the brass ring, and the Olympic Gold Medal all in one utterance. Hall's was a commercial orchard, across the street from where The Gang lived, that provided the guys with hours of employment picking apples or mostly picking "drops." Drops were apples that had fallen off of the tree. The Gang got to pick them from the ground to be sold as seconds at Hall's Store. Most importantly was the lower field of the Hall's property which was where games were played, but mostly baseball. BASE-BALL—the giant of all sports.

BASEBALL and WIFFLE BALL: that is an entire chapter in itself, to be told another day. The hour was getting late, the bar keep was wiping down the tables, the music box had Frank on it, singing "One for My Baby and One for The Road." Time to call it quits. Time to head home. Time to pay the piper. In modern 21st Century style out came the "plastic." The barkeep pointed to a small neon sign flashing over the cash register that read "In God We Trust. All Others Pay Cash." The gin mill was like The Gang and the memories . . . Great things from the past. Nothing wrong with a great past, glad to have been part of it. As Bob said, happy to have the "lasting friendships" that endure even to today.

That's **OLD YARDLEY**. The way we lived it and the way we remember it. – **MIKE, BUD and BOB**

SHORT CAREER – Terry Nau, bottom right in first row, saw his Major League baseball dreams crushed on Opening Day of the Fairless Hills Little League season in 1959.

CHAPTER 45
Our World Is Always Changing

By TERRY NAU

Two of my earliest memories predate living in Lower Bucks County. In 1951, when our family of six still resided in Munhall, a suburb of Pittsburgh, I came down with a case of pneumonia, putting me in the hospital for at least two nights. I had just turned four years old. What I remember is looking out the window at the highway off in the distance, seeing those automobile headlights beaming in the dark and hoping my parents were in one of those cars, coming to take me home. Home was a two-deck house on Margaret Street that my parents rented from an aunt.

The other memory is of kindergarten class. The kids were all napping when my mother came into the room and took me out to a waiting car, packed with gear, for our long trip across the state to a new town being built over 300 miles away in a place called Fairless Hills. I was five years old and had no clue what was going on. My parents knew. They were picking up stakes, leaving their hometown, with four boys aged 10 to just 18 months in tow. It was December 1952.

Dan and Olive Nau grew up near Pittsburgh during the Depression. They wanted a better life for their children, and themselves. They wanted to live in their own home. Mom and dad made a courageous decision to uproot their four young sons and move 315 miles east, leaving the grit and grime of Munhall for a brand new community that would rise from the farmlands around a steel mill being built on the Delaware River. We moved into a three-bedroom house located at 248 Cardiff Road. Construction of roads and homes had begun only in the last year. We lived in one of the first semi-completed sections.

Dad settled into a good job as a First Helper on an Open Hearth furnace in the hottest and grimiest part of the new U.S. Steel plant, which was known as Fairless Works. Once youngest son Larry turned five and enrolled in kindergarten, mom went to work on an assembly line at the General Motors factory in Trenton. She would eventually move into accounting jobs at Strick Trailer and U.S. Steel. Mom and dad had a long-range goal of sending all four sons to college. They would both work full-time to make this dream come true.

I look back on those early years with great fondness, as do my surviving brothers Dan and Tim, who have also written chapters for this book. Our stories are slightly different because of age differences. Except for one thing. We all had red hair, just like our mother! Danny, born four days after Pearl Harbor in 1941, was the oldest, a good three-plus years ahead of Tim, and 5 ½ years more ancient than me. Dan had his own set of friends who seemed light years older than us. Tim had more than two years on me, which was huge when we were young.

Larry, the only non-redhead, was three years younger than me and had to find his own friends. Which wasn't hard to do in a town where houses were spaced barely 10 feet apart. Our next door neighbor, Wayne Marsden, became Larry's best friend for life. There is a long-held story, probably fictional, that Wayne once sneaked into our garage and licked the icing off a birthday cake. Which he denies, to this day.

What do I remember about growing up? Hunting and fishing with dad and my brothers in the 1950s. Family picnics at Ralph Stover Park with our parents' friends and their kids, not to mention our cousins from Fallsington – Ron, Tom and Kathie Nau. Playing Little League baseball and midget football with friends in Fairless Hills. Putting up with school in my pre-teen years.

My brothers and I loved the outdoors, roaming through woods located just 150 yards from our home, taking our hunting dogs in search of rabbits and pheasants. When we each reached 12 years of age, dad would train us to use a shotgun and sign us up for hunting licenses. We would jump into the station wagon with him and at least one hunting dog, an English setter named Dinah or a beagle we called Queenie, and flush out pheasants, knocking them from the sky with our shotguns and then bringing the carcasses home to be cleaned by the boys and cooked for dinner by our mother. Dad had grown up hunting for dinner during the Depression and he never forgot those days. We often ate rabbit and pheasant for dinner and if dad was fortunate enough to bag a deer up in the Poconos during big game season, we would eat venison until the freezer went empty in the spring.

All four boys had newspaper routes at one point or another. You could clear four or five dollars a week delivering the Philadelphia Bulletin in the afternoon, or the Inquirer in the morning before school. That was a lot of money in those days. We could also pick apples off neighbors' trees on pre-dawn paper routes. One neighbor reported this thievery to our mother, who was deeply disappointed in Tim and me . . . for about five minutes. She knew: Boys will be boys!

Tim and I saved $35 between us in 1960 and purchased our own hunting dog, the aforementioned Queenie. We could take her into the woods after school and listen to Queenie's melodic howling as she tracked rabbits back to us. We couldn't fire guns in those woods so near to houses. We just enjoyed nature while listening to Queenie croon her song to the rabbits.

My baseball dreams ended at age 12 when I was tabbed to pitch on Opening Day of Little League by a desperate manager who had been impressed in practice by my sidearm curve ball. This pitch existed only on worn-out baseballs with high seams that I could pinch to spin the ball. Alas, on Opening Day, they gave us new baseballs. No high seams to grip. I was warming up on the sidelines when an 8-year-old kid leaned over the fence and asked me, "Is that all the harder you throw?" We lost 23-2 to a team led by slugging Butch Coutts, who lived on the other side of Fairless Hills. Butch and I would become lifelong friends, but he hardly recalls my trauma of getting knocked out of the box in the first inning, before hundreds of fans, including that smart-ass kid with the sharp eye for pitching talent.

Our father bonded with each of his sons, especially me, over baseball. Dad learned to love baseball while growing up in Munhall and nearby Homestead, where the Negro Leagues had a franchise called the Grays that featured future Hall of Famers Josh Gibson and Satchel Paige. Dad loved the Pittsburgh Pirates, too, but the Grays were a cheaper ticket for kids growing up in the Depression. Color didn't matter. Baseball did. Dad threw lefty and sometimes played catch with us in the front yard. Watching us playing ball over at the local field, he would tell us to "swing at the high balls because they go further." Danny, who grew to over six feet, could hit the ball a long way.

Most of all, dad loved to watch baseball on television, or listen to it on the radio. He took great pains to install a powerful antenna on the roof of our home so that we could pull in the New York channels and see his Pirates play the Giants or Dodgers. Dad also would watch the evil Yankees. I became a "Damn Yankees" fan in 1955 while watching the World Series with dad, who was rooting for the Yankees only because he hated the Dodgers. (Brooklyn always beat up on Pittsburgh.) In the spring of 1956, I latched on to the Yankees because of Mickey Mantle, the charismatic switch-hitting slugger who would win the Triple Crown that season. Dad went along with my misguided team selection because he sensed I was a quiet kid who needed some kind of interest, even if it involved rooting for the Yankees.

I would eventually become a sportswriter because of my father. He read three or four newspapers each day, focusing on the sports sections. I waited until he was done and then grabbed those papers for myself, memorizing batting averages and polishing my own math skills because of the example dad set for me. He was forever dividing numbers in his head to update batting averages. Dad dropped out of school in 8th grade to help support his widowed mother, but he could add up numbers in his head like a math wizard.

One night in May 1959, dad burst into the bedroom where Tim, Larry, and I slept in bunk beds. He had been listening to Harvey Haddix's perfect game pitching performance for Pittsburgh on the radio. We could hear the radio through the walls, so it was no surprise when dad came into our room. He was very excited. We sat there for an hour, listening to the final few innings. Haddix remained perfect into the 13th inning before an error and Joe Adcock's home run ended the game on a losing note for the Pirates. It was nearly midnight when dad switched off his transistor radio. We learned from this experience that baseball can lift your heart and break it all in the same evening.

Knowing by age 12 that I would never make it as a big league ball player, I took solace in eighth grade when an English teacher read my book report on a baseball novel called "The Long Season" and said I had a flair for writing. So with the urging of dad and my teacher, Royce Walters, I began drifting towards a career writing about sports.

Life became more complicated in January 1961 when dad returned home early one evening from his steel mill work shift. Looking pale, he retired to bed. He should have headed to the mill's medical center but instead came home to his three youngest sons, "walking through" what became a massive heart attack that destroyed half of his heart muscle. We began to understand over the following year that dad's life would always hang by a thread. We lived with the constant dread of losing our father. Danny, 19 years old, came home from college to work in the steel mill and help mom with house finances while dad recuperated in the back room of our compact Fairless Hills home. We all pitched in, but these were difficult times, especially for our mother. Our neighbors kept an eye on us, too. When things got tough in Lower Bucks, people looked out for each other.

So that was our family's struggle during the 1960s. Dad would regain most of his strength, although on hunting trips to the Poconos he tended to cook breakfast and stay indoors while his three younger sons braved the cold in search of deer.

Danny went back to college in 1962 and resumed working on his college degree. Tim joined the Air Force in 1963, right after graduating from high school. He didn't want mom and dad worrying about paying part of his college bills. The GI Bill would take care of that.

Larry and I held the fort at home. We were not great students! I was more worried about dad than anything else. He would take us to Phillies games at Connie Mack Stadium and I would hold back, walking as slowly as he did from the parking lot, because dad often suffered chest pains when he walked too fast.

The size of our high school (1500 students in grades 11 and 12) quieted my earlier penchant for being a smart aleck in class. My idea of social interaction in high school was to argue with Tom DiIorio over who was better, Mickey Mantle or Willie Mays. The halls of Pennsbury High were packed between classes. We would graduate 725 students in June 1965. I got so lost in that crowd, they had to send out a search party to find me for graduation. But it wasn't just me. A lot of us came to school each day, tried to learn what we could, and went home right after the school bell rang. We were latch-key kids who had family duties, like feeding the dog, or thawing out that night's dinner because mom was still at work. Sometimes I raced home to watch the Yankees, too. When I turned 17 and my baseball playing career officially ended, I took up a new sport with my friend Joe Baron at the Fairless Hills Golf Course. Joe got me a job there in exchange for free golf, cleaning out the clubhouse and making small talk with the clubhouse manager, John Mack, who jokingly told us that when growing up in DuBois, "I had to walk uphill both ways to school." When I got old, I used that line a few times myself.

Our innocent days of youth gradually gave way to more serious pursuits. Very few of us heard the distant drums of war beating halfway around the world. I took a year off after graduation to work in the steel mill and save money for college. Mom bought me an electric typewriter in anticipation of heading off to Penn State in September 1966. She gave me lessons on how to type with some speed and accuracy.

Always the optimist, it was my mother who called me during Orientation Week in late September with the news that the President of the United States had sent me a letter, requesting my services in the Army. Mom thought because I was in college, I qualified for a deferment, but I was still in Orientation Week. I came home and appealed to the Bristol Draft Board, lost in a hurry, and reported to the Induction Center on Oct. 26, 1966.

In January 1968, while I was serving with an artillery unit in the Republic of Vietnam, news came from home that our neighbor, Bobby Seanor, had been killed in a motorcycle accident. On Feb. 20, Army PFC Rick Guest, who grew up one street over on Collingswood Road, died in Vietnam when an ammo trailer rolled over and trapped him underneath. Four months later, Marine

Corps PFC Eddie Beers, who lived two streets in the other direction on Guilford Road, was killed by small arms fire in Quang Tri Province, RVN. This was the same year Martin Luther King and Bobby Kennedy were assassinated. In our neighborhood, the focus was on three young men who died way too soon.

Dad would die of a heart attack on March 9, 1969 — six months after I came home from Vietnam. Many years later, Larry died at age 61 in 2012 — a painful loss for his brothers, wife Trish, family and friends. Larry was the last of the four brothers to attain a college degree. He graduated from Penn State in 1975 with a degree in Horticulture and worked as a landscape architect for nearly 40 years. The four Nau boys had fulfilled their parents' goal.

It's just Dan, Tim and me now, surprised that we have lived this long, grateful that we have, and wondering when we will see each other again. Makes me think about how as kids we rarely gave thought to the passage of time. Maybe that's why childhood memories are so dear to our hearts. Time didn't matter when we were kids. Those wonderful moments and memories are frozen in our minds, easily accessed in our senior years.

My brothers and I each stopped hunting as we grew older, preferring to admire nature rather than kill it. Dad might demand an explanation. We would explain to him how our world changed, how the population of our country doubled over the last 60 years, creating an explosion of people in the suburbs of major cities. More people, more housing, more everything. Our hunting fields disappeared as housing and business developments crowded them out, just as Fairless Hills and Levittown replaced the gentle farmland of Lower Bucks County in the 1950s.

The world is always changing.

GOOD HUNTING – Larry Nau, left, and Terry Nau hold up two pheasants apiece following a hunting trip with their father in 1963.

ACKNOWLEDGMENTS

It takes a village of old friends to publish a book. I have so many Lower Bucks County pals to thank for volunteering to write a chapter about their "growing up" years. We have heard from 49 voices in this book. It's an oral history, told in the words of people who came of age in the suburbs of Philadelphia. We just wanted to validate our childhood and youthful adult experiences by putting them inside a book, many years later.

I want to also thank Merrily Evans and Liza Hamill, two of my Pennsbury Class of 1965 colleagues, for helping to edit this book. And a special thanks to another classmate, Lorraine Goodwin, who provided a surge of energy late in the process. Lorraine enlisted our Chapter 1 writer, Beverly Briegel Sanders, who added historical context to our story.

My deepest gratitude goes to my brothers, Dan and Tim, for putting their thoughts into this book. Somewhere our parents and brother Larry are smiling.

– **TERRY NAU**

CPSIA information can be obtained
at www.ICGtesting.com
Printed in the USA
LVHW051158290921
699019LV00003B/159